SOCIAL CONTRACT

SOCIAL CONTRACT

ESSAYS BY

LOCKE, HUME, and ROUSSEAU

With an Introduction by

SIR ERNEST BARKER

OXFORD UNIVERSITY PRESS

LONDON   OXFORD   NEW YORK

This volume was first published in The World's Classics, no. 511, by
Oxford University Press, London, 1947
First issued as an Oxford University Press paperback, 1960

printing, last digit: 49 48 47 46 45 44 43 42 41 40

Printed in the United States of America

CONTENTS

INTRODUCTION

BY

Sir Ernest Barker

I

The general idea of the Social Contract, which has haunted
the generations (it was current in the days of Plato, during the
fourth century B.C., and it still flutters in the pages of Herbert
Spencer's *The Man versus the State* at the end of the nineteenth century of our era), may be criticized on various
grounds. The critic may urge that it was mechanical, and not
organic, in its interpretation of political life; juristic, and not
ethical, in its rationale of political obligation; *a priori*, and not
historical, in its explanation of political society and political
authority. The criticisms have their justice. The theory of the
Social Contract could flourish only in an age, or 'climate,' of
thought in which the historical sense (the legacy left by the
Romantic movement to the historians of the nineteenth century) was still imperfect and undeveloped. But if it was unhis-
torical, the theory was still historic — and historic in more than
one sense. Not only could it show a long and continuous history, from the days of the struggles of Popes and Emperors at
the end of the eleventh century: it had also been a factor in the
process of historic causation — a factor making for freedom,
whether it was applied, as it was by the Huguenots after 1570,
to defend the cause of religious liberty, or employed, as it was
by the English Whigs in 1688 and afterwards, to buttress the
cause of civil liberty. Historic continuity, religious belief, and
legal argument could all be pleaded in its favor; and if it were
judged by its fruits, on a pragmatic test of truth, it could bring
to the bar of judgment a record of rich achievement. Even if
there had never been a contract, men actually behaved 'as if'
there had been such a thing; and behaving and acting in terms
of quasi-contract — or what the lawyers call 'contract implied
in law,' an idea which may be extended to cover the case of
'contract implied in government' — they made those terms of

quasi-contract serve good and admirable purposes. The theory of the Social Contract might be mechanical, juristic, and *a priori*. But it was none the less a way of expressing two fundamental ideas or values to which the human mind will always cling — the value of Liberty, or the idea that will, not force, is the basis of government, and the value of Justice, or the idea that right, not might, is the basis of all political society and of every system of political order.[1]

Sir Robert Filmer, in the *Patriarcha*, speaks of the theory of contract as 'first hatched in the schools, and fostered by all succeeding papists for good divinity.' There is warrant for his view. Manegold, a papalist pamphleteer who wrote about A.D. 1080, already held that 'if in any wise the king transgresses the contract by virtue of which he is chosen, he absolves the people from the obligation of submission.' But it is in the writings of St. Thomas Aquinas that the theory of Contract is finally hatched (*circa* A.D. 1250). 'St. Thomas,' Lord Acton once wrote, 'had a very large element of political liberalism.' That very large element of political liberalism was based on a conflation of three sources — the teaching of the Bible, the doctrines of Roman Law, and the principles of Aristotle's *Politics*. The Bible taught that the powers that be are ordained of God; but it also taught that David made a covenant with his people. It was the doctrine of Roman Law that *quod principi placuit legis habet vigorem*; but it was also the doctrine of Roman Law that the reason why this was so was that 'the people, by the *Lex Regia* passed in regard to his authority, confers upon him and into his hands all *its* authority and power.'[2] The principles of Aristotle's *Politics* might seem to favor a monarchy of the one best man; but they also favored a clear distinction between the king and the tyrant, and they endorsed the right of the masses not only to elect the magistrate but also to call him to account. Here was material for a

---

1. The writer would refer, in this connection, to the argument in his *Political Thought in England from 1848 to 1914* (pp. 165–6), and to Professor Buckland's criticism of that argument in *Some Reflections on Jurisprudence* (pp. 63–6).
2. We have to remember that in the theory of Roman Law any *lex* must proceed from the people: *lex est quod populus Romanus . . . constituebat*.

balanced view; and the view of St. Thomas is balanced accordingly. He draws a distinction between three ideas of authority — the idea of its *principium*; the idea of its *modus*; and the idea of its *exercitium*. On the basis of this distinction he argues (1) that the *principium* or essential substance of authority is ordained of God, but (2) that its *modus* or constitutional form (be it monarchy, aristocracy, democracy, or a mixed form) is determined by the people, and (3) that its *exercitium* or actual enjoyment is conferred — and as it is conferred may also be withdrawn — by the people. Developing the third proposition he writes, in the *De Regimine Principum*, that government is instituted by the community, and may be revoked or limited by the community if it be tyrannical; and he even adds that a tyrannical ruler *meruit . . . quod ei* pactum *a subditis non reservetur*.

This general view became the general property of the Middle Ages; and it descended from the Middle Ages to Hooker, and through Hooker to Locke. (It is for this reason that 'the identity of the first Whig' has been discovered in St. Thomas.) The view accorded well with the conditions and 'climate' of the Middle Ages. On the one hand it suited the temper, and the general system of ideas, of feudal society. Feudalism generally was a system of contract, under which each man could say to his lord, 'I will be to you faithful and true . . . *on condition that* you keep me as I am willing to deserve, and all that fulfil that our *agreement* was, when I to you submitted and chose your will.' [3] It was part of this general system of contract that the feudal king, at his coronation, entered into an implicit contract with his feudatories, when he exchanged a coronation oath, pledging him on his side to good government, for their reciprocal oath of homage and fealty. On the other hand the contractual view also suited the temper and the system of ideas of the medieval clergy. It imposed a limit on secular government: it was a guarantee of the rights of the clergy and of *libertas ecclesiae*; and the right of the people

3. From a Wessex document 'Of Oaths' (*circa* A.D.920), in Stubbs, *Select Charters*, 9th edition, p. 74.

to deprive the king of authority for breach of contract could supplement (as it could also be supplemented by) the right of the Pope to deprive the king, by excommunication, of the divinely given *principium* of authority for offenses against its Giver. We may add that a prevalent belief in the ultimate sovereignty of Natural Law formed an atmosphere of ideas favorable to the contractual view. If there was Natural Law, there must also be natural rights; if there were any limitations imposed on natural rights, those limitations must be due to a voluntary contract made by the possessors of such rights; and if the question were raised, 'What is the sanction of such a contract?', the answer could readily be given, 'The sanction is Natural Law.' There was always a close and intimate connection between the idea of Social Contract and the idea of Natural Law; and the connection is particularly evident in the theory of Locke.

When it passed from the Middle Ages into the thought of the sixteenth century (and of the first half of the seventeenth), the theory of the Social Contract continued to show a large clerical tinge. In an age of religious struggles it became the theory of minority confessions, serving to justify their resistance against any government which sought to impose the religion of the majority. In this way it could equally serve the cause of minority Calvinism or the cause of minority Romanism, and indeed it was equally adopted by both. Sir Robert Filmer noted, in a pithy apophthegm, that 'Cardinal Bellarmine and Calvin both look asquint this way.' Either side, it is true, professed to be primarily and essentially a believer in the divine ordainment of the powers that be; and either side sought to attribute to the other, and to disclaim for itself, the audacious radicalism of championing resistance and buttressing it by a doctrine of contract. But both sides, in the last resort, and when it came to the pinch of oppression, were equally contractarian. On the Calvinist side there is Languet, defending the cause of the French Huguenots in the *Vindiciae contra Tyrannos* of 1581 (a work translated and printed in English in the significant year 1648, and afterwards reprinted in the no less significant year 1689); and there is also the German Althusius, expounding the genius of Dutch Calvinism — and, with it, a theory of contract — in his *Politica methodice digesta* of 1605. On the Catholic side there is the Jesuit Suarez, developing a subtle and scholarly theory of contract in his *Tractatus de Legibus* of 1611; there is the Jesuit Mariana, a more radical contractarian (who was ready to allow to the individual the right of tyrannicide), in his *De Rege et Regis Institutione* of 1599; and still more radical, and even more ready to allow the right of tyrannicide, there are the French Catholic theorists of the League which opposed the right of succession of the Protestant Henry of Navarre. In the age of the Wars of Religion and down to the Peace of Westphalia in 1648, the Social Contract was a weapon of religion — religion, it is true, which was mixed and confused with politics, but which was essentially struggling, in the midst of all the confusion, to vindicate the cardinal rights of religious liberty.

A new age ensued in the century which lies between the publication of Hobbes's *Leviathan* in 1651 and the publication of Rousseau's *Du Contrat Social* in 1762. This is the great age of the doctrine of the Social Contract; the age of a purer and less turbulent philosophy of political principles, expressed by thinkers of the order of Hobbes, Spinoza, Locke, and Rousseau; the age in which the general background of Natural Law (which always stands behind the doctrine of the Social Contract) is firmly constructed and systematically illuminated by the thinkers of the great School of Natural Law, which runs from Grotius and Pufendorf to Fichte and Kant.[4] Here, and before we turn to the specific theories of the Social Contract advanced by Locke and Rousseau, we may pause to consider the general nature and the general implications of the doctrine. Hitherto we have been concerned with the genesis of the idea. We must now consider it analytically, resolving it

4. The writer would refer to his translation of Gierke's *Natural Law and the Theory of Society*, and to pp. xli–l of the translator's introduction. Space here forbids any attempt to give an account of the School of Natural Law; but the proper understanding of Locke and Rousseau demands a knowledge of the theory of that School.

into its elements, and noticing, as we do so, that the elements are mixed.

In effect, the idea of the Social Contract is composed of two ideas, which, if they are closely connected, must also be distinguished. There is the idea of the contract of government, the *pacte de gouvernement*, the *Herrschaftsvertrag*. There is the idea of the contract of society, the *pacte d'association*, the *Gesellschaftsvertrag*. The theory of a contract of government is a theory that the State, *in the sense of the government*, is based on a contract between ruler and subjects. It is possible to stop at this point, as many thinkers did; but if we continue to reflect, we shall begin to see that though we have come to a stopping-point we have not yet reached the stopping-place. The theory of a contract of government really postulates, as a prior condition, the theory of a contract of society. There must already be something in the nature of an organized community — in other words, a potential body of subjects, already cohering in virtue of a common social will, as well as a potential ruler, ready to assume the burden of government in agreement with that will — before there can be any contract between ruler and subjects. We must therefore hold, if we are thinking in terms of contract, that besides the contract of government, and prior to the contract of government, there is also a contract of society, a social contract proper (in the strict sense of the word 'social'); and we must conclude that the State, *in the sense of a political community, and as an organized society*, is based on a social contract — or rather on myriads of such contracts — between each and every member of that community or society. We shall therefore say that the contract of government creates *potestas*, but only *potestas*; we shall say that the contract of society creates *societas* itself; and we shall recognize that *societas* is greater than *potestas*, or at any rate prior to *potestas*.

It is on the contract of government that the medieval schoolmen, and most of the Catholic and Calvinist theorists of the latter half of the sixteenth and the early years of the seventeenth century (not all — Althusius and Suarez both went deeper, and they both recognized that the idea of contract was double), laid an exclusive emphasis. It is on the contract of society that Locke and Rousseau, like Hobbes, laid all their emphasis; and we may even say that none of the three (though there are peculiarities in the theory of Hobbes which may qualify the statement) was concerned with the contract of government. Indeed it is obvious that while we can hardly believe in a contract of government without believing, at any rate implicitly, in a contract of society, it is possible to believe in the second without believing in the first. The community once formed by a contract of society may be self-governing, without any distinction of rulers and subject, and therefore without any possibility of their making a contract with one another. This was the theory of Rousseau. Again the community, once it is formed, may appoint a 'fiduciary' or trustee government with which it makes no contract, but which it may dismiss for breach of trust on its own interpretation of the nature of the trust. This was the theory of Locke. Finally the community, once it is formed, may empty itself of every right and every power into a sovereign Leviathan, which makes no contract with it and is therefore subject to none of the limits of a contract of government. This, we may say, was the theory of Hobbes.[5]

Some few words may be added, in conclusion of this section of the argument, about the present bearing and contemporary value of the idea of contract. (1) *Society* is not constituted, and never was constituted, on any basis of contract. Society is an all-purposes association — 'in all science . . . in all art . . . in every virtue and in all perfection' — which transcends

---

5. On the other hand we have to notice (1) that in the theory of Hobbes every subject covenants with every other, in one and the same act, to form a society *and to obey a government*, and a subject will therefore break a sort of contract of government (not with the ruler, but with other subjects) if he refuses to obey; (2) that in the theory of Hobbes, as it eventually develops, the ruler is bound to give protection to the lives of his subjects, and if he fails to do so they may rebel — so that after all there *is* an implicit contract between ruler and subjects, which the ruler himself may break. (These are the peculiarities in the theory of Hobbes which qualify the statement that he was not concerned with the idea of a contract of government.)

the notion of law, and has grown and exists of itself. In the strict sense of the word 'social,' there is not, and never has been, a social contract. (2) On the other hand, the State, as distinct from society, may fairly be conceived in terms of contract; and we may regard it as constituted on the basis of contract — though seldom (except after revolutions, or, again, in the case of federations) created by an act of contract. The State, as such, is a legal association, constituted by the action of its members in making a constitution (such action sometimes, as in Great Britain, being along a line of time, rather than at a point of time) and therein and thereby contracting themselves into a body politic. The constitution of a State is the articles of a contract which constitutes the State. From this point of view we may speak, if not of a social, at any rate of a 'political contract,' expressed in the articles of the constitution, whether those articles have been gradually formed or have been precipitated in a single act. But (3) there is no need in our time to invoke or apply the idea of a 'governmental contract,' by which one part of the State, called the ruler or rulers, has convenanted with another, called the subjects. The one political contract — which unites us all (rulers and subjects alike) in terms of the constitution, and under the constitution, according to our respective capacities as defined in the constitution — this one contract is enough, and it is the only contract. In days when government was still held to be *sui generis*, and to stand over against subjects as something of a separate order, it was natural to think that there was, or should be, a contract between them which fixed their mutual limits. Today the government is not *sui generis*; it is just a part of the legal association, as the body of general citizens is equally a part; and its rights and duties are fixed, like those of the citizens generally, under and by the one and only contract of the constitution.[6]

6. The ideas here summarily stated may (it is hoped) be developed and explained by the writer in a work on *Political Terms and Values* based on his Cambridge lectures.

II

Somerset is one of the old and essential English counties; and the clothing industry of Somerset is an old and honourable industry. It was in Somerset, and from a family engaged in the cloth trade, that John Locke was born, three hundred years ago to-day.[7] He began his life about the time when John Hampden was contesting the legitimacy of ship-money; he ended it in the year in which John Churchill was winning the battle of Blenheim, when the Bill of Rights and the Act of Settlement had been securely written in our Statute-book. It was the good but well-deserved fortune of this modest Englishman, one of the incarnations of the judgematical good sense of his country, to become the accredited prophet of a not ignoble cause — the cause of Civil and Religious Liberty, to which many a good glass of port was drunk in the course of the eighteenth century. It was a cause which Milton and Sidney had preached before him; but the perspicacity of his thought, and the appeal of a style which was all the more convincing because it was unpretending and unadorned, combined with the circumstances of his life and the conjuncture of the times to give him finally the national ear. For fifteen years he lived in close association with Shaftesbury, the fiery founder of the Whig Party; for another five, which were spent in voluntary exile, he lived in Holland, among the liberal or 'Remonstrant' Dutch Calvinists, and in the company of Huguenot refugees who had fled there from France in 1685. When William of Orange landed in England, in November, 1688, Locke soon followed; and in the course of 1690 there appeared from his pen three works which have become a part of the English heritage. One was a *Letter on Toleration*, which had, indeed, appeared in Latin a year before from a Dutch printing press; another was the *Two Treatises on Government*; a third was the *Essay on the Human Understanding*. Add to these two other works, which appeared during the next few years — one on *Education*, and another on the *Reasonableness of Christianity* — and the bequest of Locke to English thought has been enumerated. It was a rich and various bequest. It touched religion, both in its practice and in its principles; it touched, and

7. The first two paragraphs of this section are reprinted from an article contributed by the writer to *The Times* on 29 August 1932 — the tercentenary of Locke's birth. The reader is also referred to an article on John Locke in *The Times Literary Supplement* of 25 August 1932.

perhaps it touched most particularly, politics; it touched the theory of knowledge and the principles of metaphysics; it touched, and it affected for long years to come, the methods of instruction of the young.

It was the political theory of Locke which affected the nation at large most deeply. Nor did it only affect England. It penetrated into France, and passed through Rousseau into the French Revolution; it penetrated into the North American Colonies, and passed through Samuel Adams and Thomas Jefferson into the American Declaration of Independence. We are generally prone to think of Locke as the exponent of the Social Contract. It would be more just to think of him as the exponent of the sovereignty of Natural Law. He put into plain English, and he dressed in an English dress of sober grey cloth, doctrines which ultimately go back to the Porch and the Stoic teachers of antiquity. There is, he taught, a Natural Law rooted and grounded in the reasonable nature of man; there are Natural Rights, existing in virtue of such law, among which the right of property, in things with which men have mixed their labour, is cardinal; and finally there is a natural system of government, under which all political power is a trust for the benefit of the people (to ensure their living by natural law, and in the enjoyment of natural rights), and the people themselves are at once the creators and the beneficiaries of that trust. These may sound abstract doctrines; but abstract doctrines can form a creed, and a political creed can fire and inspire a political party. The doctrines of Locke became the creed of a great party, and of a succession of great statesmen (for the Whigs, with all their defects, deserve that appellation) who between 1688 and 1832 worked out a system of Parliamentary Government that may justly be called the great contribution of England to Europe, and, beyond Europe, to other continents.

The beginning of the reflections on government which eventually appeared in the *Two Treatises* of 1690 may be dated as early as 1667, when Locke, who was a physician as well as a philosopher, and a physician before he became a philosopher, was first associated through his profession with the Earl of Shaftesbury. It was in this way that he acquired some practical experience of politics and a sense of political realities. He served under his patron as secretary of the

Board or Council of Trade (1673–5), and was thus immersed in problems of colonial administration; and he drafted a constitution for Carolina (of which Shaftesbury was one of the 'lords proprietors') which combined the fine principle of toleration with an express acquiescence in Negro slavery. But the period of the definite germination of the *Two Treatises* may be said to begin about 1679. Locke was still associated with Shaftesbury, and lived occasionally with him at Thanet House, in Aldersgate, where he had made his headquarters in order to keep in touch with his Whig friends in the City of London. But it was a troubled time — the time of the agitation for the Exclusion Bill, of Petitioners and Abhorrers, and of generally inflamed tempers — and Shaftesbury had become 'a daring pilot in extremity.' Locke thought it wise to spend most of his time in Oxford, where he had long been a senior student of Christ Church. (He had been educated at Westminster, destined to become the great Whig school, and he had followed the natural course — still followed by Westminster scholars today — which led from Westminster to Christ Church.) The Oxford of those days, like England generally, was much agitated by political problems which ran up into high questions of theory; and indeed the University, in July 1683, solemnly burned in the Bodleian quadrangle a number of books on political theory. It was at this time that Locke may have studied Hooker's *Ecclesiastical Polity* and thus begun to follow the line of thought which runs back to St. Thomas Aquinas, and beyond him to Aristotle.

But two books had recently appeared in 1680 which would whet reflections on politics. One was a reprint of Philip Hunton's *Treatise of Monarchy*, which had originally appeared in 1643. Some scholars have thought that Locke's opinions were largely formed by this *Treatise*; and in any case Hunton (a member of Wadham College) had been considered by Sir Robert Filmer as worthy of being bracketed for attack with Hobbes and Milton and Grotius in his *Observations concerning the Original of Government*, first published in 1652. The other book which appeared in 1680 was a posthumous work of Filmer himself — the famous *Patriarcha*, to which Locke afterwards devoted the first of the *Two Treatises of Government* which were germinating during this period of his life.[8]

At this point, in 1684, Locke was deprived of his senior studentship by the Dean of Christ Church, Dr. Fell, acting under pressure from Lord Sunderland, one of Charles II's Secretaries of State. He retired to Holland, the home of toleration and the free printing press; and there, as has already been noticed, he forgathered with the more liberal of the Dutch Calvinists and with the Huguenots who flocked into the country after the Revocation of the Edict of Nantes. In this company he could steep his mind again in the great traditions of Puritanism — natural law; individual rights; the State limited by fundamentals; toleration for the conscience of man. He had been bred in Puritanism (a strong force in the county of Somerset); and while he was living in Holland (1684–9) *antiquam exquisivit matrem.* When he wrote the *Two Treatises*, finished the long-meditated *Essay on the Human Understanding*, and composed the first *Letter on Toleration* (to which others were subsequently added) — all during his period of residence in Holland —

he had in him the great Puritan sense of the supreme importance of the individual soul; the Puritan feeling for the soul's right to determine its own relations to God, and to enjoy, at the least, toleration from the State and from all authority in so doing; the Puritan instinct for setting bounds to the State — 'thus far, and no farther'; the Puritan echo of the plea of Antigone when she cites the higher law, which is the law of Nature and God, against the edicts of Creon. True, these nobler elements were mixed in Locke, as they were mixed in the nonconformity of the English middle class, with ignobler things. The sacred right of property was somehow included among the sanctities; and an individualism based on religion was made to trail clouds of ingloriousness. That is the penalty of

8. Quoted from the article in *The Times Literary Supplement* mentioned above. It may be added here that the First Treatise, 'in which the false principles and foundation of Sir Robert Filmer and his followers are detected and overthrown,' is not reprinted in this volume. The reader will find only the Second Treatise, entitled 'an Essay concerning the true original, extent and end of Civil Government.'

making the solitary individual the pivot of all your thought. It was
a penalty paid not only in England, but also in America. The Declaration of Independence, with its initial appeal to 'the Laws of
Nature and of Nature's God,' shows one side of Locke, who lived
in American thought in 1776 even more than he lived in England.
The deep sense of property evident in American thought, including
even property in the person of others, showed another. The two
sides had already been conjoined in Locke's draft of a constitution,
for Carolina. The figure of the Individual — seated on his desert
pillar — this, in brief, is the symbol with which we are left, alike
by the *Essay* and the *Two Treatises*. In the *Essay*, as Professor
Alexander has said, 'knowledge, as Locke conceives it, is part of
the life-history of an individual.' In the *Treatises*, as he has also
said, 'the body politic is an aggregate of consenting individuals.'
Thought, in its march, has now left behind the Individual on his
desert pillar. But it is perhaps not amiss to look back. There is no
peril of our being turned into a pillar of salt if we do so, and we need
not fear. On the contrary we may even hope. In these crowded and
gregarious days of community we may recover by such retrospect
something of the salt savour of life — some sense that individual
personality is after all the unique intrinsic value we know upon this
earth. It may be that there is too much salt in Locke's philosophy.
If it be so, the centuries have added their qualifications and
antidotes.[9]

In bui'ding his political philosophy Locke starts, like
Hobbes, from the conception of a state of nature, in which
men are living as equal and separate units. But whereas in
Hobbes each unit claims a natural right (which is more properly a natural power or *potentia*) to do as he likes irrespective of
others, in Locke each unit recognizes limitations on his own
will, especially the two limitations of a right of property, vested
in his fellow-units, and of a right of punishment of transgressors of natural law, vested in each and all (§ 7). There is a right
of property, because each man has property in his person, and
therefore in his labor, and therefore in the things with which
he has inextricably mixed his labor (§ 27). Thus Locke pla-
cates the propertied classes among the Whigs, arguing for a

9. Quoted from the same article.

natural and inherent right of property, not created by the recognition and guarantee of a community, but existing before the community; whereas Hobbes — really more radical (and similar, in this respect, to Rousseau) — holds that property, like all other rights of the subject, is the creation of government, and subject, as such, to the control of its creator. Again there is also a right of punishment — indeed there is a double right: 'there are two distinct rights, the one of punishing the crime, for restraint and preventing the like offence, which . . . is in everybody, the other of taking reparation, which belongs only to the injured party' (§ 11). Such a right of punishment is the necessary corollary of the right of property; but the difficulty of such a pre-political condition as Locke describes is that it is really political. Locke's state of nature, with its régime of recognized rights, is already a political society.

He seeks to meet this difficulty, and to distinguish the state of nature from a state of organized society, by noting the imperfections present in a state of nature. When men are judges in their own case, as in such a state they are, three imperfections ensue — partial judgments; inadequate force for the execution of judgments; and variety in the judgments passed by different men in similar cases. There are therefore three things needed to remedy these imperfections — a judicature to administer law impartially; an executive to enforce the decisions of the judicature; and a legislature to lay down a uniform rule of judgment (§§ 124–6). In order to secure these remedies, men 'give up every one his single power of punishing [not, as Hobbes argued, *all* their powers, and certainly not their power over property] to be exercised by such alone as shall be appointed to it amongst them [that is to say, an executive], and by such rules as the community, or those authorized by them to that purpose, shall agree on [in other words, a legislature, composed either of the people itself or of its representatives]' (§ 127). But while Hobbes had conceived of the contract of surrender, by which a society is formed, as one with the institution of government, Locke distinguishes two separate acts. By the first, men having 'consented to make one community or government, they are thereby presently incorporated, and make one body politic, wherein the majority have a right to act and conclude the rest' (§ 95).[10] By the second, 'the majority' resolve 'upon the placing of the supreme power, which is the legislative' (§ 132); and here we may note Locke's exaltation — somewhat qualified, as will presently appear, in his later argument — of the supremacy of the legislative power. But from the first he regards the legislative, even if it be the supreme power, as 'limited to the public good of the society' (§ 132). It is 'only a *fiduciary* power to act for certain ends,' and 'there remains still in the people a supreme power [another and higher 'supreme power'] to remove or alter the legislative, when they find the legislative act contrary to the *trust* reposed in them' (§ 149).

Here, in the conception of trust, Locke is drawing on the English law of equity, as he had previously drawn (and generally draws) on the different and yet cognate idea of a general Law of Nature. But before we pursue the idea of trust, there is something to be said about Locke's general conception of the powers of government — not only the legislative, but also the other powers. We have seen that his account of the imperfections of the state of nature suggests three remedies for those imperfections, and that these three remedies would appear to be an executive, a judicial, and a legislative power. Actually, however, he proceeds to argue in terms of *two* powers rather than three. These two are (1) the legislative, and (2) the executive, which would seem to include the judicial and to be mainly concerned with the internal problem of dispensing justice under the laws promulgated by the legislative. He notes of the former that 'there is no need that the legislative should be always in being,' and of the latter that 'it is necessary there should be a power always in being which should see to the execution of the laws'; and he concludes that on this ground — the discontinuity of the one, and the continuity of the other — 'the legislative and the executive power come

10. Locke's enunciation of the majority principle and his defense of that principle in §§ 96–9 is a notable, if imperfect, study of a fundamental problem.

often to be separated' (§§ 143–4).[11] But Locke has a third power still to produce (so that, in the event, he speaks after all in terms of *three* powers); and he calls this power by the name of the 'federative' — in other words the power that makes *foedera*, or treaties, and is thus concerned with external relations. We must not, however, lay too much stress on this new distinction which produces a 'federative' power in addition to the executive. These two powers, 'though . . . really distinct in themselves . . . are hardly to be separated,' and 'are almost always united.' We may thus come to two conclusions about Locke's conception of the powers of governments. The first is that though, like Montesquieu, he speaks of three powers, his three powers (the legislative, executive, and 'federative') are different from the three powers distinguished by Montesquieu; and it was Montesquieu who first established the executive, legislative, and judicial powers as the current classification. The second is that though Locke incidentally speaks of the legislative and the executive as 'coming often to be separated,' he does not emphasize their separation (and still less that of the judicial power); and he generally seems to regard sovereignty — so far as he has any theory of sovereignty (a problem still to be discussed) — as something unitary.

We may now return to the conception of trust, and to its bearing on Locke's general theory of contract. Early in 1689 — the year before the publication of the *Two Treatises* — even the House of Lords, as a part of the Convention Parliament, had agreed by 55 votes to 46 that there was an original contract between the king and the people; and the practical consequences drawn from that premise had been (1) the parliamentary deposition (euphemistically termed 'abdication') of the king, (2) a vacancy of the throne, and (3) the parliamentary institution of a new king — or, more exactly, of a new king and queen (William and Mary) reigning conjointly. Locke accepted and justified the consequences; but he did not accept the premise. He did not, like Parliament, think in terms

11. This would appear to be as far as Locke goes in the direction of any doctrine of 'separation of powers.'

of a contract of government: he thought in terms of a contract of society, followed by the creation of a fiduciary sovereign under and by a trust-deed. It may be argued that the notion of trust implies a contract; and it may be urged in support of the argument that trust is the *mandatum* of Roman law, and that *mandatum*, in Roman law, is a form of consensual contract. If this argument were accepted, there would be two contracts in Locke — a formal contract of society and a later consensual contract of government. But this is not really Locke's view; nor is it a view which can be properly drawn from the English conception of trust, which may be like, but is not the same as, the Roman conception of *mandatum*. Trust implies three parties — the creator of the trust, or trustor; the trustee; and the beneficiary of the trust. *Vis-à-vis* the trustor, a trustee may be said to enter into a contract that he will undertake an obligation towards a third party; but *vis-à-vis* that third party (the beneficiary of the trust) the trustee does not enter into a contract — he simply accepts an obligation, and accepts it unilaterally. If we now apply the conception of trust to politics and political theory, we must notice that here there are only two parties — the community, which is both trustor and beneficiary of the trust; and the government, which is trustee. As trustor, the community may be said to enter into a contract with the trustee — that is to say, with the government; as beneficiary — *and Locke regards it principally as beneficiary* — it enters into no contract. From this point of view, the government makes no contract with the community for which it is trustee; it accepts an obligation, and it accepts it unilaterally, knowing the bounds set by the trust and by the law of God and Nature which stands behind the trust (§ 142).

Political trusteeship accordingly means a burden of obligation; its most prominent aspect is liability for abuse, or even neglect, of the powers held in trust — a liability which extends to removal for action contrary to the trust (§ 149). The trust-conception of government — not only adopted in Locke's theory, but also accepted in parliamentary practice afterwards ('in the course of the eighteenth century it became a parliamentary commonplace that all political power is a trust')[12] — is thus more unfavorable to government than the conception of an original contract between government and the people. Contract implies an agreement between two independent parties, each of which has rights of its own, and each of which surrenders some of those rights for a consideration received. The trustee, in regard to the beneficiary, is not such an independent party. There is no mutual surrender of rights for mutual receipt of consideration. The trustee has duties and not rights as against the beneficiary; the beneficiary has rights and not duties as regards the trustee. We may thus conclude that Locke dismisses the notion of a contract of government because it is too favorable to government, which would thereby be recognized as an independent party confronting the community — whereas, in his view, it only exists in, through, and for the community. Hobbes, on the other hand, though he too dismisses the notion of a contract of government, does so for an opposite reason: because it is too favorable to the community, which would thereby be recognized as an independent party confronting Leviathan, whereas, in his view, it only exists in and through Leviathan. (Even Hobbes, however, could hardly say that the community existed *for* Leviathan — on the contrary he said, or implied, the opposite — and here his argument begins to swirl among rapids.)[13]

Three other elements in the theory of Locke may be noted in conclusion of the argument.

1. He believes that the people become a corporate body through their own association, and of themselves: 'when any number of men have so consented to make one community or government, they are thereby presently incorporated,' and can thenceforth act by the majority principle (§ 95). Hobbes, on the contrary, holds that a corporate body can only be formed in the person of the sovereign, who, by receiving into

12. Maitland, Introduction to Gierke's *Political Theories of the Middle Age*, p. xxxvi. The reader is referred to the general argument of pp. xxviii–xxxvii of Maitland's Introduction, and to the essay on 'Trust and Corporation' in the volume of his *Selected Essays*.

13. See above, p. xiii, note 5.

his person all the persons (that is to say the rights, or rather the powers) of his subjects, first makes them one person or body politic in himself. Locke regards the incorporation of a society as something internal, and as consisting in the voluntary coherence of its members; Hobbes regards it as something external, and as consisting in the cohesive force applied by the head to the members. For Hobbes, there can be no corporation apart from the head; for Locke, there can be a corporate society even without a trustee. There is some warrant in the statute book after 1689 for Locke's view. 'The Public,' apart from the king and without the king, is treated in law as a corporate body responsible for the national debt. The king, as Charles II had shown at the time of the Stop of the Exchequer (1672), was not a punctual debtor; and though he might be trustee for the community, the community itself commended itself most as a responsible body to anxious creditors. The community, under the style of 'the Public,' accordingly becomes enough of a corporation to borrow from its members and pay them their interest: it even enters into financial transactions with the East India Company.[14]

2. On the other hand, Locke has no clear view of the nature or residence of sovereignty. He speaks at one time of the supreme power of the people, or in other words the community; he speaks at another of the supreme power of the legislative — which may, it is true, be the community, but may also be a body of representatives appointed by the community; and in still another context he remarks that 'where . . . the executive is vested in a single person who has also a share in the legislative, then that single person, in a very tolerable sense, may also be called the supreme power' (§ 151). 'Under *which* king, Bezonian,' one is tempted to ask — community; legislative; or single person? Locke has no certain answer. His thought turns less on sovereignty than on the rights of the individual and the limits set by those rights to the sovereign, whoever he may be. Behind these rights, as their

14. Maitland, Introduction to Gierke's *Political Theories of the Middle Age,* p. xxxvi.

stay and pillar, stands the majesty of Natural Law; and we may almost say that the ultimate control, or final sovereign, is neither the legislative nor even the community behind the legislative, but a system of Natural Law upholding natural rights. When the community acts, in the last resort, in some rare and great event of oppression, as master of its own fate, it acts in the name, and on behalf, of this final majesty.

3. There is, however, an anticipation in Locke's *Second Treatise* of Rousseau's idea of the permanent and permanently acting sovereignty of the community. In one passage, already quoted, he speaks of the rules of law agreed on *either* by the community *or* by those authorized by them to that purpose (§ 127); and in another and more explicit passage he suggests that 'the majority having . . . the whole power of the community naturally in them, may employ all that power in making laws for the community . . . and executing those laws by officers of their own appointing; and then the form of the government is a perfect democracy' (§ 132). But though he attains the idea of the permanent and permanently acting sovereignty of the community, Locke does not press the idea. He stands on the whole for the Whig grandees, entrenched in the House of Lords and influencing the House of Commons. He leaves the supreme power in the hands of the king in parliament (but it is to be a reformed parliament, and in §§ 157–8 he has a notable passage on the crying need of parliamentary reform); and he conceives the ultimate power of the community (or shall we say 'penultimate,' remembering that Natural Law is the last and farthest ultimate?) as only emerging when the legislative has to be removed or altered for acting contrary to the trust (§ 149) — when government is dissolved, and the people are at liberty to provide for themselves (§ 220) — when supreme power 'upon the forfeiture of their rulers . . . reverts to the society, and the people have a right to act as supreme' (§ 243). It is 'rarely, rarely' that the will of the community acts — only on those rare occasions when government is dissolved and revolution requires its remedy. Bosanquet has justly argued in his *Philosophical*

Theory of the State,[15] that though Locke attains the conception of the sovereignty of a general will, the will is general, but not actual. Similarly — but also conversely — though Hobbes attains the conception for a moment (in his version of the original contract of society), he throws it overboard as soon as it is attained, and plumps for a will — the will of Leviathan — which is actual, but not general. Rousseau may be said to attempt a reconciliation, by arguing for a general will which is as actual as the will of Leviathan is for Hobbes, and as general as the will of the community is for Locke. But did he succeed in his attempt?

III

Rousseau was not a philosopher — at any rate in the sense in which Hobbes, Locke, and Hume were philosophers. He was rather a *littérateur* of genius and an acute sensibility, who drew ideas from the surrounding air by the magnet of his intuition, and proceeded to make himself their incomparable exponent. Nor had he acquired, as Locke had acquired through his association with Shaftesbury, any practical experience of political affairs, except what he drew from his observation of the affairs of Geneva. He was an *à priori* theorist; and belonging to the age of the *Encyclopédie* he could theorize readily in many fields. He adorned and illuminated (or dazzled) the field of political theory with a large number of writings. The greatest was the *Du Contrat Social* of 1762; but it had been preceded by the *Discours sur l'Égalité* of 1755, by the 'Économie politique' (an article in the *Encyclopédie*) of the same year, and by two brief treatises of the year 1756 which analyze and criticize the international schemes of the Abbé de Saint-Pierre; and as it had had three predecessors, so it was followed by three successors — the last four of the *Lettres Écrites de la Montagne* (dealing partly with criticisms of the *Contrat Social*, but mainly with the constitutional problems raised by the action of the Genevan Government against himself and his writings), which appeared in 1764, the *Projet de Constitution pour la*

15. Pp. 104–6.

Corse of 1765, and the *Considérations sur le Gouvernement de Pologne* published posthumously in 1782 but written some ten years earlier.[16]

In the volume of his writings, and still more in the appeal of his style, Rousseau transcended Locke. Writing in French, the universal language of the eighteenth century, he appealed, as Locke never did, to a European public. In independence of thought, in power of philosophic reflection, and in maturity of judgment, he was inferior to Locke. He drew, in the main, on the current theory of the School of Natural Law, as it had been expounded in the seventeenth century by Grotius and Pufendorf, and as it was being expounded, in his own time, by two Swiss writers — Jacques Jean Burlamaqui (sometime member of the Council of State at Geneva) who published in 1747 his *Principes du Droit Naturel* and whose *Principes du Droit Politique* was published posthumously in 1751, and Emmerich de Vattel, of Neuchâtel, who published in 1758 his *Le Droit des gens, ou Principes de la Loi Naturelle*. It is in terms of the current theory of the School of Natural Law that Rousseau should properly be interpreted. It is true that at points — and those of the first importance — he departed from that theory. But it is also true that he was, in the main, its literary exponent; and it is also true that his very language and terminology are those of the School of Natural Law. When he writes, for instance, of the contract of society as producing *un corps moral et collectif*, he is reproducing the *corpus morale collectivum* of the Latin original from the authors of the School of Natural Law who wrote in Latin.[17]

The authors of the School of Natural Law had made their subject include three several branches of theory — a theory of society; a theory of the State; and a theory of the relations of States, or, in other words, a theory of international law and relations. Generally, it was the last of these branches of theory

16. *The Political Writings of Jean-Jacques Rousseau*, by C. E. Vaughan (Cambridge University Press, 1915), is a full edition of all the works mentioned, with introductions and notes.

17. See the writer's translation of Gierke's *Natural Law and the Theory of Society*, p. 324, n. 197, and also the Introduction, pp. xliii–vi.

which principally engaged their attention. But Vattel, if he
devoted three of the four books of his treatise to 'the nation
considered in its relation to others,' devoted the first of the
four to 'the nation considered in itself,' by which he meant a
theory of the State and of society generally. Rousseau would
appear to have intended to follow the same design. The four
books which now form the *Du Contrat Social* were intended,
like Vattel's first book, to contain an account of 'the nation
considered in itself'; but they were to be followed, as we learn
from a concluding sentence, by an account of 'the nation considered in its relation to others,' or, in other words, by a
theory of *le droit des gens*. 'After laying down the true principles of *droit politique*,' Rousseau wrote, 'and attempting to
establish the State on its basis, it will remain for us to consoli-
date it by its external relations, and that will comprise *le droit
des gens*.' But he found the theme too vast; and his treatise *Du
Contrat Social* is a propylaeum which leads into nothing
further.[18]

We may thus attach Rousseau to the School of Natural Law;
but we must also dissociate him from it. It is a significant
thing that the first draft of the *Contrat Social* contained a long
chapter, originally entitled 'Du droit naturel et de la Société
générale,' which was meant to refute the idea of natural law.
It is also a significant thing, and suggestive of an oscillating
mind, that the whole of this chapter is omitted in the final
draft and the printed version. Where did Rousseau actually
stand in regard to the idea of natural law? He hardly knew.
On the one hand he needed it — for how could there be a legal
thing like a contract of society unless there were a natural law
in terms and under the sanction of which a contract could be
made? — and he also found it in his authorities. On the other
hand he disliked it; and he felt in his bones that the nation

18. In his *Confessions* Rousseau speaks of having conceived the design of a general
work on *Institutions politiques* (external as well as internal?) as early as 1744,
when he was a secretary to the French Ambassador in Venice, and of having
detached the *Contrat Social* from what he had written of this work and 'resolved to burn all the rest.' See C. E. Vaughan's edition, vol. ii, pp. 1–2, and
vol. i, p. 438, n. 1.

made law, and not law the nation. How can we solve the antinomy?

The truth is that Rousseau was a romantic caught in the toils of a classical conception (if the idea of natural law may be called classical), in which he had dressed himself but in which he did not believe. He is two things in one, and he may be said both to belong and not to belong to the School of Natural Law.

On the one hand he has the individualism of that school, and he has also its universalism. He believes in the free individual, who is everywhere born free; he believes in a universal system of *droit politique*, which rests on a ubiquitous basis of individual liberty. If he had followed this line of belief to its ultimate conclusion, he would have been a votary of the natural rights of man and an apostle of undiluted liberalism. But there is another side to his teaching — a side which is at once very different, and, in its ultimate influence, far more important. The final sovereign of Rousseau is not an individual or a body of individuals. The final norm of social life is not a body of Natural Law, issuing in a system of natural rights, which proceeds from the reason of the individual, and is everywhere the same because that reason is everywhere identical. The sovereign of which he speaks is a 'moral person,' and the final norm is the 'general will' of that person. Now it is true that *persona moralis* was a term of art in the School of Natural Law, by which it was used to signify the nature of a corporate body as a 'person' which was something other than a physical person; and it is also true that the idea of the will of *omnes ut universi*, as distinct from the will of *omnes ut singuli*, was an idea also current in that school.[19] But it is equally true that the 'moral person' and 'general will' of Rousseau are ideas which transcend the limits of natural-law thought. Rousseau was a romantic before Romanticism; and he prepared the way for the new style of German thought which was to divinize the Folk-person and to historicize law as the expression in time of the general will or consciousness of right which proceeds from that person. Hegelianism and the Historical School of Law can find their nutriment in him, as he himself found his nutriment in the

19. Here again, in the distinction of *volonté de tous* and *volonté générale*, as well as in the use of the term *corps moral et collectif*, Rousseau reproduces in French what had been said in Latin before him.

School of Natural Law; and while the springs of the past flow into his teaching, the springs of the future also issue from it.[20]

This was the general setting, and the general influence, of the *Contrat Social*. A book so Janus-like can easily be interpreted in opposite senses. For a long time, and by most thinkers (as well as by the general public), it was interpreted as a paean on individualism. Its first sentence was a sufficient cue: 'man was born free, and everywhere he is in chains.' (But read only a few pages farther, and you will find, at the end of the first paragraph of the eighth chapter, that 'man ought to bless without ceasing the happy moment' — the moment of the social contract — which snatched him forever from the state of nature in which he was born, and 'turned a stupid and limited animal into an intelligent being and a man.' The pendulum swings rapidly.) But there were other excuses than a cursory reading of the opening words of the *Contrat Social* to justify this line of interpretation. Though the argument of the *Contrat Social*, if studied more closely, shows a rapid transition from an initial individualism towards collectivism, the earlier discourse on the *Origin and Foundations of Inequality*, which was written for, but failed to win, a prize offered by the Academy of Dijon, was more of a single piece, more purely a gospel of return to nature, and more of a paean on individualism. But it is not what Rousseau wrote before the *Contrat Social* — it is rather what followed after, in the days of the French Revolution — which explains the individualistic and emotional explanation of the philosophy of the *Contrat Social*, as a gospel of return to nature and the natural rights of man. It was easy to interpret the revolutionary *Declaration des Droits de l'Homme et du Citoyen*, first drafted in 1789, as a doctrine suckled on the milk of Rousseau; and when that was once done, it was easy to take the converse step, and to interpret Rousseau in the light of the *Declaration*, on the principle that he could best be known by the fruits supposed to be his. Actually, the influence of Rousseau's teaching on the French Revolution was far less

20. Quoted from the writer's introduction to his translation of Gierke's *Natural Law and the Theory of Society*, p. xlv.

than it has been supposed to be. Actually, too, his philosophy is far less a philosophy congenial to the France of 1789, and far more a philosophy congenial to the Germany of twenty and thirty years later (the Germany of Fichte and Hegel), than its individualist interpreters guessed. In effect, the philosophy of the *Contrat Social* is a 'philosophy of the bridge.' It marks the transition from natural law to an idealization of the national state. It may begin with Locke. But it ends by going back to the idealization of the Polis proclaimed in Plato's *Republic* (that, and not 'a return to nature,' is the real return of Rousseau), and in that act of going back to Plato it also goes forward into the future and becomes the *praeparatio evangelii Hegeliani*.

Three propositions may be advanced about the theory implicit in Rousseau's *Contrat Social*. In the first place, he regards the State as a progressive force which lifts man gradually upward from his primitive condition. Far from suggesting any return to a state of nature, he holds that the state of nature was unstable and became intolerable. The need of self-preservation dictated a contract, formed by the free will of all; and the society so created resulted in the establishment of justice and the attainment of a higher (because rational and self-conscious) morality. He believes in the miracle of the true State, rationally constructed and continuing to act by rational self-control — the miracle that turns a stupid and limited animal into an intelligent being. The State which he attacks — and he does attack the State — is only the perverted or despotic State, irrational because it is not the expression and organ of a free rational will.

The second proposition, which follows on the first, is that Rousseau is not a sentimentalist of nature, but the austere rationalist of political society. He objects to a patriarchal theory of the State, as he objects to a theory which bases it on force, because neither supplies a rational basis for political obligation. The only basis of the State which he will admit is the rational basis of a reasonable will. So far we may applaud his theory; but we may add that he would have escaped from a mist of confusion, and avoided the inexplicable miracle of a sudden contractual emergence from a primitive and stupid condition into a civilized blaze of enlightenment, if he had stopped to draw a distinction between society and the State. The society of the nation is a given fact of historical evolution, not created by any contract of society, but simply there. The State based on that society may be, or may become at a given moment of time (as France sought to do in 1789), the result of a creative act performed by the members of the society, acting through some assembly or convention for the purpose of making a constitution under which, and in terms of which, they are resolved to live for the future as a legal association.[21] In that case, and in that sense, a sort of contract may be said to underlie the State; but there is none which underlies the nation or the fact of national society.

The third proposition, which supplements and elucidates the second, is that Rousseau refuses to base the State on mere will, and insists that it must be based on a will of a particular quality — a general will directed to the attainment of the general good. When he speaks of this general will, or *volonté générale*, he uses the adjective to indicate the *quality* of the 'object' sought, and not the *quantity* of the 'subjects' or persons by whom it is sought. He rejects the mere will of all (*omnes ut singuli*); he argues for a will of a general intention (the will of *omnes ut universi*), which, far from being felt or expressed by all, may have to be expressed by a single man — the 'legislator' — who grasps its demand. The distinction here drawn between the will of all and the general will is, as we have already noticed, a distinction current among the writers of the School of Natural Law. But it receives a new edge in the theory of Rousseau; and it becomes in his hand a keen two-edged sword which seems to defend democracy (and primary democracy at that), but ends by arming Leviathan. Was not the Napoleon of the Code an admirable 'legislator'?

We touch at this point on a cardinal difficulty in Rousseau's thought. He wants to use his two-edged sword in defense of

21. See above, pp. xiii–xiv.

primary democracy, with no representatives, without any parties, and within the confines of the small State which primary democracy demands. He rejects representative government, or *parliamentary* democracy. But he only does so to find in the issue that he has rejected democracy itself. The unguided democracy of a primary assembly without any parties is a *souverain fainéant*. A 'mayor of the palace' must be provided; and we are left in the issue with Pepin of Heristal acting as 'legislator' for the *souverain*.

Rousseau belonged by origin to the city-state of Geneva, to whose 'magnificent, most honoured, and sovereign seigneurs' he dedicated his *Discours sur l'Égalité*. The free institutions and the civic life of Geneva affected his thought. We may almost say that they Hellenized his views into a belief in primary democracy, making him at once the votary of the contemporary Swiss canton and the apostle of the ancient civic republics of Athens and Sparta. We may also say, in another phrase, that they hypostatized his abstract idea of a sovereign general will, and turned it into a mundane matter of government by a primary assembly. There is much to be said in favor of the idea of the general will, taken in and by itself. The problem is the translation of the idea; its application in actual life; the discovery of the organ through which it acts. It is here that Rousseau sails into troubled waters; and it is here that we have to study the tacks and shifts of his thought.

We must begin our study with his version of the contract. He is like Hobbes in that he postulates the entire surrender of himself by each individual in the moment of the contract: he is unlike in that he regards each individual as surrendering himself to no man, but 'alienating himself with all his rights to the whole community' (I, c. 6). All, in the sense of all the individuals surrendering, form the *état*; all, in the sense of the community to which surrender is made, form the *souverain*; and all are thus, at one and the same time, a passive body of subjects and an active body of sovereigns. Here Rousseau enunciates his famous paradox, 'Each, giving himself to all gives himself to nobody': in other words, each gives himself

to himself, and each is still his own master. The paradox con-
ceáls a paralogism. I surrender all myself — and I surrender
it all to 999 others as well as myself: I only receive a fraction
of the sovereignty of the community; and ultimately I must
reflect that if I am the thousandth part of a tyrant, I am also
the whole of a slave. Leviathan is still Leviathan, even when
he is corporate.

There is a further difference, however, between the Leviathan of Hobbes and the Leviathan of Rousseau, over and
above the difference that the one Leviathan is a sole person
and the other a community of persons. The Leviathan of
Hobbes is at once a legislative and an executive, uniting all the
powers. The community which forms Rousseau's Leviathan
is purely a legislative, confining itself to the generalities of
legislation. For particular acts of authority the community institutes a *gouvernement*, an intermediary body for the execution of the laws which it makes, standing between itself as
souverain and itself in its capacity of *état* (III, c. 1). This government, however, is only a temporary and limited commission: while the sovereign community exists of itself, and its
sovereignty is inalienable and indivisible, the government exists by grace of the sovereign, and its power can be resumed
or divided at will by the sovereign. There is thus no contract
of government for Rousseau; he will only recognize the one
contract of society: 'there is only one contract in the State,
that of association, and it excludes all others' (III, c. 16).

But though the community may thus alienate executive
power to a commission (temporarily, and subject to the re-
sumption or division of such power as it may will), it never
alienates legislative power to representatives. That would be
to alienate sovereignty, which is impossible. Here Rousseau
differs fundamentally from Locke, who, if he had envisaged
the possibility of the community acting itself as legislative,
had also assumed that it would normally act through its representatives. Rousseau dismisses with a cavalier gesture any idea
of parliamentary democracy: representation is derived from
the iniquitous and absurd system of feudal government; rep-

resentatives in counsel are like mercenaries in war; the English people thinks it is free, and deceives itself greatly — it is only free during a general election (III, c. 15).[22] Banishing parliamentary democracy, he accordingly preaches the doctrine of a primary legislative, sovereign over an executive which serves as its *commissaire*.

There is an old lesson of politics — the principle of balance (John Stuart Mill could even call it the principle of antagonism) — which teaches us that, in actual life, States need a strong executive as well as a strong legislative. There is also another lesson of politics — perhaps more recent, but certainly no less important — which teaches us that a strong executive and a strong legislative must not simply confront one another, on a system of division of powers, but must also cooperate with one another, in a system of reciprocity and mutual confidence. Rousseau paid little heed to the first of these lessons; and we can hardly blame him (after all he was writing in 1762, and a developed cabinet system of reciprocity between the executive and the legislative power still lay in the future) for not thinking of the second. He was hardly concerned with practical necessities: he was hot in pursuit of the logical symmetry of an ideal scheme of popular sovereignty. We may therefore limit our criticism to an inquiry into its logic. Was it, after all, symmetrical; and was it a consistent scheme?

On his scheme the generality was to be the sovereign body, in the capacity of a legislative; and the reason was that the generality, and only the generality, could be trusted to will a general will, and to rise superior to particular and sectional interests. Was this a well-founded trust? Hardly; for when his journey begins the traveler finds that he has to traverse ranges — and they are somewhat mountainous ranges — of logical

22. This attitude to English parliamentarianism was inherited, or at any rate shared, by Kant and Hegel. Kant regarded the English constitution as an oligarchy, with parliament acting not only as legislative but also, through its ministers, as executive — and that in the interests of a party, or even of individuals. Hegel regarded parliament as an institution of *die bürgerliche Gesellschaft* — bourgeois or tradesmen society — concerned to advance particular interests, and therefore inferior to a monarch who stood above the play of society.

difficulty. In the first place he has to distinguish a real general will from a mere will of all — the will of a true collectivity from a mere aggregate of wills. How is this to be done? Rousseau answers, 'By the presence or absence of party-lines in voting' (II, c. 3). If party is present, and a great clique carries the day, the general good will be sacrificed; if there are no parties, and each individual votes individually, the individual selfishnesses in voting will cancel one another, and the general good will be the residuum. In an age which still interpreted party as faction (the age, for example, of Bolingbroke and the theory of the superiority of *la patrie* to *le parti*) this was perhaps a natural view; and yet it is hardly logical to argue that individualism in voting is the royal road which leads to collectivism in decision. Party, after all, is a necessary means of precipitating in a set form a program of the general good, and of realizing that program in the strength of concerted action; and Burke was wiser than Rousseau when he argued at the end of his pamphlet on *The Present Discontents* (published eight years after the *Contrat Social*) that party was 'a body of men united for promoting . . . the *national* interest upon some particular principle.' The true freedom of the citizen consists in the citizens' choice; and where is the citizen's choice unless there are alternative programs, presented by different parties, between which choice can be made? It is not the absence, but the presence, of party — if party is only organized as a body of opinion about the national interest and the general good, and not corrupted into a sum of personal interests — which is the true criterion of the existence of a general will.

In the second place — and here we reach another range of logical difficulty — the question arises whether the whole people, if it be set to legislate for itself, can ever discover for itself the general good which, *ex hypothesi*, it really wishes to enact. To distil the requirements of the general good in an actual measure of legislation is something which requires both an intellectual effort of sustained reflection (or, better, sustained discussion) and a moral effort of abstinence from private and sinister interests: it will not come of itself, through the automatic cancellation of private interests by one another. Rousseau himself is aware of the necessity of distillation; but he will not trust representatives to do this necessary work. He accordingly introduces a wise legislator — antique in idea, but contemporary history has shown us that he may be terribly modern in practice — as a *deus ex machina* to tell the people what they ought to will. 'Of itself, the people always wishes the good; of itself, it does not always see it' (II, c. 6). Here emerges the 'leader' and 'guide . . .' Here too, as we have already noticed, the sword of Rousseau turns round in his hand, and shows its other edge.

In effect, and in the last resort, Rousseau is a totalitarian. We need not exaggerate the importance of the 'legislator' to arrive at this result. Omit the legislator altogether: the result is still there. Imagine Rousseau a perfect democrat: his perfect democracy is still a multiple autocrat. He leaves no safeguard against the omnipotence of the *souverain*. It is significant that the *Contrat Social* ends with the suggestion of religious persecution. The man who has publicly acknowledged the articles of the civil faith, which it belongs to the sovereign to determine, and who has then acted as if he did not believe in those articles — *qu'il soit puni de mort*. Rousseau was so far from believing in *les droits de l'homme* that he went to the other extreme. He was so convinced that it was enough for the individual to enjoy political rights (as a fraction of the collectivity) that he forgot the necessity of his enjoying the rights of 'civil and religious liberty.' The English Whigs and their philosopher Locke, with all their faults, were wiser in their generation.

There is still a third range of logical difficulty, less terrible than the second, but still sufficiently formidable. How can the great state of modern times reconcile its size to a primary legislative? Rousseau himself realized that this theory suited only the small community, such as Greece had known and Switzerland still knew; and he would have reconciled it to the greater size of the modern state either by advocating a movable metropolis, if a state had many towns, or by suggesting some system of federalism. The suggestion of federalism remained merely a suggestion: [23] the advocacy of a movable metropolis may remind us of an early phase in the history of Trade Unionism (described in the first chapter, entitled 'Primitive Democracy,' of the Webbs' book on *Industrial Democracy*), when trade union branches in different towns were made in rotation the 'governing branch' of the whole of that union for a fixed period. The phase soon passed; and the later development of Trade Unionism admirably shows (though sometimes with lapses back to 'the primitive') the impracticability of Rousseauism, and the need of representative institutions in any large society which seeks to follow the arduous path of true self-government.

Here we may leave the *Contrat Social*. One may say of it, in an old medieval distich,

> Hic liber est in quo quaerit sua dogmata quisque,
> Invenit et pariter dogmata quisque sua.

You can find your own dogmas in Rousseau, whether you belong to the Left (and especially to the left of the Left) or whether you belong to the Right (and especially to the right of the Right). The only dogmas which it is difficult to find are those of the Center — the Center to which the English Whigs, whom a later generation called Liberals, have really always belonged, though they have always professed to belong to the Left. There is no comfort for the Center in all the shot fabric of Rousseau's book. That is why it is natural, and even permissible, to prefer the hodden gray of Locke's cloth to the brilliant but parti-colored silk of Rousseau . . . Yet what a magic has style — above all when the language is French. It makes the tour of the world, and it carries with it everywhere the ideas which it has adorned. It is curious to reflect what would have happened to Rousseau's ideas if they

---

23. Federalism is only mentioned in a single sentence of the *Contrat Social*, but there is a story that Rousseau wrote sixteen chapters on the subject, which he entrusted in manuscript to a friend who destroyed them at the beginning of the French Revolution. See Vaughan's edition of *The Political Writings of Rousseau*, vol. i, pp. 95–102, and vol. ii, pp. 135–6.

had been given, about 1760, to an English writer in Cambridge, or a German writer in the University of Halle, and he had been told to express them to the best of his ability. Would the English writer have set the Cam on fire — let alone the Thames? Or the German the Saale — let alone the Rhine?

IV

Locke and Rousseau, if in different ways and different degrees, accepted the idea of the social contract: Hume, more historically minded, and more conservative in his convictions, was its critic. His skeptical intellect led him to approach political theories — the theory of divine right as well as the theory of social contract, but more especially the latter — with a touch of acid realism, which was mingled with a half-ironical suavity. 'There is something,' he seems to say, 'in your different theories; but less, much less, than you think.'

The essay 'Of the original contract' was first published (along with an essay 'Of passive obedience' and a suggestive essay 'Of national characters') in the new edition of *Essays Moral and Political* which appeared in 1748. It starts from the proposition that the theory of divine right and that of original contract are both the constructions of a party — a proposition which implies that they were built by the English Whigs and Tories, and built in the course of the last hundred years. The proposition may be disputed. Both theories have a wider range than England; and both go back to the Middle Ages, or even earlier. When Hume ends his essay by noting that 'scarce any man, till very lately, ever imagined that government was founded on compact,' and makes this an argument for concluding that 'it is certain that it cannot, in general, have any such foundation,' he is on erroneous ground.

Leaving this error on one side, we may proceed to ask what sort of contract Hume has in his mind. It would appear to be the contract of government, and not the contract of society — the original contract between the king and the people which had been approved by the Convention Parliament in 1689. It is a contract 'by which the subjects have tacitly reserved the power of resisting their sovereign, whenever they find themselves aggrieved by that authority with which they have, for certain purposes, voluntarily entrusted him.' This theory of contract stands opposed to the other theory which makes authority a divine commission — not a popular trust — and, as such, sacred and inviolate. Both theories, to Hume, have some truth; but neither is wholly true. He has little to say of the theory of divine right, except that, by the same logic by which it covers the sovereign power, it must equally cover every petty jurisdiction, and 'a constable, therefore, no less than a king, acts by a divine commission.' His real theme is the theory of original contract; and here he allows that government, 'if we trace it to its first origin in the woods and deserts,' certainly *originated* in consent — but he equally denies that in the world of today it *exists* by consent. The original contract has long been obliterated by a thousand changes of government: almost all governments now existing are founded on usurpation, or conquest, or both. There may still be some rare disorderly popular elections of government; if there are, they are to be deprecated; and in any case the English Revolution of 1688 was not one of them — 'it was only the majority of seven hundred who determined that change [in Hume's view, merely a change of the succession] for near ten millions.' The most that can be allowed is that the consent of the people is *one* just foundation of government; but 'it has very seldom had place in any degree, and never almost in its full extent.' To suppose *all* government based on consent is to suppose 'all men possessed of so perfect an understanding as always to know their own interests' — 'but this state of perfection is likewise much superior to human nature.' And if you take refuge in the argument that at any rate there is tacit consent, or implied consent, and support your argument by saying that a man gives such consent merely by staying in a country when he could leave it if he so desired — well, the answer is that there is no consent, of any sort, unless there is freedom of choice, and there is actually no such freedom. Why, you cannot even emigrate without permission if the prince chooses so to ordain.

Hitherto the argument of Hume has rested on an appeal to the evidence of history and the observation of facts. In the second part of the essay he attempts a more philosophical refutation of the idea of contract. Distinguishing the moral duties to which we are instinctively impelled (such as pity for the unfortunate) from those to which we are impelled by a sense of obligation 'when we consider the necessities of human society,' he proceeds to consider three duties which belong to the latter category. There is justice, or a regard to the property of others; there is fidelity, or the observance of promises; there is the political or civil duty of allegiance. These duties flow, he argues, *and flow independently*, from the sense of obligation imposed by the necessities of human society. Why base allegiance on fidelity, as the contractarians do when they refer the duties of subjects (and with them the duties of sovereigns) to the foundation of observance of promises supposed to be expressed in a contract? We must keep allegiance and fidelity separate. 'The obligation to allegiance being of like force and authority with the obligation to fidelity, we gain nothing by resolving the one into the other. The general interests or necessities of society are sufficient to establish both.'

The answer which Hume thus gives to the problem of political obligation may be briefly summarized. 'Obey the powers that be. It is true that they are ordained by usurpation, or force, or both; but you must none the less pay them obedience for the simple reason that society could not otherwise subsist.' It is hardly a satisfactory answer. There is something, after all, in the idea of fidelity which goes deeper than the idea of allegiance, and which is really the basis of allegiance. There is such a thing (to use Burke's phrase) as an 'engagement or pact of the constitution,' [24] which demands the fidelity both of rulers and subjects; under which both equally stand; and to which both are equally bound. What is the proof of this en-

24. The reader is referred to the argument at the end of the first section, pp. xiii–xiv.

gagement or pact? Well, there is one sort of proof which Hume himself is bound, upon his own showing, to admit. He ends the essay 'Of original contract' by 'an appeal to general opinion.' 'In all questions with regard to morals,' he writes, 'there is really no other standard by which any controversy can be decided.' What then was the general opinion of Hume's own country (if, like him, we may confine our view within the four seas) about the problem of political obligation? Surely it was in his day, as it had been before his day and continued to be after his day, an opinion that obligation was not unilateral; that it embraced both sovereign and subject in a common pact or engagement; that both, in a word, were equally bound by the law of the constitution. The opinion is as old as Magna Carta: it is also as recent as the most recent theory of the sovereignty of the constitution — the constitution which, in its essence, may be called the political contract.

Here we may leave the idea of contract. Historians have not loved the idea; they know the records of history, and they do not believe that there ever was such a thing. Lawyers have not loved the idea: they know what actual contracts are, how lawyers draft them and courts enforce them, and they do not believe that the social contract is anything more than a sham — a *quasi* or an *als ob*. Where historians and lawyers are agreed, a mere layman may think it wise to be silent. And yet there must be some 'soul of truth' in so old and inveterate an idea,

> Would men observingly distil it out.

Perhaps enough has already been said, in the course of the argument, to suggest where this soul of truth may be sought. Meanwhile it is not inapposite — though it may also be a mere offering on the altar of pragmatism — to end by recurring to the good service which the doctrine of contract (and the doctrine of natural law which is behind it, or above it) has rendered to the cause of liberty, and to the general cause of political progress. Its fruits do not prove its truth. But they deserve to be remembered. The English Revolution of 1688 was cradled in contract, and the American Revolution of 1776 had the same ancestry. In both the idea of contract can plead some title to have contributed to the cause of liberty. It may seem more paradoxical — perhaps purely paradoxical — to argue that the idea of contract has contributed to the cause of political progress. Is not a deed of contract a dead hand on political development, and is not a belief in 'historical growth' the true philosophy for the progressive? Perhaps we may answer that things are not always what they seem. A deed, if we conceive it broadly enough, may be a beckoning hand to progress rather than a dead hand on development. The idea of an original contract and a deed of political association may have its restrictive side. This was the argument of Tom Paine when he opened the *Rights of Man* by denouncing Burke for seeking to lay the dead hand of 1689 on the living present of 1791, and for saying as it were to the Convention Parliament and its antique notion of contract, 'O Parliament, live for ever.' But the idea of contract and the deed has also its constructive side. It implies that political development is not an automatic growth; that it springs from human will, and the act and deed of men; and that it must continue to spring from, and must even be accelerated by, the same creative force. It may be a paradox, but it is also a truth, that those who cling to the idea of growth may sometimes oppose a new growth, having only too much of the historic sense — and equally that those who cling to the idea of an original deed of creation may often encourage reform and progress, even though (or perhaps because) they have little of the sense of historic growth.

1946

NOTE. One half of this volume is a new translation of Rousseau's *Du Contrat Social*. Locke's *Second Treatise* and Hume's *Essay* (the texts of which have been carefully checked with the original editions) are added as English counterparts and complements. The writer of the Introduction would venture to suggest that the collocation may furnish the reader with an admirable exercise in thought. He would also draw the reader's attention to the clarity of Mr. Hopkins's translation, which seems to him to provide a version faithful not only to Rousseau's thought, but also to his style.

E. B.

John Locke

1632 – 1704

AN ESSAY CONCERNING THE TRUE ORIGINAL, EXTENT AND END OF CIVIL GOVERNMENT

1. It having been shewn in the foregoing discourse,

    1. That Adam had not, either by natural right of father-hood, nor by positive donation from God, any such authority over his children, or dominion over the world, as is pretended.

    2. That if he had, his heirs yet had no right to it.

    3. That if his heirs had, there being no law of nature nor positive law of God that determines which is the right heir in all cases that may arise, the right of succession, and consequently of bearing rule, could not have been certainly determined.

    4. That if even that had been determined, yet the knowledge of which is the eldest line of Adam's posterity being so long since utterly lost, that in the races of mankind and families of the world, there remains not to one above another, the least pretence to be the eldest house, and to have the right of inheritance.

All these premises having, as I think, been clearly made out, it is impossible that the rulers now on earth should make any benefit, or derive any the least shadow of authority from that, which is held to be the fountain of all power, *Adam's private dominion and paternal jurisdiction*; so that he that will not give just occasion to think that all government in the world is the product only of force and violence, and that men live together by no other rules but that of beasts, where the strongest carries it, and so lay a foundation for perpetual disorder and mischief, tumult, sedition, and rebellion (things that the followers of that hypothesis so loudly cry out against), must of necessity find out another rise of government, another original of political power, and another way of designing and knowing the persons that have it, than what Sir Robert Filmer hath taught us.

    2. To this purpose, I think it may not be amiss, to set down what I take to be political power; that the power of a magis-

trate over a subject may be distinguished from that of a father
over his children, a master over his servant, a husband over
his wife, and a lord over his slave. All which distinct powers
happening sometimes together in the same man, if he be considered under these different relations, it may help us to distinguish these powers one from another, and shew the difference betwixt a ruler of a commonwealth, a father of a family,
and a captain of a galley.

3. Political power, then, I take to be a right of making laws
with penalties of death, and consequently all less penalties, for
the regulating and preserving of property, and of employing
the force of the community, in the execution of such laws, and
in the defence of the commonwealth from foreign injury; and
all this only for the public good.

(((II)))

OF THE STATE OF NATURE

4. To understand political power aright, and derive it from
its original, we must consider, what state all men are naturally
in, and that is, a state of perfect freedom to order their actions,
and dispose of their possessions and persons, as they think fit,
within the bounds of the law of nature, without asking leave,
or depending upon the will of any other man.

A state also of equality, wherein all the power and jurisdiction is reciprocal, no one having more than another; there
being nothing more evident, than that creatures of the same
species and rank, promiscuously born to all the same advantages of nature, and the use of the same faculties, should also
be equal one amongst another without subordination or subjection, unless the lord and master of them all should, by any
manifest declaration of his will, set one above another, and
confer on him, by an evident and clear appointment, an undoubted right to dominion and sovereignty.

5. This equality of men by nature, the judicious Hooker
looks upon as so evident in itself, and beyond all question,

that he makes it the foundation of that obligation to mutual love amongst men, on which he builds the duties they owe one another, and from whence he derives the great maxims of justice and charity. His words are:

'The like natural inducement hath brought men to know that it is no less their duty, to love others than themselves; for seeing those things which are equal, must needs all have one measure; if I cannot but wish to receive good, even as much at every man's hands, as any man can wish unto his own soul, how should I look to have any part of my desire herein satisfied, unless myself be careful to satisfy the like desire, which is undoubtedly in other men. We all being of one and the same nature; to have any thing offered them repugnant to this desire, must needs in all respects grieve them as much as me; so that if I do harm, I must look to suffer, there being no reason that others should shew greater measure of love to me, than they have by me shewed unto them; my desire therefore to be loved of my equals in nature, as much as possible may be, imposeth upon me a natural duty of bearing to themward fully the like affection; from which relation of equality between ourselves and them that are as ourselves, what several rules and canons natural reason hath drawn, for direction of life, no man is ignorant.' *Eccl. Pol.*, lib. i.

6. But though this be a state of liberty, yet it is not a state of licence: though man in that state have an uncontrollable liberty to dispose of his person or possessions, yet he has not liberty to destroy himself, or so much as any creature in his possession, but where some nobler use than its bare preservation calls for it. The state of nature has a law of nature to govern it, which obliges every one, and reason, which is that law, teaches all mankind, who will but consult it, that being all equal and independent, no one ought to harm another in his life, health, liberty, or possessions: for men being all the workmanship of one omnipotent, and infinitely wise maker; all the servants of one sovereign master, sent into the world by his order, and about his business; they are his property,

whose workmanship they are, made to last during his, not one another's pleasure: and being furnished with like faculties, sharing all in one community of nature, there cannot be supposed any such subordination among us, that may authorize us to destroy one another, as if we were made for one another's uses, as the inferior ranks of creatures are for ours. Every one, as he is bound to preserve himself, and not to quit his station wilfully, so by the like reason, when his own preservation comes not in competition, ought he as much as he can to preserve the rest of mankind, and not unless it be to do justice on an offender, take away, or impair the life, or what tends to the preservation of the life, the liberty, health, limb or goods of another.

7. And that all men may be restrained from invading others rights, and from doing hurt to one another, and the law of nature be observed, which willeth the peace and preservation of all mankind, the execution of the law of nature is, in that state, put into every man's hands, whereby every one has a right to punish the transgressors of that law to such a degree, as may hinder its violation. For the law of nature would, as all other laws that concern men in this world, be in vain, if there were nobody that in the state of nature had a power to execute that law, and thereby preserve the innocent and restrain offenders. And if any one in the state of nature may punish another for any evil he has done, every one may do so: for in that state of perfect equality where naturally there is no superiority or jurisdiction of one over another, what any may do in prosecution of that law, every one must needs have a right to do.

8. And thus, in the state of nature, one man comes by a power over another; but yet no absolute or arbitrary power, to use a criminal, when he has got him in his hands, according to the passionate heats, or boundless extravagancy of his own will; but only to retribute to him, so far as calm reason and conscience dictates, what is proportionate to his transgression, which is so much as may serve for reparation and restraint: for these two are the only reasons why one man may

lawfully do harm to another, which is that we call punishment. In transgressing the law of nature, the offender declares himself to live by another rule than that of reason and common equity, which is that measure God has set to the actions of men for their mutual security, and so he becomes dangerous to mankind, the tie, which is to secure them from injury and violence, being slighted and broken by him, which being a trespass against the whole species, and the peace and safety of it, provided for by the law of nature, every man upon this score, by the right he hath to preserve mankind in general, may restrain, or where it is necessary, destroy things noxious to them, and so may bring such evil on any one, who hath transgressed that law, as may make him repent the doing of it, and thereby deter him, and, by his example others, from doing the like mischief. And in this case, and upon this ground, every man hath a right to punish the offender, and be executioner of the law of nature.

9. I doubt not but this will seem a very strange doctrine to some men; but before they condemn it, I desire them to resolve me, by what right any prince or state can put to death, or punish an alien, for any crime he commits in their country. 'Tis certain their laws, by virtue of any sanction they receive from the promulgated will of the legislative, reach not a stranger: they speak not to him, nor, if they did, is he bound to hearken to them. The legislative authority, by which they are in force over the subjects of that commonwealth, hath no power over him. Those who have the supreme power of making laws in England, France or Holland, are to an Indian, but like the rest of the world, men without authority: and therefore, if by the law of nature every man hath not a power to punish offences against it, as he soberly judges the case to require, I see not how the magistrate of any community can punish an alien of another country; since, in reference to him, they can have no more power than what every man naturally may have over another.

10. Besides the crime which consists in violating the law, and varying from the right rule of reason, whereby a man so

far becomes degenerate, and declares himself to quit the principles of human nature and to be a noxious creature, there is commonly injury done, and some person or other, some other man receives damage by his transgression; in which case he who hath received any damage, has, besides the right of punishment common to him with other men, a particular right to seek reparation from him that has done it: and any other person, who finds it just, may also join with him that is injured, and assist him in recovering from the offender so much as may make satisfaction for the harm he has suffered.

11. From these two distinct rights, the one of punishing the crime for restraint, and preventing the like offence, which right of punishing is in everybody; the other of taking reparation, which belongs only to the injured party, comes it to pass that the magistrate, who by being magistrate hath the common right of punishing put into his hands, can often, where the public good demands not the execution of the law, remit the punishment of criminal offences by his own authority, but yet cannot remit the satisfaction due to any private man for the damage he has received. That, he who has suffered the damage has a right to demand in his own name, and he alone can remit: the damnified person has this power of appropriating to himself the goods or service of the offender, by right of self-preservation, as every man has a power to punish the crime, to prevent its being committed again, by the right he has of preserving all mankind, and doing all reasonable things he can in order to that end: and thus it is, that every man, in the state of nature, has a power to kill a murderer, both to deter others from doing the like injury, which no reparation can compensate, by the example of the punishment that attends it from every body, and also to secure men from the attempts of a criminal, who having renounced reason, the common rule and measure God hath given to mankind, hath, by the unjust violence and slaughter he hath committed upon one, declared war against all mankind, and therefore may be destroyed as a lion or a tiger, one

of those wild savage beasts, with whom men can have no society nor security: and upon this is grounded that great law of nature, *Whoso sheddeth man's blood, by man shall his blood be shed*. And Cain was so fully convinced, that every one had a right to destroy such a criminal, that after the murder of his brother, he cries out, *Every one that findeth me shall slay me;* so plain was it writ in the hearts of all mankind.

12. By the same reason may a man in the state of nature punish the lesser breaches of that law. It will perhaps be demanded, with death? I answer, each transgression may be punished to that degree, and with so much severity, as will suffice to make it an ill bargain to the offender, give him cause to repent, and terrify others from doing the like. Every offence, that can be committed in the state of nature, may in the state of nature be also punished equally, and as far forth as it may, in a commonwealth: for though it would be besides my present purpose, to enter here into the particulars of the law of nature, or its measures of punishment; yet, it is certain there is such a law, and that too as intelligible and plain to a rational creature, and a studier of that law, as the positive laws of commonwealths: nay, possibly plainer; as much as reason is easier to be understood, than the fancies and intricate contrivances of men, following contrary and hidden interests put into words; for so truly are a great part of the municipal laws of countries, which are only so far right, as they are founded on the law of nature, by which they are to be regulated and interpreted.

13. To this strange doctrine, *viz.* That in the state of nature every one has the executive power of the law of nature, I doubt not but it will be objected, that it is unreasonable for men to be judges in their own cases, that self-love will make men partial to themselves and their friends: and on the other side, ill-nature, passion and revenge will carry them too far in punishing others; and hence nothing but confusion and disorder will follow; and that therefore God hath certainly appointed government to restrain the partiality and violence of men. I easily grant that civil government is the proper

remedy for the inconveniences of the state of nature, which must certainly be great where men may be judges in their own case, since 'tis easy to be imagined, that he who was so unjust as to do his brother an injury, will scarce be so just as to condemn himself for it; but I shall desire those who make this objection, to remember, that absolute monarchs are but men; and if government is to be the remedy of those evils, which necessarily follow from men's being judges in their own cases, and the state of nature is therefore not to be endured, I desire to know what kind of government that is, and how much better it is than the state of nature, where one man commanding a multitude, has the liberty to be judge in his own case, and may do to all his subjects whatever he pleases, without the least question or control of those who execute his pleasure? and in whatsoever he doth, whether led by reason, mistake or passion, must be submitted to? which men in the state of nature are not bound to do one to another. And if he that judges, judges amiss in his own, or any other case, he is answerable for it to the rest of mankind.

14. 'Tis often asked as a mighty objection, where are, or ever were there any men in such a state of nature? To which it may suffice as an answer at present, that since all princes and rulers of *independent* governments all through the world, are in a state of nature, 'tis plain the world never was, nor never will be, without numbers of men in that state. I have named all governors of *independent* communities, whether they are, or are not, in league with others: for 'tis not every compact that puts an end to the state of nature between men, but only this one of agreeing together mutually to enter into one community, and make one body politic; other promises, and compacts, men may make one with another, and yet still be in the state of nature. The promises and bargains for truck, etc. between the two men in the desert island, mentioned by Garcilasso de la Vega, in his history of Peru; or between a Swiss and an Indian, in the woods of America, are binding to them, though they are perfectly in a state of nature, in reference to one another: for truth and keeping of

faith belongs to men as men, and not as members of society.

15. To those that say, there were never any men in the state of nature, I will not only oppose the authority of the judicious Hooker, *Eccl. Pol.* lib. i. *sect.* 10, where he says, 'the laws which have been hitherto mentioned, *i.e.*, the laws of nature, do bind men absolutely, even as they are men, although they have never any settled fellowship, never any solemn agreement amongst themselves what to do, or not to do: but forasmuch as we are not by ourselves sufficient to furnish ourselves with competent store of things, needful for such a life as our nature doth desire, a life fit for the dignity of man; therefore to supply those defects and imperfections which are in us, as living singly and solely by ourselves, we are naturally induced to seek communion and fellowship with others: this was the cause of men uniting themselves at first in politic societies.' But I moreover affirm, that all men are naturally in that state, and remain so, till by their own consents they make themselves members of some politic society; and I doubt not in the sequel of this discourse, to make it very clear.

(((III)))

OF THE STATE OF WAR

16. The state of war is a state of enmity and destruction; and therefore declaring by word or action, not a passionate and hasty, but sedate, settled design upon another man's life, puts him in a state of war with him against whom he has declared such an intention, and so has exposed his life to the other's power to be taken away by him, or any one that joins with him in his defence, and espouses his quarrel, it being reasonable and just I should have a right to destroy that which threatens me with destruction; for by the fundamental law of nature, man being to be preserved, as much as possible, when all cannot be preserved, the safety of the innocent is to be preferred; and one may destroy a man who makes war upon him, or has discovered an enmity to his be-

ing, for the same reason that he may kill a wolf or a lion, because such men are not under the ties of the common law of reason, have no other rule but that of force and violence, and so may be treated as beasts of prey, those dangerous and noxious creatures that will be sure to destroy him whenever he falls into their power.

17. And hence it is that he who attempts to get another man into his absolute power does thereby put himself into a state of war with him; it being to be understood as a declaration of a design upon his life. For I have reason to conclude that he who would get me into his power without my consent would use me as he pleased when he had got me there, and destroy me too when he had a fancy to it; for nobody can desire to have me in his absolute power unless it be to compel me by force to that which is against the right of my freedom — *i.e.* make me a slave. To be free from such force is the only security of my preservation, and reason bids me look on him as an enemy to my preservation who would take away that freedom which is the fence to it; so that he who makes an attempt to enslave me thereby puts himself into a state of war with me. He that in the state of nature would take away the freedom that belongs to any one in that state must necessarily be supposed to have a design to take away everything else, that freedom being the foundation of all the rest; as he that in the state of society would take away the freedom belonging to those of that society or commonwealth must be supposed to design to take away from them everything else, and so be looked on as in a state of war.

18. This makes it lawful for a man to kill a thief who has not in the least hurt him, nor declared any design upon his life, any farther than by the use of force, so to get him in his power as to take away his money, or what he pleases, from him; because using force, where he has no right to get me into his power, let his pretence be what it will, I have no reason to suppose that he who would take away my liberty would not, when he had me in his power, take away everything else. And therefore it is lawful for me to treat him as

one who has put himself into a state of war with me — *i.e.*, kill him if I can; for to that hazard does he justly expose himself whoever introduces a state of war, and is aggressor in it.

19. And here we have the plain difference between the state of nature and the state of war, which however some men have confounded, are as far distant as a state of peace, goodwill, mutual assistance, and preservation; and a state of enmity, malice, violence and mutual destruction are one from another. Men living together according to reason without a common superior on earth, with authority to judge between them, are properly in the state of nature. But force, or a declared design of force upon the person of another, where there is no common superior on earth to appeal to for relief, is the state of war; and 'tis the want of such an appeal gives a man the right of war even against an aggressor, though he be in society and a fellow-subject. Thus, a thief whom I cannot harm, but by appeal to the law, for having stolen all that I am worth, I may kill when he sets on me to rob me but of my horse or coat, because the law, which was made for my preservation, where it cannot interpose to secure my life from present force, which if lost is capable of no reparation, permits me my own defence and the right of war, a liberty to kill the aggressor, because the aggressor allows not time to appeal to our common judge, nor the decision of the law, for remedy in a case where the mischief may be irreparable. Want of a common judge with authority puts all men in a state of nature; force without right upon a man's person makes a state of war both where there is, and is not, a common judge.

20. But when the actual force is over, the state of war ceases between those that are in society and are equally on both sides subjected to the fair determination of the law; because then there lies open the remedy of appeal for the past injury, and to prevent future harm; but where no such appeal is, as in the state of nature, for want of positive laws, and judges with authority to appeal to, the state of war, once begun, continues with a right to the innocent party to de-

stroy the other whenever he can, until the aggressor offers
peace, and desires reconciliation on such terms as may repair
any wrongs he has already done, and secure the innocent for
the future; nay, where an appeal to the law and constituted
judges lies open, but the remedy is denied by a manifest
perverting of justice, and a barefaced wresting of the laws to
protect or indemnify the violence or injuries of some men or
party of men, there it is hard to imagine any thing but a state
of war: for wherever violence is used, and injury done,
though by hands appointed to administer justice, it is still
violence and injury, however coloured with the name, pretences, or forms of law, the end whereof being to protect and
redress the innocent, by an unbiassed application of it, to
all who are under it; wherever that is not *bona fide* done, war
is made upon the sufferers, who having no appeal on earth
to right them, they are left to the only remedy in such cases,
an appeal to Heaven.

21. To avoid this state of war (wherein there is no appeal
but to heaven, and wherein every the least difference is apt
to end, where there is no authority to decide between the
contenders) is one great reason of men's putting themselves
into society, and quitting the state of nature. For where there
is an authority, a power on earth from which relief can be
had by appeal, there the continuance of the state of war is
excluded, and the controversy is decided by that power. Had
there been any such court, any superior jurisdiction on earth,
to determine the right between Jephtha and the Ammonites,
they had never come to a state of war, but we see he was
forced to appeal to Heaven. *The Lord the judge* (says he) *be
judge this day between the Children of Israel, and the Children
of Ammon. Judges* xi. 27, and then prosecuting and relying
on his appeal, he leads out his army to battle. And therefore
in such controversies, where the question is put, *who shall
be judge?* it cannot be meant, who shall decide the controversy; every one knows what Jephtha here tells us, that *the
Lord the judge* shall judge. Where there is no judge on earth,
the appeal lies to God in heaven. That question then cannot

mean, Who shall judge whether another hath put himself in a state of war with me, and whether I may, as Jephtha did, appeal to Heaven in it? Of that I myself can only be judge in my own conscience, as I will answer it at the one great day, to the supreme Judge of all men.

(((IV)))

OF SLAVERY

22. The natural liberty of man is to be free from any superior power on earth, and not to be under the will or legislative authority of man, but to have only the law of Nature for his rule. The liberty of man in society is to be under no other legislative power but that established by consent in the commonwealth, nor under the dominion of any will, or restraint of any law, but what the legislative shall enact according to the trust put in it. Freedom, then, is not what Sir Robert Filmer tells us, *O.A.* 55. *A liberty for every one to do what he lists, to live as he pleases, and not to be tied by any laws*; but freedom of men under government is to have a standing rule to live by, common to every one of that society, and made by the legislative power erected in it. A liberty to follow my own will in all things where the rule prescribes not, not to be subject to the inconstant, uncertain, unknown, arbitrary will of another man, as freedom of nature is to be under no other restraint but the law of nature.

23. This freedom from absolute, arbitrary power is so necessary to, and closely joined with, a man's preservation, that he cannot part with it but by what forfeits his preservation and life together. For a man, not having the power of his own life, cannot, by compact or his own consent, enslave himself to any one, nor put himself under the absolute, arbitrary power of another to take away his life when he pleases. Nobody can give more power than he has himself, and he that cannot take away his own life cannot give another power over it. Indeed, having by his fault forfeited his own life by

some act that deserves death, he to whom he has forfeited it may, when he has him in his power, delay to take it, and make use of him to his own service; and he does him no injury by it. For, whenever he finds the hardship of his slavery outweigh the value of his life, 'tis in his power, by resisting the will of his master, to draw on himself the death he desires.

24. This is the perfect condition of slavery, which is nothing else but the state of war continued between a lawful conqueror and a captive. For, if once compact enter between them, and make an agreement for a limited power on the one side, and obedience on the other, the state of war and slavery ceases as long as the compact endures; for, as has been said, no man can by agreement pass over to another that which he hath not in himself, a power over his own life.

I confess, we find among the Jews, as well as other nations, that men did sell themselves; but 'tis plain this was only to drudgery, not to slavery; for it is evident the person sold was not under an absolute, arbitrary, despotical power. For the master could not have power to kill him at any time, whom at a certain time he was obliged to let go free out of his service; and the master of such a servant was so far from having an arbitrary power over his life that he could not at pleasure so much as maim him, but the loss of an eye or tooth set him free, *Exod*. xxi.

(((V)))

OF PROPERTY

25. Whether we consider natural reason, which tells us that men, being once born, have a right to their preservation, and consequently to meat and drink and such other things as Nature affords for their subsistence, or *revelation*, which gives us an account of those grants God made of the world to Adam, and to Noah and his sons, 'tis very clear that God, as King David says, *Psalm* cxv. 16, *has given the earth to the children of men*, given it to mankind in common. But, this being supposed, it seems to some a very great difficulty how

any one should ever come to have a property in anything, I will not content myself to answer, that, if it be difficult to make out *property* upon a supposition that God gave the world to Adam and his posterity in common, it is impossible that any man but one universal monarch should have any *property* upon a supposition that God gave the world to Adam and his heirs in succession, exclusive of all the rest of his posterity; but I shall endeavour to shew how men might come to have a property in several parts of that which God gave to mankind in common, and that without any express compact of all the commoners.

26. God, who hath given the world to men in common, hath also given them reason to make use of it to the best advantage of life and convenience. The earth and all that is therein is given to men for the support and comfort of their being. And though all the fruits it naturally produces, and beasts it feeds, belong to mankind in common, as they are produced by the spontaneous hand of nature, and no body has originally a private dominion exclusive of the rest of mankind in any of them, as they are thus in their natural state, yet being given for the use of men, there must of necessity be a means to appropriate them some way or other before they can be of any use, or at all beneficial, to any particular man. The fruit or venison which nourishes the wild Indian, who knows no enclosure, and is still a tenant in common, must be his, and so his — *i.e.*, a part of him, that another can no longer have any right to it before it can do him any good for the support of his life.

27. Though the earth and all inferior creatures be common to all men, yet every man has a *property* in his own *person*. This nobody has any right to but himself. The *labour* of his body and the *work* of his hands, we may say, are properly his. Whatsoever, then, he removes out of the state that nature hath provided and left it in, he hath mixed his labour with it, and joined to it something that is his own, and thereby makes it his property. It being by him removed from the common state nature placed it in, it hath by this labour

something annexed to it that excludes the common right of other men. For this labour being the unquestionable property of the labourer, no man but he can have a right to what that is once joined to, at least where there is enough, and as good left in common for others.

28. He that is nourished by the acorns he picked up under an oak, or the apples he gathered from the trees in the wood, has certainly appropriated them to himself. Nobody can deny but the nourishment is his. I ask, then, when did they begin to be his? when he digested? or when he ate? or when he boiled? or when he brought them home? or when he picked them up? And 'tis plain, if the first gathering made them not his, nothing else could. That labour put a distinction between them and common. That added something to them more than Nature, the common mother of all, had done, and so they became his private right. And will any one say he had no right to those acorns or apples he thus appropriated because he had not the consent of all mankind to make them his? Was it a robbery thus to assume to himself what belonged to all in common? If such a consent as that was necessary, man had starved, notwithstanding the plenty God had given him. We see in commons, which remain so by compact, that 'tis the taking any part of what is common, and removing it out of the state Nature leaves it in, which begins the property, without which the common is of no use. And the taking of this or that part does not depend on the express consent of all the commoners. Thus, the grass my' horse has bit, the turfs my servant has cut, and the ore I have digged in any place, where I have a right to them in common with others, become my property without the assignation or consent of any body. The labour that was mine, removing them out of that common state they were in, hath fixed my property in them.

29. By making an explicit consent of every commoner necessary to any one's appropriating to himself any part of what is given in common, children or servants could not cut the meat which their father or master had provided for

them in common without assigning to every one his peculiar part. Though the water running in the fountain be every one's, yet who can doubt but that in the pitcher is his only who drew it out? His labour hath taken it out of the hands of Nature where it was common, and belonged equally to all her children, and hath thereby appropriated it to himself.

30. Thus this law of reason makes the deer that Indian's who hath killed it; 'tis allowed to be his goods who hath bestowed his labour upon it, though, before, it was the common right of every one. And amongst those who are counted the civilized part of mankind, who have made and multiplied positive laws to determine property, this original law of nature for the beginning of property, in what was before common, still takes place, and by virtue thereof, what fish any one catches in the ocean, that great and still remaining common of mankind; or what ambergris any one takes up here is by the labour that removes it out of that common state nature left it in, made his property who takes that pains about it. And even amongst us, the hare that any one is hunting is thought his who pursues her during the chase. For being a beast that is still looked upon as common, and no man's private possession, whoever has employed so much labour about any of that kind as to find and pursue her has thereby removed her from the state of nature wherein she was common, and hath begun a property.

31. It will perhaps be objected to this, that if gathering the acorns or other fruits of the earth, etc., makes a right to them, then any one may engross as much as he will. To which I answer, Not so. The same law of nature that does by this means give us property, does also bound that property too. *God has given us all things richly*, 1 *Tim*. vi. 12. Is the voice of reason confirmed by inspiration? But how far has he given it us, *to enjoy*? As much as any one can make use of to any advantage of life before it spoils, so much he may by his labour fix a property in. Whatever is beyond this is more than his share, and belongs to others. Nothing was made by God for man to spoil or destroy. And thus considering the

plenty of natural provisions there was a long time in the world, and the few spenders, and to how small a part of that provision the industry of one man could extend itself and engross it to the prejudice of others, especially keeping within the bonds set by reason of what might serve for his use, there could be then little room for quarrels or contentions about property so established.

32. But the chief matter of property being now not the fruits of the earth and the beasts that subsist on it, but the earth itself, as that which takes in and carries with it all the rest, I think it is plain that property in that too is acquired as the former. As much land as a man tills, plants, improves, cultivates, and can use the product of, so much is his property. He by his labour does, as it were, enclose it from the common. Nor will it invalidate his right to say, Every body else has an equal title to it, and therefore he cannot appropriate, he cannot enclose, without the consent of all his fellow-commoners, all mankind. God, when he gave the world in common to all mankind, commanded man also to labour, and the penury of his condition required it of him. God and his reason commanded him to subdue the earth — i.e., improve it for the benefit of life and therein lay out something upon it that was his own, his labour. He that, in obedience to this command of God, subdued, tilled, and sowed any part of it, thereby annexed to it something that was his property, which another had no title to, nor could without injury take from him.

33. Nor was this appropriation of any parcel of land, by improving it, any prejudice to any other man, since there was still enough and as good left, and more than the yet unprovided could use. So that, in effect, there was never the less left for others because of his enclosure for himself. For he that leaves as much as another can make use of does as good as take nothing at all. No body could think himself injured by the drinking of another man, though he took a good draught, who had a whole river of the same water left him

to quench his thirst. And the case of land and water, where there is enough of both, is perfectly the same.

34. God gave the world to men in common, but since he gave it them for their benefit and the greatest conveniences of life they were capable to draw from it, it cannot be supposed he meant it should always remain common and uncultivated. He gave it to the use of the industrious and rational (and labour was to be his title to it); not to the fancy or covetousness of the quarrelsome and contentious. He that had as good left for his improvement as was already taken up needed not complain, ought not to meddle with what was already improved by another's labour; if he did 'tis plain he desired the benefit of another's pains, which he had no right to, and not the ground which God had given him, in common with others, to labour on, and whereof there was as good left as that already possessed, and more than he knew what to do with, or his industry could reach to.

35. 'Tis true, in land that is common in England or any other country, where there are plenty of people under government who have money and commerce, no one can enclose or appropriate any part without the consent of all his fellow-commoners; because this is left common by compact, i.e., by the law of the land, which is not to be violated. And, though it be common in respect of some men, it is not so to all mankind, but is the joint property of this country, or this parish. Besides, the remainder, after such enclosure, would not be as good to the rest of the commoners as the whole was, when they could all make use of the whole; whereas in the beginning and first peopling of the great common of the world it was quite otherwise. The law man was under was rather for appropriating. God commanded, and his wants forced him to labour. That was his property, which could not be taken from him wherever he had fixed it. And hence subduing or cultivating the earth and having dominion, we see, are joined together. The one gave title to the other. So that God, by commanding to subdue, gave authority so far to appropriate.

And the condition of human life, which requires labour and materials to work on, necessarily introduce private possessions.

36. The measure of property nature has well set by the extent of men's labour and the conveniency of life. No man's labour could subdue or appropriate all, nor could his enjoyment consume more than a small part; so that it was impossible for any man, this way, to entrench upon the right of another or acquire to himself a property to the prejudice of his neighbour, who would still have room for as good and as large a possession (after the other had taken out his) as before it was appropriated. Which measure did confine every man's possession to a very moderate proportion, and such as he might appropriate to himself without injury to any body in the first ages of the world, when men were more in danger to be lost, by wandering from their company, in the then vast wilderness of the earth, than to be straitened for want of room to plant in. And the same measure may be allowed still, without prejudice to any body, as full as the world seems. For, supposing a man or family, in the state they were at first, peopling of the world by the children of Adam or Noah; let him plant in some inland vacant places of America, we shall find that the possessions he could make himself, upon the measures we have given, would not be very large, nor, even to this day, prejudice the rest of mankind or give them reason to complain or think themselves injured by this man's encroachment, though the race of men have now spread themselves to all corners of the world, and do infinitely exceed the small number was at the beginning. Nay, the extent of ground is of so little value without labour that I have heard it affirmed that in Spain itself a man may be permitted to plough, sow, and reap, without being disturbed, upon land he has no other title to, but only his making use of it. But, on the contrary, the inhabitants think themselves beholden to him who, by his industry on neglected, and consequently waste land, has increased the stock of corn, which they wanted. But be this as it will, which I lay no stress on, this I

dare boldly affirm, that the same rule of propriety (*viz.*), that every man should have as much as he could make use of, would hold still in the world, without straitening any body, since there is land enough in the world to suffice double the inhabitants, had not the invention of money, and the tacit agreement of men to put a value on it, introduced (by consent) larger possessions and a right to them; which, how it has done, I shall by and by shew more at large.

37. This is certain, that in the beginning, before the desire of having more than man needed had altered the intrinsic value of things, which depends only on their usefulness to the life of man, or had agreed that a little piece of yellow metal, which would keep without wasting or decay, should be worth a great piece of flesh or a whole heap of corn, though men had a right to appropriate by their labour, each one to himself, as much of the things of nature as he could use, yet this could not be much, nor to the prejudice of others, where the same plenty was still left, to those who would use the same industry.

Before the appropriation of land, he who gathered as much of the wild fruit, killed, caught, or tamed as many of the beasts as he could — he that so employed his pains about any of the spontaneous products of nature as any way to alter them from the state nature put them in, by placing any of his labour on them, did thereby acquire a propriety in them; but if they perished in his possession without their due use — if the fruits rotted or the venison putrified before he could spend it, he offended against the common law of nature, and was liable to be punished: he invaded his neighbour's share for he had no right farther than his use called for any of them, and they might serve to afford him conveniences of life.

38. The same measures governed the possession of land, too. Whatsoever he tilled and reaped, laid up and made use of before it spoiled, that was his peculiar right; whatsoever he enclosed, and could feed and make use of, the cattle and product was also his. But if either the grass of his enclosure

rotted on the ground, or the fruit of his planting perished
without gathering and laying up, this part of the earth, notwithstanding his enclosure, was still to be looked on as
waste, and might be the possession of any other. Thus, at the
beginning, Cain might take as much ground as he could till
and make it his own land, and yet leave enough to Abel's
sheep to feed on: a few acres would serve for both their possessions. But as families increased and industry enlarged
their stocks, their possessions enlarged with the need of
them; but yet it was commonly without any fixed property
in the ground they made use of till they incorporated, settled
themselves together, and built cities, and then, by consent,
they came in time to set out the bounds of their distinct territories and agree on limits between them and their neighbours, and by laws within themselves settled the properties
of those of the same society. For we see that in that part of
the world which was first inhabited, and therefore like to be
best peopled, even as low down as Abraham's time, they
wandered with their flocks and their herds, which was their
substance, freely up and down — and this Abraham did in a
country where he was a stranger. Whence it is plain that,
at least, a great part of the land lay in common, that the inhabitants valued it not, nor claimed property in any more
than they made use of; but when there was not room enough
in the same place for their herds to feed together, they, by
consent, as Abraham and Lot did, *Gen.* xiii. 5, separated and
enlarged their pasture where it best liked them. And for the
same reason, Esau went from his father and his brother, and
planted in Mount Seir, *Gen.* xxxvi. 6.

39. And thus, without supposing any private dominion
and property in Adam over all the world, exclusive of all
other men, which can no way be proved, nor any one's property be made out from it, but supposing the world, given as
it was to the children of men in common, we see how labour
could make men distinct titles to several parcels of it for their
private uses, wherein there could be no doubt of right, no
room for quarrel.

40. Nor is it so strange as perhaps before consideration, it may appear, that the property of labour should be able to overbalance the community of land, for 'tis labour indeed that puts the difference of value on every thing; and let any one consider what the difference is between an acre of land planted with tobacco or sugar, sown with wheat or barley, and an acre of the same land lying in common without any husbandry upon it, and he will find that the improvement of labour makes the far greater part of the value. I think it will be but a very modest computation to say, that of the products of the earth useful to the life of man, nine-tenths are the effects of labour: nay, if we will rightly estimate things as they come to our use, and cast up the several expenses about them, what in them is purely owing to nature and what to labour, we shall find that in most of them ninety-nine hundredths are wholly to be put on the account of labour.

41. There cannot be a clearer demonstration of any thing than several nations of the Americans are of this, who are rich in land and poor in all the comforts of life; whom nature, having furnished as liberally as any other people with the materials of plenty, i.e., a fruitful soil, apt to produce in abundance what might serve for food, raiment, and delight; yet, for want of improving it by labour, have not one hundredth part of the conveniences we enjoy. And a king of a large and fruitful territory there feeds, lodges, and is clad worse than a day labourer in England.

42. To make this a little clearer, let us but trace some of the ordinary provisions of life, through their several progresses, before they come to our use, and see how much they receive of their value from humane industry. Bread, wine, and cloth are things of daily use and great plenty; yet notwithstanding acorns, water, and leaves, or skins must be our bread, drink and clothing, did not labour furnish us with these more useful commodities. For whatever bread is more worth than acorns, wine than water, and cloth or silk than leaves, skins or moss, that is wholly owing to labour and industry. The one of these being the food and raiment which

unassisted nature furnishes us with; the other provisions
which our industry and pains prepare for us, which how
much they exceed the other in value, when any one hath
computed, he will then see how much labour makes the far
greatest part of the value of things we enjoy in this world;
and the ground which produces the materials is scarce to be
reckoned in as any, or at most, but a very small part of it; so
little, that even amongst us, land that is left wholly to nature,
that hath no improvement of pasturage, tillage, or planting,
is called, as indeed it is, waste; and we shall find the benefit
of it amount to little more than nothing.

43. An acre of land that bears here twenty bushels of
wheat, and another in America, which, with the same husbandry, would do the like, are, without doubt, of the same
natural, intrinsic value. But yet the benefit mankind receives
from one in a year is worth five pounds, and the other possibly not worth a penny; if all the profit an Indian received
from it were to be valued and sold here, at least I may truly
say, not one thousandth. 'Tis labour, then, which puts the
greatest part of value upon land, without which it would
scarcely be worth any thing; 'tis to that we owe the greatest
part of all its useful products; for all that the straw, bran,
bread, of that acre of wheat, is more worth than the product
of an acre of as good land which lies waste is all the effect of
labour. For 'tis not barely the ploughman's pains, the reaper's
and thresher's toil, and the baker's sweat, is to be counted
into the bread we eat; the labour of those who broke the oxen,
who digged and wrought the iron and stones, who felled and
framed the timber employed about the plough, mill, oven,
or any other utensils, which are a vast number, requisite to
this corn, from its sowing to its being made bread, must all
be charged on the account of labour, and received as an effect
of that: nature and the earth furnished only the almost
worthless materials as in themselves. 'Twould be a strange
catalogue of things that industry provided and made use of
about every loaf of bread before it came to our use if we
could trace them; iron, wood, leather, bark, timber, stone,

bricks, coals, lime, cloth, dyeing-drugs, pitch, tar, masts, ropes, and all the materials made use of in the ship that brought any of the commodities made use of by any of the workmen, to any part of the work, all which 'twould be almost impossible, at least too long, to reckon up.

44. From all which it is evident, that though the things of nature are given in common, man (by being master of himself, and proprietor of his own person, and the actions or labour of it) had still in himself the great foundation of property; and that which made up the great part of what he applied to the support or comfort of his being, when invention and arts had improved the conveniences of life, was perfectly his own, and did not belong in common to others.

45. Thus labour, in the beginning, gave a right of property, wherever any one was pleased to employ it, upon what was common, which remained a long while, the far greater part, and is yet more than mankind makes use of. Men at first, for the most part, contented themselves with what unassisted nature offered to their necessities; and though afterwards, in some parts of the world, where the increase of people and stock, with the use of money, had made land scarce, and so of some value, the several communities settled the bounds of their distinct territories, and, by laws, within themselves, regulated the properties of the private men of their society, and so, by compact and agreement, settled the property which labour and industry began; and the leagues that have been made between several states and kingdoms, either expressly or tacitly disowning all claim and right to the land in the other's possession, have, by common consent, given up their pretences to their natural common right, which originally they had to those countries; and so have, by positive agreement, settled a property amongst themselves, in distinct parts of the world; yet there are still great tracts of ground to be found, which the inhabitants thereof, not having joined with the rest of mankind in the consent of the use of their common money, lie waste, and are more than the

people who dwell on it, do, or can make use of, and so still
lie in common; though this can scarce happen amongst that
part of mankind that have consented to the use of money.

46. The greatest part of things really useful to the life of
man, and such as the necessity of subsisting made the first
commoners of the world look after, as it doth the Americans
now, are generally things of short duration, such as, if they
are not consumed by use, will decay and perish of themselves. Gold, silver, and diamonds are things that fancy or
agreement hath put the value on, more than real use and the
necessary support of life. Now of those good things which
nature hath provided in common, every one had a right (as
hath been said) to as much as he could use, and had a property in all that he could effect with his labour; all that his
industry could extend to, to alter from the state nature had
put it in, was his. He that gathered a hundred bushels of
acorns or apples had thereby a property in them, they were
his goods as soon as gathered. He was only to look that he
used them before they spoiled, else he took more than his
share, and robbed others. And, indeed, it was a foolish thing,
as well as dishonest, to hoard up more than he could make
use of. If he gave away a part to any body else, so that it
perished not uselessly in his possession, these he also made
use of. And if he also bartered away plums that would have
rotted in a week, for nuts that would last good for his eating
a whole year, he did no injury; he wasted not the common
stock; destroyed no part of the portion of goods that belonged to others, so long as nothing perished uselessly in his
hands. Again, if he would give his nuts for a piece of metal,
pleased with its colour, or exchange his sheep for shells, or
wool for a sparkling pebble or a diamond, and keep those by
him all his life, he invaded not the right of others; he might
heap up as much of these durable things as he pleased; the
exceeding of the bounds of his just property not lying in the
largeness of his possession, but the perishing of anything
uselessly in it.

47. And thus came in the use of money, some lasting

thing that men might keep without spoiling, and that, by mutual consent, men would take in exchange for the truly useful but perishable supports of life.

48. And as different degrees of industry were apt to give men possessions in different proportions, so this invention of money gave them the opportunity to continue and enlarge them. For supposing an island, separate from all possible commerce with the rest of the world, wherein there were but a hundred families, but there were sheep, horses, and cows, with other useful animals, wholesome fruits, and land enough for corn for a hundred thousand times as many, but nothing in the island, either because of its commonness or perishableness, fit to supply the place of money. What reason could any one have there to enlarge his possessions beyond the use of his family, and a plentiful supply to its consumption, either in what their own industry produced, or they could barter for like perishable, useful commodities with others? Where there is not something both lasting and scarce, and so valuable to be hoarded up, there men will not be apt to enlarge their possessions of land, were it never so rich, never so free for them to take. For I ask, what would a man value ten thousand or an hundred thousand acres of excellent land, ready cultivated and well stocked, too, with cattle, in the middle of the inland parts of America, where he had no hopes of commerce with other parts of the world, to draw money to him by the sale of the product? It would not be worth the enclosing, and we should see him give up again to the wild common of Nature whatever was more than would supply the conveniences of life, to be had there for him and his family.

49. Thus, in the beginning, all the world was America, and more so than that is now; for no such thing as money was any where known. Find out something that hath the use and value of money amongst his neighbours, you shall see the same man will begin presently to enlarge his possessions.

50. But since gold and silver, being little useful to the life of man, in proportion to food, raiment, and carriage, has its

value only from the consent of men, whereof labour yet makes in great part the measure, it is plain that the consent of men have agreed to a disproportionate and unequal possession of the earth, I mean out of the bounds of society and compact; for in governments the laws regulate it; they having, by consent, found out and agreed in a way how a man may rightfully, and without injury, possess more than he himself can make use of by receiving gold and silver, which may continue long in a man's possession without decaying for the overplus, and agreeing those metals should have a value.

51. And thus, I think, it is very easy to conceive, without any difficulty, how labour could at first begin a title of property in the common things of nature, and how the spending it upon our uses bounded it; so that there could then be no reason of quarrelling about title, nor any doubt about the largeness of possession it gave. Right and conveniency went together. For as a man had a right to all he could employ his labour upon, so he had no temptation to labour for more than he could make use of. This left no room for controversy about the title, nor for encroachment on the right of others. What portion a man carved to himself was easily seen; and it was useless as well as dishonest to carve himself too much, or take more than he needed.

(((VI)))

OF PATERNAL POWER

52. It may perhaps be censured as an impertinent criticism in a discourse of this nature to find fault with words and names that have obtained in the world. And yet possibly it may not be amiss to offer new ones when the old are apt to lead men into mistakes, as this of paternal power probably has done, which seems so to place the power of parents over their children wholly in the father, as if the mother had no share in it; whereas if we consult reason or revelation, we

shall find she hath an equal title, which may give one reason to ask whether this might not be more properly called parental power? For whatever obligation nature and the right of generation lays on children, it must certainly bind them equal to both the concurrent causes of it. And accordingly we see the positive law of God every where joins them together without distinction, when it commands the obedience of children: *Honour thy father and thy mother, Exod.* xx. 12; *Whosoever curseth his father or his mother, Lev.* xx. 9; *Ye shall fear every man his mother and his father, Lev.* xix. 3; *Children, obey your parents, Eph.* etc. vi. 1, is the style of the Old and New Testament.

53. Had but this one thing been well considered without looking any deeper into the matter, it might perhaps have kept men from running into those gross mistakes they have made about this power of parents, which however, it might without any great harshness bear the name of absolute dominion and regal authority, when under the title of *paternal power*, it seemed appropriated to the father; would yet have sounded but oddly, and in the very name shown the absurdity, if this supposed absolute power over children had been called parental, and thereby discovered that it belonged to the mother too; for it will but very ill serve the turn of those men who contend so much for the absolute power and authority of the fatherhood, as they call it, that the mother should have any share in it. And it would have but ill supported the monarchy they contend for, when by the very name it appeared that the fundamental authority from whence they would derive their government of a single person only was not placed in one, but two persons jointly. But to let this of names pass.

54. Though I have said above (*Chap.* 2) *That all men by nature are equal*, I cannot be supposed to understand all sorts of *equality*: Age or virtue may give men a just precedency. Excellency of parts and merit may place others above the common level. Birth may subject some, and alliance or benefits others, to pay an observance to those to whom Nature,

gratitude, or other respects, may have made it due; and yet all this consists with the equality which all men are in in respect of jurisdiction or dominion one over another, which was the equality I there spoke of as proper to the business in hand, being that equal right that every man hath to his natural freedom, without being subjected to the will or authority of any other man.

55. Children, I confess, are not born in this full state of equality, though they are born to it. Their parents have a sort of rule and jurisdiction over them when they come into the world, and for some time after, but it is but a temporary one. The bonds of this subjection are like the swaddling clothes they are wrapt up in and supported by in the weakness of their infancy. Age and reason as they grow up loosen them, till at length they drop quite off, and leave a man at his own free disposal.

56. Adam was created a perfect man, his body and mind in full possession of their strength and reason, and so was capable from the first instant of his being to provide for his own support and preservation, and govern his actions according to the dictates of the law of reason God had implanted in him. From him the world is peopled with his descendants, who are all born infants, weak and helpless, without knowledge or understanding. But to supply the defects of this imperfect state of maturity till the improvement of growth and age had removed them, Adam and Eve, and after them all parents were, by the law of nature, under an obligation to preserve, nourish, and educate the children they had begotten, not as their own workmanship, but the workmanship of their own Maker, the Almighty, to whom they were to be accountable for them.

57. The law that was to govern Adam was the same that was to govern all his posterity, the law of reason. But his offspring having another way of entrance into the world, different from him, by a natural birth, that produced them ignorant, and without the use of reason, they were not presently under that law. For no body can be under a law

that is not promulgated to him; and this law being promulgated or made known by reason only, he that is not come to the use of his reason cannot be said to be under this law; and Adam's children being not presently as soon as born under this law of reason, were not presently free. For law, in its true notion, is not so much the limitation as the direction of a free and intelligent agent to his proper interest, and prescribes no farther than is for the general good of those under the law. Could they be happier without it, the law, as a useless thing, would of itself vanish; and that ill deserves the name of confinement which hedges us in only from bogs and precipices. So that however it may be mistaken, the end of law is not to abolish or restrain, but to preserve and enlarge freedom; for in all the states of created beings capable of laws, where there is no law there is no freedom; for liberty is to be free from restraint and violence from others, which cannot be where there is no law; and is not, as we are told, *a liberty for every man to do what he lists*. (For who could be free, when every other man's humour might domineer over him?) But a liberty to dispose and order freely as he lists his person, actions, possessions, and his whole property within the allowance of those laws under which he is, and therein not to be subject to the arbitrary will of another, but freely follow his own.

58. The power, then, that parents have over their children arises from that duty which is incumbent on them, to take care of their offspring during the imperfect state of childhood. To inform the mind, and govern the actions of their yet ignorant nonage, till reason shall take its place and ease them of that trouble, is what the children want, and the parents are bound to. For God having given man an understanding to direct his actions, has allowed him a freedom of will and liberty of acting, as properly belonging thereunto, within the bounds of that law he is under. But whilst he is in an estate wherein he has no understanding of his own to direct his will, he is not to have any will of his own to follow. He that understands for him must will for him too; he must

prescribe to his will, and regulate his actions, but when he comes to the estate that made his father a freeman, the son is a freeman too.

59. This holds in all the laws a man is under, whether natural or civil. Is a man under the law of nature? What made him free of that law? what gave him a free disposing of his property, according to his own will, within the compass of that law? I answer, a state of maturity wherein he might be supposed capable to know that law, that so he might keep his actions within the bounds of it. When he has acquired that state, he is presumed to know how far that law is to be his guide, and how far he may make use of his freedom, and so comes to have it; till then, some body else must guide him, who is presumed to know how far the law allows a liberty. If such a state of reason, such an age of discretion made him free, the same shall make his son free too. Is a man under the law of England? What made him free of that law? That is, to have the liberty to dispose of his actions and possessions, according to his own will, within the permission of that law? A capacity of knowing that law. Which is supposed, by that law, at the age of twenty-one, and in some cases sooner. If this made the father free, it shall make the son free too. Till then, we see the law allows the son to have no will, but he is to be guided by the will of his father or guardian, who is to understand for him. And if the father die, and fail to substitute a deputy in this trust, if he hath not provided a tutor to govern his son during his minority, during his want of understanding, the law takes care to do it: some other must govern him and be a will to him till he hath attained to a state of freedom, and his understanding be fit to take the government of his will. But after that the father and son are equally free, as much as tutor and pupil after nonage, equally subjects of the same law together, without any dominion left in the father over the life, liberty, or estate of his son, whether they be only in the state and under the law of nature, or under the positive laws of an established government.

60. But if through defects that may happen out of the

ordinary course of nature, anyone comes not to such a degree of reason wherein he might be supposed capable of knowing the law, and so living within the rules of it, he is never capable of being a free man, he is never let loose to the disposure of his own will, because he knows no bounds to it, has not understanding, its proper guide; but is continued under the tuition and government of others all the time his own understanding is incapable of that charge. And so lunatics and idiots are never set free from the government of their parents: *Children who are not as yet come unto those years whereat they may have; and innocents, which are excluded by a natural defect from ever having;* Thirdly, *Madmen, which, for the present, cannot possibly have the use of right reason to guide themselves, have, for their guide, the reason that guideth other men which are tutors over them, to seek and procure their good for them,* says Hooker, *Eccl. Pol.,* lib. i, sect. 7. All which seems no more than that duty which God and nature has laid on man, as well as other creatures, to preserve their offspring till they can be able to shift for themselves, and will scarce amount to an instance or proof of parents' regal authority.

61. Thus we are born free as we are born rational; not that we have actually the exercise of either: age that brings one, brings with it the other too. And thus we see how natural freedom and subjection to parents may consist together, and are both founded on the same principle. A child is free by his father's title, by his father's understanding, which is to govern him till he hath it of his own. The freedom of a man at years of discretion, and the subjection of a child to his parents, whilst yet short of that age, are so consistent and so distinguishable, that the most blinded contenders for monarchy, *by right of fatherhood*, cannot miss this *difference*, the most obstinate cannot but allow their consistency. For were their doctrine all true, were the right heir of Adam now known, and, by that title, settled a monarch in his throne, invested with all the absolute unlimited power Sir Robert Filmer talks of, if he should die as soon as his heir was born, must not the child, notwithstanding he were never so free, never

so much sovereign, be in subjection to his mother and nurse, to tutors and governors, till age and education brought him reason and ability to govern himself and others? The necessities of his life, the health of his body, and the information of his mind would require him to be directed by the will of others and not his own; and yet will anyone think that this restraint and subjection were inconsistent with, or spoiled him of, that liberty or sovereignty he had a right to, or gave away his empire to those who had the government of his nonage? This government over him only prepared him the better and sooner for it. If any body should ask me when my son is of age to be free, I shall answer, just when his monarch is of age to govern. *But at what time*, says the judicious Hooker, *Eccl. Pol.*, lib. i, sect. 6, *a man may be said to have attained so far forth the use of reason as sufficeth to make him capable of those laws whereby he is then bound to guide his actions; this is a great deal more easy for sense to discern than for anyone, by skill and learning, to determine.*

62. Commonwealths themselves take notice of, and allow that there is a time when men are to begin to act like free men, and therefore, till that time, require not oaths of fealty or allegiance, or other public owning of, or submission to, the government of their countries.

63. The freedom then of man and liberty of acting according to his own will, is grounded on his having reason, which is able to instruct him in that law he is to govern himself by, and make him known how far he is left to the freedom of his own will. To turn him loose to an unrestrained liberty, before he has reason to guide him, is not the allowing him the privilege of his nature to be free, but to thrust him out amongst brutes, and abandon him to a state as wretched and as much beneath that of a man as theirs. This is that which puts the authority into the parents' hands to govern the minority of their children. God hath made it their business to employ this care on their offspring, and hath placed in them suitable inclinations of tenderness and concern to temper this

power, to apply it as his wisdom designed it, to the children's good as long as they should need to be under it.

64. But what reason can hence advance this care of the parents due to their offspring into an absolute, arbitrary dominion of the father, whose power reaches no farther than by such a discipline as he finds most effectual to give such strength and health to their bodies, such vigour and rectitude to their minds, as may best fit his children to be most useful to themselves and others, and, if it be necessary to his condition, to make them work when they are able for their own subsistence. But in his power the mother, too, has her share with the father.

65. Nay, this power so little belongs to the father by any peculiar right of nature, but only as he is guardian of his children, that when he quits his care of them he loses his power over them, which goes along with their nourishment and education, to which it is inseparably annexed, and belongs as much to the foster-father of an exposed child as to the natural father of another. So little power does the bare act of begetting give a man over his issue, if all his care ends there, and this be all the title he hath to the name and authority of a father. And what will become of this paternal power in that part of the world where one woman hath more than one husband at a time? or in those parts of America where, when husband and wife part, which happens frequently, the children are all left to the mother, follow her, and are wholly under her care and provision? And if the father die whilst the children are young, do they not naturally everywhere owe the same obedience to their mother, during their minority, as to their father, were he alive? And will anyone say that the mother hath a legislative power over her children that she can make standing rules which shall be of perpetual obligation, by which they ought to regulate all the concerns of their property, and bound their liberty all the course of their lives? Or can she enforce the observation of them with capital punishments? For this is the proper power of the magis-

trate, of which the father hath not so much as the shadow.
His command over his children is but temporary, and
reaches not their life or property. It is but a help to the
weakness and imperfection of their nonage, a discipline necessary to their education. And though a father may dispose
of his own possessions as he pleases when his children are
out of danger of perishing for want, yet his power extends
not to the lives or goods which either their own industry,
or another's bounty, has made theirs, nor to their liberty
neither, when they are once arrived to the enfranchisement
of the years of discretion. The father's empire then ceases,
and he can from thence forwards no more dispose of the
liberty of his son than that of any other man. And it must
be far from an absolute or perpetual jurisdiction, from which
a man may withdraw himself, having licence from Divine
authority to *leave father and mother and cleave to his wife*.

66. But though there be a time when a child comes to be
as free from subjection to the will and command of his father
as he himself is free from subjection to the will of any body
else, and they are each under no other restraint but that
which is common to them both, whether it be the law of
nature or municipal law of their country, yet this freedom
exempts not a son from that honour which he ought, by the
law of God and nature, to pay his parents, God having made
the parents instruments in his great design of continuing the
race of mankind and the occasions of life to their children.
As he hath laid on them an obligation to nourish, preserve,
and bring up their offspring, so he has laid on the children
a perpetual obligation of honouring their parents, which,
containing in it an inward esteem and reverence to be shown
by all outward expressions, ties up the child from anything
that may ever injure or affront, disturb, or endanger the happiness or life of those from whom he received his, and engages him in all actions of defence, relief, assistance, and
comfort of those by whose means he entered into being and
has been made capable of any enjoyments of life. From this
obligation no state, no freedom, can absolve children. But

this is very far from giving parents a power of command over their children, or an authority to make laws and dispose as they please of their lives or liberties. It is one thing to owe honour, respect, gratitude, and assistance; another to require an absolute obedience and submission. The honour due to parents a monarch in his throne owes his mother, and yet this lessens not his authority nor subjects him to her government.

67. The subjection of a minor places in the father a temporary government which terminates with the minority of the child; and the honour due from a child places in the parents a perpetual right to respect, reverence, support, and compliance too, more or less, as the father's care, cost, and kindness in his education has been more or less, and this ends not with minority, but holds in all parts and conditions of a man's life. The want of distinguishing these two powers which the father hath in the right of tuition, during minority and the right of honour all his life, may perhaps have caused a great part of the mistakes about this matter. For to speak properly of them, the first of these is rather the privilege of children and duty of parents than any prerogative of paternal power. The nourishment and education of their children is a charge so incumbent on parents for their children's good, that nothing can absolve them from taking care of it. And though the power of commanding and chastising them go along with it, yet God hath woven into the principles of human nature such a tenderness for their offspring, that there is little fear that parents should use their power with too much rigour; the excess is seldom on the severe side, the strong bias of nature drawing the other way. And therefore God Almighty, when he would express his gentle dealings with the Israelites, he tells them that though he chastened them, *he chastened them as a man chastens his son*, Deut. viii. 5, i.e., with tenderness and affection, and kept them under no severer discipline than what was absolutely best for them, and had been less kindness to have slackened. This is that power to which children are commanded obedience, that

the pains and care of their parents may not be increased or ill-rewarded.

68. On the other side, honour and support, all that which gratitude requires to return for the benefits received by and from them is the indispensable duty of the child and the proper privilege of the parents. This is intended for the parents' advantage, as the other is for the child's; though education, the parents' duty, seems to have most power, because the ignorance and infirmities of childhood stand in need of restraint and correction, which is a visible exercise of rule and a kind of dominion. And that duty which is comprehended in the word *honour* requires less obedience, though the obligation be stronger on grown than younger children. For who can think the command, *Children, obey your parents*, requires in a man that has children of his own the same submission to his father as it does in his yet young children to him; and that by this precept he were bound to obey all his father's commands, if, out of a conceit of authority, he should have the indiscretion to treat him still as a boy?

69. The first part, then, of paternal power, or rather duty, which is education, belongs so to the father that it terminates at a certain season. When the business of education is over it ceases of itself, and is also alienable before. For a man may put the tuition of his son in other hands; and he that has made his son an apprentice to another has discharged him, during that time, of a great part of his obedience, both to himself and to his mother. But all the duty of honour, the other part, remains nevertheless entire to them; nothing can cancel that. It is so inseparable from them both, that the father's authority cannot dispossess the mother of this right, nor can any man discharge his son from honouring her that bore him. But both these are very far from a power to make laws, and enforcing them with penalties that may reach estate, liberty, limbs, and life. The power of commanding ends with nonage; and though after that honour and respect, support and defence, and whatsoever gratitude can oblige a man to for the highest benefits he is naturally capable of, be al-

ways due from a son to his parents, yet all this puts no sceptre into the father's hand, no sovereign power of commanding. He has no dominion over his son's property or actions, nor any right that his will should prescribe to his son's in all things; however, it may become his son in many things, not very inconvenient to him and his family, to pay a deference to it.

70. A man may owe honour and respect to an ancient or wise man, defence to his child or friend, relief and support to the distressed, and gratitude to a benefactor, to such a degree that all he has, all he can do, cannot sufficiently pay it; but all these give no authority, no right of making laws to any one over him from whom they are owing. And 'tis plain all this is due not only to the bare title of father, not only because, as has been said, it is owing to the mother too; but because these obligations to parents, and the degrees of what is required of children, may be varied by the different care and kindness, trouble and expense, is often employed upon one child more than another.

71. This shews the reason how it comes to pass that parents in societies, where they themselves are subjects, retain a power over their children and have as much right to their subjection as those who are in the state of nature, which could not possibly be if all political power were only paternal, and that, in truth, they were one and the same thing: for then, all paternal power being in the prince, the subject could naturally have none of it. But these two powers, political and paternal, are so perfectly distinct and separate, and built upon so different foundations, and given to so different ends, that every subject that is a father has as much a paternal power over his children as the prince has over his. And every prince that has parents owes them as much filial duty and obedience as the meanest of his subjects do to theirs, and can therefore contain not any part or degree of that kind of dominion which a prince or magistrate has over his subject.

72. Though the obligation on the parents to bring up their children, and the obligation on children to honour their par-

ents, contain all the power, on the one hand, and submission on the other, which are proper to this relation, yet there is another power ordinarily in the father, whereby he has a tie on the obedience of his children, which, though it be common to him with other men, yet the occasions of showing it, almost constantly happening to fathers in their private families and the instances of it elsewhere being rare, and less taken notice of, it passes in the world for a part of *paternal jurisdiction*. And this is the power men generally have to bestow their estates on those who please them best. The possession of the father being the expectation and inheritance of the children ordinarily, in certain proportions, according to the law and custom of each country, yet it is commonly in the father's power to bestow it with a more sparing or liberal hand, according as the behaviour of this or that child hath comported with his will and humour.

73. This is no small tie to the obedience of children; and there being always annexed to the enjoyment of land a submission to the government of the country of which that land is a part, it has been commonly supposed that a father could oblige his posterity to that government of which he himself was a subject, that his compact held them; whereas, it being only a necessary condition annexed to the land which is under that government, reaches only those who will take it on that condition, and so is no natural tie or engagement, but a voluntary submission; for every man's children being, by nature, as free as himself or any of his ancestors ever were, may, whilst they are in that freedom, choose what society they will join themselves to, what commonwealth they will put themselves under. But if they will enjoy the inheritance of their ancestors, they must take it on the same terms their ancestors had it, and submit to all the conditions annexed to such a possession. By this power, indeed, fathers oblige their children to obedience to themselves even when they are past minority, and most commonly, too, subject them to this or that political power. But neither of these by any peculiar right of *fatherhood*, but by the reward they have in their

hands to enforce and recompense such a compliance; and is no more power than what a Frenchman has over an Englishman, who, by the hopes of an estate he will leave him, will certainly have a strong tie on his obedience; and if when it is left him, he will enjoy it, he must certainly take it upon the conditions annexed to the possession of land in that country where it lies, whether it be France or England.

74. To conclude, then, though the father's power of commanding extends no farther than the minority of his children, and to a degree only fit for the discipline and government of that age; and·though that honour and respect, and all that which the Latins called piety, which they indispensably owe to their parents all their lifetimes, and in all estates, with all that support and defence, is due to them, gives the father no power of governing, i.e., making laws and exacting penalties on his children; though by this he has no dominion over the property or actions of his son, yet 'tis obvious to conceive how easy it was in the first ages of the world, and in places still where the thinness of people gives families leave to separate into unpossessed quarters, and they have room to remove and plant themselves in yet vacant habitations, for the father of the family to become the prince of it; [2] he had been a ruler from the beginning of the infancy of his children; and when they were grown up, since without some government it would be hard for them to live together, it was

2. 'It is no improbable opinion, therefore, which the archphilosopher was of, That the chief person in every household was always, as it were, a king; so when numbers of households joined themselves in civil societies together, kings were the first kind of governors among them, which is also, as it seemeth, the reason why the name of fathers continued still in them, who of fathers were made rulers; as also the ancient custom of governors to do as Melchizedec; and being kings, to exercise the office of priests, which fathers did, at the first, grew, perhaps, by the same occasion. Howbeit, this is not the only kind of regiment that has been received in the world. The inconveniencies of one kind have caused sundry other to be devised, so that, in a word, all public regiment, of what kind soever, seemeth evidently to have risen from the deliberate advice, consultation and composition between men, judging it convenient and behoveful, there being no impossibility in Nature, considered by itself, but that man might have lived without any public regiment.' — Hooker's *Eccl. Pol.*, lib. i, sect. 10.

likeliest it should, by the express or tacit consent of the children, be in the father, where it seemed, without any change, barely to continue. And when, indeed, nothing more was required to it than the permitting the father to exercise alone in his family that executive power of the law of nature which every free man naturally hath, and by that permission resigning up to him a monarchical power whilst they remained in it. But that this was not by any paternal right, but only by the consent of his children, is evident from hence, that nobody doubts but if a stranger, whom chance or business had brought to his family, had there killed any of his children, or committed any other fact, he might condemn and put him to death, or otherwise have punished him as well as any of his children, which was impossible he should do by virtue of any paternal authority over one who was not his child, but by virtue of that executive power of the law of nature, which, as a man, he had a right to; and he alone could punish him in his family where the respect of his children had laid by the exercise of such a power, to give way to the dignity and authority they were willing should remain in him above the rest of his family.

75. Thus 'tis easy and almost natural for children, by a tacit and almost natural consent, to make way for the father's authority and government. They had been accustomed in their childhood to follow his direction, and to refer their little differences to him; and when they were men, who fitter to rule them? Their little properties and less covetousness seldom afforded greater controversies; and when any should arise, where could they have a fitter umpire than he, by whose care they had every one been sustained and brought up, and who had a tenderness for them all? 'Tis no wonder that they made no distinction betwixt minority and full age, nor looked after one-and-twenty, or any other age, that might make them the free disposers of themselves and fortunes, when they could have no desire to be out of their pupilage. The government they had been under, during it, continued still to be more their protection than restraint; and

they could nowhere find a greater security to their peace, liberties, and fortunes than in the rule of a father.

76. Thus the natural fathers of families, by an insensible change, became the politic monarchs of them too; and as they chanced to live long, and leave able and worthy heirs for several successions or otherwise, so they laid the foundations of hereditary or elective kingdoms under several constitutions and manors, according as chance, contrivance, or occasions happened to mould them. But if princes have their titles in the father's right, and it be a sufficient proof of the natural right of fathers to political authority, because they commonly were those in whose hands we find, *de facto*, the exercise of government, I say, if this argument be good, it will as strongly prove that all princes, nay, princes only, ought to be priests, since 'tis as certain that in the beginning *the father of the family was priest, as that he was ruler in his own household.*

(((VII)))

OF POLITICAL OR CIVIL SOCIETY

77. God, having made man such a creature that, in his own judgement, it was not good for him to be alone, put him under strong obligations of necessity, convenience, and inclination, to drive him into society, as well as fitted him with understanding and language to continue and enjoy it. The first society was between man and wife, which gave beginning to that between parents and children, to which, in time, that between master and servant came to be added. And though all these might, and commonly did, meet together, and make up but one family, wherein the master or mistress of it had some sort of rule proper to a family, each of these, or all together, came short of *political society*, as we shall see if we consider the different ends, ties, and bounds of each of these.

78. Conjugal society is made by a voluntary compact between man and woman, and though it consist chiefly in such

a communion and right in one another's bodies as is necessary to its chief end, procreation, yet it draws with it mutual support and assistance, and a communion of interest too, as necessary not only to unite their care and affection, but also necessary to their common offspring, who have a right to be nourished and maintained by them till they are able to provide for themselves.

79. For the end of conjunction between male and female being not barely procreation, but the continuation of the species, this conjunction betwixt male and female ought to last, even after procreation, so long as is necessary to the nourishment and support of the young ones, who are to be sustained by those that got them till they are able to shift and provide for themselves. This rule, which the infinite wise Maker hath set to the works of his hands, we find the inferior creatures steadily obey. In those viviparous animals which feed on grass the conjunction between male and female lasts no longer than the very act of copulation, because the teat of the dam being sufficient to nourish the young till it be able to feed on grass, the male only begets, but concerns not himself for the female or young, to whose sustenance he can contribute nothing. But in beasts of prey the conjunction lasts longer, because the dam, not being able well to subsist herself and nourish her numerous offspring by her own prey alone (a more laborious as well as more dangerous way of living than by feeding on grass), the assistance of the male is necessary to the maintenance of their common family, which cannot subsist till they are able to prey for themselves, but by the joint care of male and female. The same is observed in all birds (except some domestic ones, where plenty of food excuses the cock from feeding and taking care of the young brood), whose young, needing food in the nest, the cock and hen continue mates till the young are able to use their wing and provide for themselves.

80. And herein, I think, lies the chief, if not the only reason, why the male and female in mankind are tied to a longer conjunction than other creatures, *viz.* because the

female is capable of conceiving, and, *de facto*, is commonly with child again, and brings forth too a new birth, long before the former is out of a dependency for support on his parents' help and able to shift for himself, and has all the assistance is due to him from his parents, whereby the father, who is bound to take care for those he hath begot, is under an obligation to continue in conjugal society with the same woman longer than other creatures, whose young, being able to subsist of themselves before the time of procreation returns again, the conjugal bond dissolves of itself, and they are at liberty till Hymen, at his usual anniversary season, summons them again to choose new mates. Wherein one cannot but admire the wisdom of the great Creator, who, having given to man an ability to lay up for the future as well as supply the present necessity, hath made it necessary that society of man and wife should be more lasting than of male and female amongst other creatures, that so their industry might be encouraged, and their interest better united, to make provision and lay up goods for their common issue, which uncertain mixture, or easy and frequent solutions of conjugal society, would mightily disturb.

81. But though these are ties upon mankind which make the *conjugal bonds* more firm and lasting in man than the other species of animals, yet it would give one reason to inquire why this compact, where procreation and education are secured and inheritance taken care for, may not be made determinable, either by consent, or at a certain time, or upon certain conditions, as well as any other voluntary compacts, there being no necessity in the nature of the thing, nor to the ends of it, that it should always be for life; I mean, to such as are under no restraint of any positive law which ordains all such contracts to be perpetual.

82. But the husband and wife, though they have but one common concern, yet having different understandings, will unavoidably sometimes have different wills too; it therefore being necessary that the last determination, i.e., the rule, should be placed somewhere, it naturally falls to the man's

share, as the abler and the stronger. But this, reaching but
to the things of their common interest and property, leaves
the wife in the full and free possession of what by contract
is her peculiar right, and at least gives the husband no more
power over her life than she has over his; the power of the
husband being so far from that of an absolute monarch that
the wife has, in many cases, a liberty to separate from him
where natural right or their contract allows it, whether that
contract be made by themselves in the state of nature or by
the customs or laws of the country they live in, and the
children, upon such separation, fall to the father or mother's
lot as such contract does determine.

83. For all the ends of marriage being to be obtained
under politic government, as well as in the state of nature,
the civil magistrate doth not abridge the right or power of
either, naturally necessary to those ends, *viz.* procreation
and mutual support and assistance whilst they are together,
but only decides any controversy that may arise between
man and wife about them. If it were otherwise, and that absolute sovereignty and power of life and death naturally belonged to the husband, and were necessary to the society
between man and wife, there could be no matrimony in any
of those countries where the husband is allowed no such
absolute authority. But the ends of matrimony requiring no
such power in the husband, the condition of conjugal society
put it not in him; it being not at all necessary to that state.
Conjugal society could subsist and attain its ends without
it; nay, community of goods, and the power over them,
mutual assistance, and maintenance, and other things belonging to conjugal society, might be varied and regulated
by that contract which unites man and wife in that society,
as far as may consist with procreation and the bringing up
of children till they could shift for themselves; nothing being
necessary to any society that is not necessary to the ends for
which it is made.

84. The society betwixt parents and children, and the distinct rights and powers belonging respectively to them, I

have treated of so largely in the foregoing chapter that I shall not here need to say anything of it; and I think it is plain that it is far different from a politic society.

85. Master and servant are names as old as history, but given to those of far different condition; for a free man makes himself a servant to another by selling him for a certain time the service he undertakes to do in exchange for wages he is to receive; and though this commonly puts him into the family of his master, and under the ordinary discipline thereof, yet it gives the master but a temporary power over him, and no greater than what is contained in the contract between 'em. But there is another sort of servants which by a peculiar name we call slaves, who being captives taken in a just war, are by the right of nature, subjected to the absolute dominion and arbitrary power of their masters. These men having, as I say, forfeited their lives and, with it, their liberties, and lost their estates, and being in the state of slavery, not capable of any property, cannot in the state be considered as any part of civil society, the chief end whereof is the preservation of property.

86. Let us therefore consider a master of a family with all these subordinate relations of wife, children, servants, and slaves, united under the domestic rule of a family, with what resemblance soever it may have in its order, offices, and number too, with a little commonwealth, yet is very far from it both in its constitution, power, and end; or if it must be thought a monarchy, and the *paterfamilias* the absolute monarch in it, absolute monarchy will have but a very shattered and short power, when 'tis plain by what has been said before, that the master of the family has a very distinct and differently limited power both as to time and extent over those several persons that are in it; for excepting the slave (and the family is as much a family, and his power as *paterfamilias* as great, whether there be any slaves in his family or no) he has no legislative power of life and death over any of them, and none too but what a mistress of a family may have as well as he. And he certainly can have no absolute

power over the whole family who has but a very limited one
over every individual in it. But how a family, or any other
society of men, differ from that which is properly political
society, we shall best see by considering wherein political
society itself consists.

87. Man being born, as has been proved, with a title to
perfect freedom and an uncontrolled enjoyment of all the
rights and privileges of the law of nature, equally with any
other man, or number of men in the world, hath by nature a
power not only to preserve his property, that is, his life,
liberty, and estate, against the injuries and attempts of other
men, but to judge of and punish the breaches of that law in
others, as he is persuaded the offence deserves, even with
death itself, in crimes where the heinousness of the fact, in
his opinion, requires it. But because no political society can
be, nor subsist, without having in itself the power to preserve
the property, and in order thereunto punish the offences of
all those of that society: there, and there only, is political
society, where every one of the members hath quitted this
natural power, resigned it up into the hands of the community in all cases that exclude him not from appealing for
protection to the law established by it. And thus all private
judgement of every particular member being excluded, the
community comes to be umpire, by settled standing rules;
indifferent, and the same to all parties: And by men having
authority from the community for the execution of those
rules, decides all the differences that may happen between
any members of that society concerning any matter of right,
and punishes those offences which any member hath committed against the society with such penalties as the law has
established; whereby it is easy to discern who are, and who
are not, in political society together. Those who are united
into one body, and have a common established law and judicature to appeal to, with authority to decide controversies
between them and punish offenders, are in civil society one
with another; but those who have no such common appeal,
I mean on earth, are still in the state of nature, each being,

where there is no other, judge for himself and executioner; which is, as I have before showed it, the perfect state of nature.

88. And thus the commonwealth comes by a power to set down what punishment shall belong to the several transgressions they think worthy of it, committed amongst the members of that society (which is the power of making laws) as well as it has the power to punish any injury done unto any of its members by anyone that is not of it (which is the power of war and peace); and all this for the preservation of property of all the members of that society, as far as is possible. But though every man entered into society has quitted his power to punish offences against the law of nature in prosecution of his own private judgement, yet with the judgement of offences which he has given up to the legislative in all cases where he can appeal to the magistrate, he has given up a right to the commonwealth to employ his force for the execution of the judgements of the commonwealth whenever he shall be called to it, which, indeed, are his own judgements, they being made by himself or his representative. And herein we have the original of the legislative and executive power of civil society, which is to judge by standing laws how far offences are to be punished when committed within the commonwealth; and also by occasional judgements founded on the present circumstances of the fact, how far injuries from without are to be vindicated, and in both these to employ all the force of all the members when there shall be need.

89. Wherever therefore any number of men are so united into one society as to quit everyone his executive power of the law of nature, and to resign it to the public, there and there only is a political or civil society. And this is done wherever any number of men, in the state of nature, enter into society to make one people, one body politic under one supreme government: or else when anyone joins himself to and incorporates with any government already made. For hereby he authorizes the society, or which is all one, the legislative

thereof, to make laws for him as the public good of the society shall require, to the execution whereof his own assistance (as to his own decrees) is due. And this puts men out of a state of nature into that of a commonwealth, by setting up a judge on earth with authority to determine all the controversies and redress the injuries that may happen to any member of the commonwealth; which judge is the legislative or magistrates appointed by it. And wherever there are any number of men, however associated, that have no such decisive power to appeal to, there they are still in the state of nature.

90. And hence it is evident that absolute monarchy, which by some men is counted for the only government in the world, is indeed inconsistent with civil society, and so can be no form of civil government at all. For the end of civil society being to avoid and remedy those inconveniences of the state of nature which necessarily follow from every man's being judge in his own case, by setting up a known authority, to which every one of that society may appeal upon any injury received, or controversy that may arise, and which everyone of the society ought to obey;[3] wherever any persons are who have not such an authority to appeal to, for the decision of any difference between them there, those persons are still in the state of nature. And so is every absolute prince in respect of those who are under his *dominion*.

91. For he being supposed to have all, both legislative and executive, power in himself alone, there is no judge to be found, no appeal lies open to anyone, who may fairly and indifferently, and with authority decide, and from whence relief and redress may be expected of any injury or inconveniency that may be suffered from him, or by his order. So that such a man, however entitled, Czar, or Grand Signior, or how you please, is as much in the state of nature, with all

3. 'The public power of all society is above every soul contained in the same society, and the principal use of that power is to give laws unto all that are under it, which laws in such cases we must obey, unless there be reason showed which may necessarily enforce that the law of reason or of God doth enjoin the contrary.' — Hooker's *Eccl. Pol.*, lib. i, sect. 16.

under his dominion, as he is with the rest of mankind. For wherever any two men are, who have no standing rule and common judge to appeal to on earth, for the determination of controversies of right betwixt them, there they are still in the state of nature, and under all the inconveniencies of it, with only this woeful difference to the subject, or rather slave of an absolute prince.[4] That whereas, in the ordinary state of nature, he has a liberty to judge of his right, and according to the best of his power, to maintain it; but whenever his property is invaded by the will and order of his monarch, he has not only no appeal, as those in society ought to have, but, as if he were degraded from the common state of rational creatures, is denied a liberty to judge of, or defend his right, and so is exposed to all the misery and inconveniences that a man can fear from one, who being in the unrestrained state of nature, is yet corrupted with flattery and armed with power.

92. For he that thinks absolute power purifies men's bloods, and corrects the baseness of human nature, need read but the history of this, or any other age, to be convinced of the contrary. He that would have been insolent and injurious in the woods of America would not probably be much better in a throne, where perhaps learning and religion shall be found out to justify all that he shall do to his subjects, and

---

4. 'To take away all such mutual grievances, injuries, and wrongs — i.e., *such as attend men in the state of nature,* there was no way but only by growing into composition and agreement amongst themselves by ordaining some kind of government public, and by yielding themselves subject thereunto, that unto whom they granted authority to rule and govern, by them the peace, tranquillity, and happy estate of the rest might be procured. Men always knew that where force and injury was offered, they might be defenders of themselves. They knew that, however men may seek their own commodity, yet if this were done with injury unto others, it was not to be suffered, but by all men and all good means to be withstood. Finally, they knew that no man might, in reason, take upon him to determine his own right, and according to his own determination proceed in maintenance thereof, in as much as every man is towards himself, and them whom he greatly affects, partial; and therefore, that strifes and troubles would be endless, except they gave their common consent, all to be ordered by some whom they should agree upon, without which consent there would be no reason that one man should take upon him to be lord or judge over another.' — Hooker's *Eccl. Pol.,* lib. i, sect. 10.

the sword presently silence all those that dare question it. For what the protection of absolute monarchy is, what kind of fathers of their countries it makes princes to be, and to what a degree of happiness and security it carries civil society, where this sort of government is grown to perfection, he that will look into the late relation of Ceylon may easily see.

93. In absolute monarchies, indeed, as well as other governments of the world, the subjects have an appeal to the law, and judges to decide any controversies, and restrain any violence that may happen betwixt the subjects themselves, one amongst another. This everyone thinks necessary, and believes he deserves to be thought a declared enemy to society and mankind who should go about to take it away. But whether this be from a true love of mankind and society, and such a charity as we owe all one to another, there is reason to doubt. For this is no more than what every man, who loves his own power, profit, or greatness, may, and naturally must do, keep those animals from hurting or destroying one another who labour and drudge only for his pleasure and advantage; and so are taken care of, not out of any love the master has for them, but love of himself, and the profit they bring him. For if it be asked what security, what fence is there in such a state against the violence and oppression of this absolute ruler, the very question can scarce be borne. They are ready to tell you that it deserves death only to ask after safety. Betwixt subject and subject, they will grant, there must be measures, laws, and judges for their mutual peace and security. But as for the ruler, he ought to be absolute, and is above all such circumstances; because he has a power to do more hurt and wrong, 'tis right when he does it. To ask how you may be guarded from harm or injury on that side, where the strongest hand is to do it, is presently the voice of faction and rebellion. As if when men, quitting the state of nature, entered into society, they agreed that all of them but one should be under the restraint of laws; but that he should still retain all the liberty of the state of nature,

increased with power, and made licentious by impunity. This is to think that men are so foolish that they take care to avoid what mischiefs may be done them by polecats or foxes, but are content, nay, think it safety, to be devoured by lions.

94. But, whatever flatterers may talk to amuse people's understandings, it hinders not men from feeling; and when they perceive that any man, in what station soever, is out of the bounds of the civil society they are of, and that they have no appeal, on earth, against any harm they may receive from him, they are apt to think themselves in the state of nature, in respect of him whom they find to be so; and to take care, as soon as they can, to have that safety and security, in civil society, for which it was first instituted, and for which only they entered into it. And therefore, though perhaps at first (as shall be showed more at large hereafter, in the following part of this discourse) some one good and excellent man having got a pre-eminency amongst the rest, had this deference paid to his goodness and virtue, as to a kind of natural authority, that the chief rule, with arbitration of their differences, by a tacit consent devolved into his hands, without any other caution but the assurance they had of his uprightness and wisdom; yet when time giving authority, and, as some men would persuade us, sacredness to customs, which the negligent and unforeseeing innocence of the first ages began, had brought in successors of another stamp, the people finding their properties not secure under the government as then it was [5] (whereas government has no other end but the preservation of property), could never be safe, nor at rest, nor think themselves in civil society, till the legisla-

5. 'At the first, when some certain kind of regiment was once appointed, it may be that nothing was then further thought upon for the manner of governing, but all permitted unto their wisdom and discretion which were to rule till, by experience, they found this for all parts very inconvenient, so as the thing which they had devised for a remedy did indeed but increase the sore which it should have cured. They saw that *to live by one man's will became the cause of all men's misery*. This constrained them to come unto laws wherein all men might see their duty beforehand, and know the penalties of transgressing them.' — Hooker's *Eccl. Pol.*, lib. i, sect. 10.

tive was placed in collective bodies of men, call them senate,
parliament, or what you please, by which means every single
person became subject equally, with other the meanest men,
to those laws, which he himself, as part of the legislative, had
established; nor could anyone, by his own authority, avoid
the force of the law, when once made, nor by any pretence of
superiority plead exemption, thereby to license his own, or
the miscarriages of any of his dependants. No man in civil
society can be exempted from the laws of it. For if any man
may do what he thinks fit and there be no appeal on earth
for redress or security against any harm he shall do, I ask
whether he be not perfectly still in the state of nature, and
so can be no part or member of that civil society, unless anyone will say the state of nature and civil society are one and
the same thing, which I have never yet found anyone so
great a patron of anarchy as to affirm.[6]

(((VIII)))

OF THE BEGINNING OF POLITICAL SOCIETIES

95. Men being, as has been said, by nature all free, equal,
and independent, no one can be put out of his estate and
subjected to the political power of another without his own
consent, which is done by agreeing with other men, to join
and unite into a community for their comfortable, safe, and
peaceable living, one amongst another, in a secure enjoyment of their properties, and a greater security against any
that are not of it. This any number of men may do, because
it injures not the freedom of the rest; they are left, as they
were, in the liberty of the state of nature. When any number
of men have so consented to make one community or government, they are thereby presently incorporated, and make
one body politic, wherein the majority have a right to act
and conclude the rest.

6. 'Civil law, being the act of the whole body politic, doth therefore overrule each
    several part of the same body.' — Hooker's *Eccl. Pol.*, lib. i, sect. 10.

96. For, when any number of men have, by the consent of every individual, made a community, they have thereby made that community one body, with a power to act as one body, which is only by the will and determination of the majority. For that which acts any community, being only the consent of the individuals of it, and it being one body, must move one way, it is necessary the body should move that way whither the greater force carries it, which is the consent of the majority, or else it is impossible it should act or continue one body, one community, which the consent of every individual that united into it agreed that it should; and so everyone is bound by that consent to be concluded by the majority. And therefore we see that in assemblies empowered to act by positive laws where no number is set by that positive law which empowers them, the act of the majority passes for the act of the whole, and of course determines as having, by the law of nature and reason, the power of the whole.

97. And thus every man, by consenting with others to make one body politic under one government, puts himself under an obligation to everyone of that society to submit to the determination of the majority, and to be concluded by it; or else this original compact, whereby he with others incorporates into one society, would signify nothing, and be no compact if he be left free and under no other ties than he was in before in the state of nature. For what appearance would there be of any compact? What new engagement if he were no farther tied by any decrees of the society than he himself thought fit and did actually consent to? This would be still as great a liberty as he himself had before his compact, or anyone else in the state of nature hath, who may submit himself and consent to any acts of it if he thinks fit.

98. For if the consent of the majority shall not in reason be received as the act of the whole, and conclude every individual, nothing but the consent of every individual can make any thing to be the act of the whole, which, considering the infirmities of health and avocations of business,

which in a number though much less than that of a commonwealth, will necessarily keep many away from the public
assembly; and the variety of opinions and contrariety of interests which unavoidably happen in all collections of men,
'tis next impossible ever to be had. And, therefore, if coming into society be upon such terms, it will be only like Cato's
coming into the theatre, *tantum ut exiret*. Such a constitution as this would make the mighty *Leviathan* of a shorter
duration than the feeblest creatures, and not let it outlast the
day it was born in, which cannot be supposed till we can
think that rational creatures should desire and constitute
societies only to be dissolved. For where the majority cannot conclude the rest, there they cannot act as one body, and
consequently will be immediately dissolved again.

99. Whosoever therefore out of a state of nature unite
into a community, must be understood to give up all the
power necessary to the ends for which they unite into society
to the majority of the community, unless they expressly
agreed in any number greater than the majority. And this is
done by barely agreeing to unite into one political society,
which is all the compact that is, or needs be, between the
individuals that enter into or make up a commonwealth.
And thus, that which begins and actually constitutes any
political society is nothing but the consent of any number of
freemen capable of a majority, to unite and incorporate into
such a society. And this is that, and that only, which did or
could give beginning to any lawful government in the world.

100. To this I find two objections made:

First, *That there are no instances to be found in story of a
company of men, independent and equal one amongst another,
that met together, and in this way began and set up a government.*

Secondly, *'Tis impossible of right that men should do so, because all men, being born under government, they are to submit
to that, and are not at liberty to begin a new one.*

101. To the first there is this to answer: That it is not at
all to be wondered that history gives us but a very little ac-

count of men that lived together in the state of nature. The inconveniencies of that condition, and the love and want of society, no sooner brought any number of them together, but they presently united and incorporated if they designed to continue together. And if we may not suppose men ever to have been in the state of nature, because we hear not much of them in such a state, we may as well suppose the armies of Salmanasser or Xerxes were never children, because we hear little of them till they were men and embodied in armies. Government is everywhere antecedent to records, and letters seldom come in amongst a people till a long continuation of civil society has, by other more necessary arts, provided for their safety, ease, and plenty. And then they begin to look after the history of their founders, and search into their original when they have outlived the memory of it. For 'tis with commonwealths as with particular persons, they are commonly ignorant of their own births and infancies; and if they know any thing of their original, they are beholding for it to the accidental records that others have kept of it. And those that we have of the beginning of any polities in the world, excepting that of the Jews, where God himself immediately interposed, and which favours not at all paternal dominion, are all either plain instances of such a beginning as I have mentioned, or at least have manifest footsteps of it.

102. He must show a strange inclination to deny evident matter of fact, when it agrees not with his hypothesis, who will not allow that the beginning of Rome and Venice were by the uniting together of several men, free and independent one of another, amongst whom there was no natural superiority or subjection. And if Josephus Acosta's word may be taken, he tells us that in many parts of America there was no government at all. *There are great and apparent conjectures,* says he, *that these men,* speaking of those of Peru, *for a long time had neither kings nor commonwealths, but lived in troops, as they do this day in* Florida — *the* Cheriquanas, *those of* Brazil, *and many other nations, which have no certain kings, but, as occasion is offered in peace or war, they choose their cap-*

tains as they please, l. i. c. 25. If it be said that every man there was born subject to his father, or the head of his family, that the subjection due from a child to a father took not away his freedom of uniting into what political society he thought fit, has been already proved; but be that as it will, these men, 'tis evident, were actually free; and whatever superiority some politicians now would place in any of them, they themselves claimed it not; but, by consent, were all equal, till, by the same consent, they set rulers over themselves. So that their politic societies all began from a voluntary union, and the mutual agreement of men freely acting in the choice of their governors and forms of government.

103. And I hope those who went away from Sparta, with Palantus, mentioned by Justin, will be allowed to have been free men independent one of another, and to have set up a government over themselves by their own consent. Thus I have given several examples out of history of people, free and in the state of nature, that, being met together, incorporated and began a commonwealth. And if the want of such instances be an argument to prove that government were not nor could not be so begun, I suppose the contenders for paternal empire were better let it alone than urge it against natural liberty; for if they can give so many instances out of history of governments begun upon paternal right, I think (though at best an argument from what has been, to what should of right be, has no great force) one might, without any great danger, yield them the cause. But if I might advise them in the case, they would do well not to search too much into the original of governments as they have begun *de facto,* lest they should find at the foundation of most of them something very little favourable to the design they promote, and such a power as they contend for.

104. But, to conclude: reason being plain on our side that men are naturally free; and the examples of history showing that the governments of the world that were begun in peace had their beginning laid on that foundation, and were made by the consent of the people; there can be little room for

doubt, either where the right is, or what has been the opinion or practice of mankind about the first erecting of governments.

105. I will not deny that if we look back, as far as history will direct us, towards the original of commonwealths, we shall generally find them under the government and administration of one man. And I am also apt to believe that where a family was numerous enough to subsist by itself, and continued entire together, without mixing with others, as it often happens, where there is much land and few people, the government commonly began in the father. For the father having, by the law of nature, the same power, with every man else, to punish, as he thought fit, any offences against that law, might thereby punish his transgressing children, even when they were men, and out of their pupilage; and they were very likely to submit to his punishment, and all join with him against the offender in their turns, giving him thereby power to execute his sentence against any transgression, and so, in effect, make him the law-maker and governor over all that remained in conjunction with his family. He was fittest to be trusted; paternal affection secured their property and interest under his care, and the custom of obeying him in their childhood made it easier to submit to him rather than any other. If therefore they must have one to rule them, as government is hardly to be avoided amongst men that live together, who so likely to be the man as he that was their common father, unless negligence, cruelty, or any other defect of mind or body, made him unfit for it? But when either the father died, and left his heir, for want of age, wisdom, courage, or any other qualities, less fit for rule, or where several families met and consented to continue together, there, 'tis not to be doubted, but they used their natural freedom to set up him whom they judged the ablest and most likely to rule well over them. Conformable hereunto we find the people of America, who, living out of the reach of the conquering swords and spreading domination of the two great empires of Peru and Mexico, enjoyed

their own natural freedom, though, *cœteris paribus*, they commonly prefer the heir of their deceased king; yet, if they find him any way weak or uncapable, they pass him by, and set up the stoutest and bravest man for their ruler.

106. Thus, though looking back as far as records give us any account of peopling the world, and the history of nations, we commonly find the government to be in one hand, yet it destroys not that which I affirm (*viz.*) that the beginning of politic society depends upon the consent of the individuals to join into and make one society, who, when they are thus incorporated, might set up what form of government they thought fit. But this having given occasion to men to mistake and think that, by nature, government was monarchical, and belonged to the father, it may not be amiss here to consider why people, in the beginning, generally pitched upon this form, which, though perhaps the father's pre-eminency might, in the first institution of some commonwealths, give a rise to and place in the beginning the power in one hand, yet it is plain that the reason that continued the form of government in a single person was not any regard or respect to paternal authority, since all petty monarchies, that is, almost all monarchies, near their original have been commonly, at least upon occasion, elective.

107. First then, in the beginning of things, the father's government of the childhood of those sprung from him, having accustomed them to the rule of one man, and taught them that where it was exercised with care and skill, with affection and love to those under it, it was sufficient to procure and preserve to men all the political happiness they sought for in society. It was no wonder that they should pitch and naturally run into that form of government which, from their infancy, they had been all accustomed to, and which, by experience, they had found both easy and safe. To which if we add, that monarchy being simple and most obvious to men, whom neither experience had instructed in forms of government, nor the ambition or insolence of empire had taught to beware of the encroachments of preroga-

tive or the inconveniences of absolute power, which monarchy, in succession, was apt to lay claim to and bring upon them; it was not at all strange that they should not much trouble themselves to think of methods of restraining any exorbitances of those to whom they had given the authority over them, and of balancing the power of government by placing several parts of it in different hands. They had neither felt the oppression of tyrannical dominion, nor did the fashion of the age, nor their possessions, or way of living, which afforded little matter for covetousness or ambition, give them any reason to apprehend or provide against it; and therefore 'tis no wonder they put themselves into such a frame of government as was not only, as I said, most obvious and simple, but also best suited to their present state and condition, which stood more in need of defence against foreign invasions and injuries than of multiplicity of laws where there was but very little property, and wanted not variety of rulers and abundance of officers to direct and look after their execution where there were but few trespasses and few offenders. Since, then, those who liked one another so well as to join into society cannot but be supposed to have some acquaintance and friendship together, and some trust one in another, they could not but have greater apprehensions of others than of one another; and, therefore, their first care and thought cannot but be supposed to be, how to secure themselves against foreign force. 'Twas natural for them to put themselves under a frame of government which might best serve to that end, and choose the wisest and bravest man to conduct them in their wars and lead them out against their enemies, and in this chiefly be their ruler.

108. Thus we see that the kings of the Indians, in America, which is still a pattern of the first ages in Asia and Europe, whilst the inhabitants were too few for the country, and want of people and money gave men no temptation to enlarge their possessions of land, or contest for wider extent of ground, are little more than generals of their armies; and though they command absolutely in war, yet at home, and

in time of peace, they exercise very little dominion, and have but a very moderate sovereignty, the resolutions of peace and war being ordinarily either in the people or in a council, though the war itself, which admits not of plurality of governors, naturally devolves the command into the king's sole authority.

109. And thus, in Israel itself, the chief business of their judges and first kings seems to have been to be captains in war and leaders of their armies, which (besides what is signified by *going out and in before the people*, which was, to march forth to war and home again in the heads of their forces) appears plainly in the story of Jephtha. The Ammonites making war upon Israel, the Gileadites, in fear, send to Jephtha, a bastard of their family, whom they had cast off, and article with him, if he will assist them against the Ammonites, to make him their ruler, which they do in these words: *And the people made him head and captain over them*, Judges xi. 11, which was, as it seems, all one as to be judge. *And he judged Israel*, Judges, xii. 7, that is, was their captain-general *six years*. So when Jotham upbraids the Shechemites with the obligation they had to Gideon, who had been their judge and ruler, he tells them: *He fought for you, and adventured his life far, and delivered you out of the hands of Midian*, Judges, ix. 17. Nothing mentioned of him but what he did as a general, and, indeed, that is all is found in his history, or in any of the rest of the judges. And Abimelech particularly is called king, though at most he was but their general. And when, being weary of the ill-conduct of Samuel's sons, the children of Israel desired a king, *like all the nations, to judge them, and to go out before them, and to fight their battles*, 1 Sam. viii. 20, God, granting their desire, says to Samuel, *I will send thee a man, and thou shalt anoint him to be captain over my people Israel, that he may save my people out of the hands of the Philistines*, c. ix. v. 16. As if the only business of a king had been to lead out their armies and fight in their defence; and, accordingly, at his inauguration, pouring a vial of oil upon him, declares to Saul that *the Lord had anointed*

him to be captain over his inheritance, c. x. v. 1. And therefore
those who, after Saul's being solemnly chosen and saluted
king by the tribes at Mispah, were unwilling to have him
their king, make no other objection but this, *How shall this
man save us?* v. 27, as if they should have said, This man is
unfit to be our king, not having skill and conduct enough in
war to be able to defend us. And when God resolved to transfer the government to David, it is in these words: *But now
thy kingdom shall not continue: the Lord hath sought him a man
after his own heart, and the Lord hath commanded him to be
captain over his people,* c. xiii. v. 14. As if the whole kingly
authority were nothing else but to be their general; and
therefore the tribes who had stuck to Saul's family, and opposed David's reign, when they came to Hebron with terms
of submission to him, they tell him, amongst other arguments, they had to submit to him as to their king, that he
was, in effect, their king in Saul's time, and therefore they
had no reason but to receive him as their king now. *Also*
(say they) *in time past, when Saul was king over us, thou wast
he that leddest out and broughtest in Israel, and the Lord said
unto thee, Thou shalt feed my people Israel, and thou shalt be a
captain over Israel.*

110. Thus, whether a family by degrees grew up into a
commonwealth, and the fatherly authority being continued
on to the elder son, every one in his turn growing up under
it, tacitly submitted to it, and the easiness and equality of it
not offending any one, every one acquiesced till time seemed
to have confirmed it and settled a right of succession by prescription; or whether several families, or the descendants of
several families, whom chance, neighbourhood, or business
brought together, united into society; the need of a general
whose conduct might defend them against their enemies in
war, and the great confidence the innocence and sincerity of
that poor but virtuous age, such as are almost all those which
begin governments that ever come to last in the world, gave
men one of another, made the first beginners of commonwealths generally put the rule into one man's hand, without

any other express limitation or restraint but what the nature of the thing and the end of government required. It was given them for the public good and safety, and to those ends, in the infancies of commonwealths, they commonly used it; and unless they had done so, young societies could not have subsisted, without such nursing fathers; without this care of the governors, all governments would have sunk under the weakness and infirmities of their infancy, the prince and the people had soon perished together.

111. But though the golden age (before vain ambition, and *amor sceleratus habendi*, evil concupiscence had corrupted men's minds into a mistake of true power and honour) had more virtue, and consequently better governors, as well as less vicious subjects; and there was then no stretching prerogative on the one side to oppress the people, nor, consequently, on the other, any dispute about privilege, to lessen or restrain the power of the magistrate; and so no contest betwixt rulers and people about governors or government.[7] Yet, when ambition and luxury, in future ages, would retain and increase the power, without doing the business for which it was given, and aided by flattery, taught princes to have distinct and separate interests from their people, men found it necessary to examine more carefully the original and rights of government, and to find out ways to restrain the exorbitances and prevent the abuses of that power, which they having entrusted in another's hands, only for their own good, they found was made use of to hurt them.

112. Thus we may see how probable it is that people that were naturally free, and by their own consent either sub-

---

7. 'At first, when some certain kind of regiment was once approved, it may be nothing was then further thought upon for the manner of governing, but all permitted unto their wisdom and discretion, which were to rule till, by experience, they found this for all parts very inconvenient, so as the thing which they had devised for a remedy did indeed but increase the sore which it should have cured. They saw that *to live by one man's will became the cause of all men's misery*. This constrained them to come unto laws wherein all men might see their duty beforehand, and know the penalties of transgressing them.' — Hooker's *Eccl. Pol.*, lib. i, sect. 10.

mitted to the government of their father, or united together, out of different families, to make a government, should generally put the rule into one man's hands, and choose to be under the conduct of a single person, without so much as by express conditions limiting or regulating his power, which they thought safe enough in his honesty and prudence; though they never dreamed of monarchy being *jure Divino*, which we never heard of among mankind till it was revealed to us by the divinity of this last age, nor ever allowed paternal power to have a right to dominion or to be the foundation of all government. And thus much may suffice to show that, as far as we have any light from history, we have reason to conclude that all peaceful beginnings of government have been laid in the consent of the people. I say *peaceful*, because I shall have occasion, in another place, to speak of conquest, which some esteem a way of beginning of governments.

The other objection, I find, urged against the beginning of polities, in the way I have mentioned, is this, viz.:

113. *That all men being born under government, some or other, it is impossible any of them should ever be free and at liberty to unite together and begin a new one, or ever be able to erect a lawful government.*

If this argument be good, I ask, How came so many lawful monarchies into the world? For if anybody, upon this supposition, can show me any one man, in any age of the world, free to begin a lawful monarchy, I will be bound to show him ten other free men at liberty, at the same time, to unite and begin a new government under a regal or any other form. It being demonstration, that if anyone born under the domination of another may be so free as to have a right to command others in a new and distinct empire, everyone that is born under the dominion of another may be so free too, and may become a ruler or subject of a distinct separate government. And so, by this their own principle, either all men, however born, are free, or else there is but one lawful prince, one lawful government in the world; and then they have nothing to do but barely to show us which that is, which, when they have done, I doubt not but all mankind will easily agree to pay obedience to him.

114. Though it be a sufficient answer to their objection to show that it involves them in the same difficulties that it doth those they use it against, yet I shall endeavour to discover the weakness of this argument a little farther.

All men, say they, *are born under government, and therefore they cannot be at liberty to begin a new one. Everyone is born a subject to his father or his prince, and is therefore under the perpetual tie of subjection and allegiance.* 'Tis plain mankind never owned nor considered any such natural subjection that they were born in, to one or to the other, that tied them, without their own consents, to a subjection to them and their heirs.

115. For there are no examples so frequent in history, both sacred and profane, as those of men withdrawing themselves and their obedience from the jurisdiction they were born under, and the family or community they were bred up in, and setting up new governments in other places, from whence sprang all that number of petty commonwealths in the beginning of ages, and which always multiplied as long as there was room enough, till the stronger or more fortunate swallowed the weaker; and those great ones, again breaking to pieces, dissolved into lesser dominions; all which are so many testimonies against paternal sovereignty, and plainly prove that it was not the natural right of the father descending to his heirs that made governments in the beginning; since it was impossible, upon that ground, there should have been so many little kingdoms but only one universal monarchy if men had not been at liberty to separate themselves from their families and the government, be it what it will that was set up in it, and go and make distinct commonwealths and other governments as they thought fit.

116. This has been the practice of the world from its first beginning to this day; nor is it now any more hindrance to the freedom of mankind, that they are born under constituted

and ancient polities that have established laws and set forms of government, than if they were born in the woods amongst the unconfined inhabitants that ran loose in them. For those who would persuade us that by being born under any government we are naturally subjects to it, and have no more any title or pretence to the freedom of the state of nature, have no other reason (bating that of paternal power, which we have already answered) to produce for it, but only because our fathers or progenitors passed away their natural liberty, and thereby bound up themselves and their posterity to a perpetual subjection to the government which they themselves submitted to. 'Tis true that whatever engagements or promises anyone made for himself, he is under the obligation of them, but cannot by any compact whatsoever bind his children or posterity. For his son, when a man, being altogether as free as the father, any act of the father can no more give away the liberty of the son than it can of anybody else. He may, indeed, annex such conditions to the land he enjoyed, as a subject of any commonwealth, as may oblige his son to be of that community, if he will enjoy those possessions which were his father's, because that estate being his father's property, he may dispose or settle it as he pleases.

117. And this has generally given the occasion to the mistake in this matter; because commonwealths not permitting any part of their dominions to be dismembered, nor to be enjoyed by any but those of their community, the son cannot ordinarily enjoy the possessions of his father but under the same terms his father did, by becoming a member of the society, whereby he puts himself presently under the government he finds there established, as much as any other subject of that commonwealth. And thus the consent of free men, born under government, which only makes them members of it, being given separately in their turns, as each comes to be of age, and not in a multitude together, people take no notice of it, and thinking it not done at all, or not necessary, conclude they are naturally subjects as they are men.

118. But 'tis plain governments themselves understand it otherwise; they claim no power over the son because of that they had over the father; nor look on children as being their subjects, by their fathers being so. If a subject of England have a child by an Englishwoman in France, whose subject is he? Not the King of England's; for he must have leave to be admitted to the privileges of it. Nor the King of France's, for how then has his father a liberty to bring him away, and breed him as he pleases; and whoever was judged as a traitor or deserter, if he left, or warred against a country, for being barely born in it of parents that were aliens there? 'Tis plain, then, by the practice of governments themselves, as well as by the law of right reason, that a child is born a subject of no country or government. He is under his father's tuition and authority till he come to age of discretion, and then he is a free man, at liberty what government he will put himself under, what body politic he will unite himself to. For if an Englishman's son born in France be at liberty, and may do so, it is evident there is no tie upon him by his father's being a subject of this kingdom, nor is he bound up by any compact of his ancestors; and why then hath not his son, by the same reason, the same liberty, though he be born anywhere else? Since the power that a father hath naturally over his children is the same wherever they be born, and the ties of natural obligations are not bounded by the positive limits of kingdoms and commonwealths.

119. Every man being, as has been showed, naturally free, and nothing being able to put him into subjection to any earthly power, but only his own consent, it is to be considered what shall be understood to be a sufficient declaration of a man's consent to make him subject to the laws of any government. There is a common distinction of an express and a tacit consent, which will concern our present case. No body doubts but an express consent of any man, entering into any society, makes him a perfect member of that society, a subject of that government. The difficulty is, what ought to be looked upon as a tacit consent, and how far

it binds, i.e., how far anyone shall be looked on to have consented, and thereby submitted to any government, where he
has made no expressions of it at all. And to this I say, that
every man that hath any possession or enjoyment of any part
of the dominions of any government doth thereby give his
tacit consent, and is as far forth obliged to obedience to the
laws of that government, during such enjoyment, as any one
under it, whether this his possession be of land to him and
his heirs for ever, or a lodging only for a week; or whether it
be barely travelling freely on the highway; and, in effect, it
reaches as far as the very being of anyone within the territories of that government.

120. To understand this the better, it is fit to consider
that every man when he at first incorporates himself into any
commonwealth, he, by his uniting himself thereunto, an-
nexes also, and submits to the community those possessions
which he has, or shall acquire, that do not already belong to
any other government. For it would be a direct contradiction
for anyone to enter into society with others for the securing
and regulating of property, and yet to suppose his land,
whose property is to be regulated by the laws of the society,
should be exempt from the jurisdiction of that government
to which he himself, the proprietor of the land, is a subject.
By the same act, therefore, whereby anyone unites his person, which was before free, to any commonwealth, by the
same he unites his possessions, which were before free, to it
also; and they become, both of them, person and possession,
subject to the government and dominion of that commonwealth as long as it hath a being. Whoever therefore, from
thenceforth, by inheritance, purchase, permission, or otherwise enjoys any part of the land so annexed to, and under the
government of that commonwealth, must take it with the
condition it is under; that is, of submitting to the government of the commonwealth, under whose jurisdiction it is,
as far forth as any subject of it.

121. But since the government has a direct jurisdiction
only over the land and reaches the possessor of it (before he

has actually incorporated himself in the society) only as he dwells upon and enjoys that, the obligation anyone is under by virtue of such enjoyment to submit to the government begins and ends with the enjoyment; so that whenever the owner, who has given nothing but such a tacit consent to the government, will, by donation, sale or otherwise, quit the said possession, he is at liberty to go and incorporate himself into any other commonwealth, or agree with others to begin a new one *in vacuis locis*, in any part of the world they can find free and unpossessed; whereas he that has once, by actual agreement and any express declaration, given his consent to be of any commonweal, is perpetually and indispensably obliged to be, and remain unalterably a subject to it, and can never be again in the liberty of the state of nature, unless by any calamity the government he was under comes to be dissolved; or else by some public act cuts him off from being any longer a member of it.

122. But submitting to the laws of any country, living quietly, and enjoying privileges and protection under them, makes not a man a member of that society; this is only a local protection and homage due to and from all those who, not being in a state of war, come within the territories belonging to any government, to all parts whereof the force of its law extends. But this no more makes a man a member of that society, a perpetual subject of that commonwealth, than it would make a man a subject to another in whose family he found it convenient to abide for some time, though, whilst he continued in it, he were obliged to comply with the laws and submit to the government he found there. And thus we see that foreigners, by living all their lives under another government, and enjoying the privileges and protection of it, though they are bound, even in conscience, to submit to its administration as far forth as any denizen, yet do not thereby come to be subjects or members of that commonwealth. Nothing can make any man so but his actually entering into it by positive engagement and express promise and compact. This is that which I think, concerning the beginning of po-

litical societies, and that consent which makes anyone a member of any commonwealth.

(((IX)))

OF THE ENDS OF POLITICAL SOCIETY AND GOVERNMENT

123. If man in the state of nature be so free as has been said; if he be absolute lord of his own person and possessions; equal to the greatest and subject to no body, why will he part with his freedom? Why will he give up this empire, and subject himself to the dominion and control of any other power? To which 'tis obvious to answer, that though in the state of nature he hath such a right, yet the enjoyment of it is very uncertain and constantly exposed to the invasion of others; for all being kings as much as he, every man his equal, and the greater part no strict observers of equity and justice, the enjoyment of the property he has in this state is very unsafe, very unsecure. This makes him willing to quit this condition which, however free, is full of fears and continual dangers; and 'tis not without reason that he seeks out and is willing to join in society with others who are already united, or have a mind to unite for the mutual preservation of their lives, liberties, and estates, which I call by the general name, property.

124. The great and chief end therefore, of men's uniting into commonwealths, and putting themselves under government, is the preservation of their property; to which in the state of nature there are many things wanting.

First, There wants an established, settled, known law, received and allowed by common consent to be the standard of right and wrong, and the common measure to decide all controversies between them. For though the law of nature be plain and intelligible to all rational creatures, yet men, being biased by their interest, as well as ignorant for want of study of it, are not apt to allow of it as a law binding to them in the application of it to their particular cases.

125. *Secondly,* In the state of nature there wants a known

and indifferent judge, with authority to determine all differences according to the established law. For everyone in that state being both judge and executioner of the law of nature, men being partial to themselves, passion and revenge is very apt to carry them too far, and with too much heat in their own cases, as well as negligence and unconcernedness, make them too remiss in other men's.

126. *Thirdly*, In the state of nature there often wants power to back and support the sentence when right, and to give it due execution. They who by any injustice offended, will seldom fail where they are able by force to make good their injustice. Such resistance many times makes the punishment dangerous, and frequently destructive to those who attempt it.

127. Thus mankind, notwithstanding all the privileges of the state of nature, being but in an ill condition while they remain in it, are quickly driven into society. Hence it comes to pass, that we seldom find any number of men live any time together in this state. The inconveniences that they are therein exposed to by the irregular and uncertain exercise of the power every man has of punishing the transgressions of others, make them take sanctuary under the established laws of government, and therein seek the preservation of their property. 'Tis this makes them so willingly give up every one his single power of punishing to be exercised by such alone as shall be appointed to it amongst them, and by such rules as the community, or those authorized by them to that purpose, shall agree on. And in this we have the original right and rise of both the legislative and executive power as well as of the governments and societies themselves.

128. For in the state of Nature to omit the liberty he has of innocent delights, a man has two powers.

The first is to do whatsoever he thinks fit for the preservation of himself and others within the permission of the law of nature; by which law, common to them all, he and all the rest of mankind are one community, make up one society distinct from all other creatures and were it not for the corruption and viciousness of degenerate men, there would be no need of any other, no necessity that men should separate from this great and natural community, and associate into less combinations.

The other power a man has in the state of nature is the power to punish the crimes committed against that law. Both these he gives up when he joins in a private, if I may so call it, or particular political society, and incorporates into any commonwelath separate from the rest of mankind.

129. The first power, *viz.* of doing whatsoever he thought fit for the preservation of himself and the rest of mankind, he gives up to be regulated by laws made by the society, so far forth as the preservation of himself and the rest of that society shall require; which laws of the society in many things confine the liberty he had by the law of nature.

130. *Secondly,* The power of punishing he wholly gives up, and engages his natural force (which he might before employ in the execution of the law of nature, by his own single authority, as he thought fit) to assist the executive power of the society as the law thereof shall require. For being now in a new state, wherein he is to enjoy many conveniences from the labour, assistance, and society of others in the same community, as well as protection from its whole strength, he is to part also with as much of his natural liberty, in providing for himself, as the good, prosperity, and safety of the society shall require, which is not only necessary but just, since the other members of the society do the like.

131. But though men when they enter into society give up the equality, liberty, and executive power they had in the state of nature into the hands of the society, to be so far disposed of by the legislative as the good of the society shall require, yet it being only with an intention in everyone the better to preserve himself, his liberty and property (for no rational creature can be supposed to change his condition with an intention to be worse), the power of the society or legislative constituted by them can never be supposed to ex-

tend farther than the common good, but is obliged to secure
everyone's property by providing against those three defects
above-mentioned that made the state of nature so unsafe
and uneasy. And so, whoever has the legislative or supreme
power of any commonwelath, is bound to govern by established standing laws, promulgated and known to the people,
and not by extemporary decrees, by indifferent and upright
judges, who are to decide controversies by those laws; and
to employ the force of the community at home only in the
execution of such laws, or abroad to prevent or redress
foreign injuries and secure the community from inroads and
invasion. And all this to be directed to no other end but the
peace, safety, and public good of the people.

(((X)))

OF THE FORMS OF A COMMONWEALTH

132. The majority having, as has been shewed, upon men's
first uniting into society, the whole power of the community
naturally in them, may employ all that power in making laws
for the community from time to time, and executing those
laws by officers of their own appointing, and then the form
of the government is a perfect democracy; or else may put
the power of making laws into the hands of a few select men,
and their heirs or successors, and then it is an oligarchy; or
else into the hands of one man, and then it is a monarchy; if
to him and his heirs, it is a hereditary monarchy; if to him
only for life, but upon his death the power only of nominat-
ing a successor to return to them, an elective monarchy. And
so accordingly of these make compounded and mixed forms
of government, as they think good. And if the legislative
power be at first given by the majority to one or more persons only for their lives, or any limited time, and then the
supreme power to revert to them again, when it is so re-
verted the community may dispose of it again anew into
what hands they please, and so constitute a new form of gov-

ernment; for the form of government depending upon the placing the supreme power, which is the legislative, it being impossible to conceive that an inferior power should prescribe to a superior, or any but the supreme make laws, according as the power of making laws is placed, such is the form of the commonwealth.

133. By *commonwealth* I must be understood all along to mean not a democracy, or any form of government, but any independent community which the Latins signified by the word *civitas*, to which the word which best answers in our language is Commonwealth, and most properly expresses such a society of men which Community does not (for there may be subordinate communities in a government), and city much less. And therefore to avoid ambiguity, I crave leave to use the word *Commonwealth* in that sense; in which sense I find the word used by King James the First, which I think to be its genuine signification, which, if anybody dislike, I consent with him to change it for a better.

(((XI)))

OF THE EXTENT OF THE LEGISLATIVE POWER

134. The great end of men's entering into society being the enjoyment of their properties in peace and safety, and the great instrument and means of that being the laws established in that society, the first and fundamental positive law of all commonwealths is the establishing of the legislative power; as the first and fundamental natural law, which is to govern even the legislative itself, is the preservation of the society, and (as far as will consist with the public good) of every person in it. This legislative is not only the supreme power of the commonwealth, but sacred and unalterable in the hands where the community have once placed it; nor can any edict of anybody else, in what form soever conceived, or by what power soever backed, have the force and obligation of a law which has not its sanction from that legislative

which the public has chosen and appointed; for without this the law could not have that which is absolutely necessary to its being a law, the consent of the society, over whom nobody can have a power to make laws [8] but by their own consent and by authority received from them; and therefore all the obedience, which by the most solemn ties anyone can be obliged to pay, ultimately terminates in this supreme power, and is directed by those laws which it enacts. Nor can any oaths to any foreign power whatsoever, or any domestic subordinate power, discharge any member of the society from his obedience to the legislative, acting pursuant to their trust, nor oblige him to any obedience contrary to the laws so enacted or farther than they do allow, it being ridiculous to imagine one can be tied ultimately to obey any power in the society which is not the supreme.

135. Though the legislative, whether placed in one or more, whether it be always in being or only by intervals, though it be the supreme power in every commonwealth, yet

First, It is not, nor can possibly be, absolutely arbitrary over the lives and fortunes of the people. For it being but the joint power of every member of the society given up to that person or assembly which is legislator, it can be no more than those persons had in a state of nature before they entered into society, and gave it up to the community. For nobody can transfer to another more power than he has in himself,

8. 'The lawful power of making laws to command whole politic societies of men, belonging so properly unto the same entire societies, that for any prince or potentate, of what kind soever upon earth, to exercise the same of himself, and not by express commission immediately and personally received from God, or else by authority derived at the first from their consent, upon whose persons they impose laws, it is no better than mere tyranny. Laws they are not, therefore, which public approbation hath not made so.' — Hooker's *Eccl. Pol.*, lib. i, sect. 10. 'Of this point, therefore, we are to note that such men naturally have no full and perfect power to command whole politic multitudes of men, therefore utterly without our consent we could in such sort be at no man's commandment living. And to be commanded, we do consent when that society, whereof we be a part, hath at any time before consented, without revoking the same after by the like universal agreement.

'Laws therefore human, of what kind soever, are available by consent.' — Hooker's *Eccl. Pol.*

and nobody has an absolute arbitrary power over himself, or over any other, to destroy his own life, or take away the life or property of another. A man, as has been proved, cannot subject himself to the arbitrary power of another; and having, in the state of nature, no arbitrary power over the life, liberty, or possession of another, but only so much as the law of nature gave him for the preservation of himself and the rest of mankind, this is all he doth, or can give up to the commonwealth, and by it to the legislative power, so that the legislative can have no more than this. Their power in the utmost bounds of it is limited to the public good of the society.⁹ It is a power that hath no other end but preservation, and therefore can never have a right to destroy, enslave, or designedly to impoverish the subjects; the obligations of the law of nature cease not in society, but only in many cases are drawn closer, and have, by human laws, known penalties annexed to them to enforce their observation. Thus the law of nature stands as an eternal rule to all men, legislators as well as others. The rules that they make for other men's actions must, as well as their own and other men's actions, be conformable to the law of nature, i.e. to the will of God, of which that is a declaration, and the fundamental law of nature being the preservation of mankind, no human sanction can be good or valid against it.

136. *Secondly*, The legislative or supreme authority cannot assume to itself a power to rule by extemporary arbi-

9. 'Two foundations there are which bear up public societies; the one a natural inclination whereby all men desire sociable life and fellowship; the other an order, expressly or secretly agreed upon, touching the manner of their union in living together. The latter is that which we call the law of a commonweal, the very soul of a politic body, the parts whereof are by law animated, held together, and set on work in such actions as the common good requireth. Laws politic, ordained for external order and regiment amongst men, are never framed as they should be, unless presuming the will of man to be inwardly obstinate, rebellious, and averse from all obedience to the sacred laws of his nature; in a word, unless presuming man to be in regard of his depraved mind little better than a wild beast, they do accordingly provide notwithstanding, so to frame his outward actions, that they be no hindrance unto the common good, for which societies are instituted. Unless they do this they are not perfect.' — Hooker's *Eccl. Pol.*, lib. i, sect. 10.

trary decrees, but is bound to dispense justice and decide the
rights of the subject by promulgated standing laws,[10] and
known authorized judges. For the law of nature being un-
written, and so nowhere to be found but in the minds of men,
they who, through passion or interest, shall miscite or mis-
apply it, cannot so easily be convinced of their mistake where
there is no established judge; and so it serves not as it ought,
to determine the rights and fence the properties of those that
live under it, especially where everyone is judge, interpreter,
and executioner of it too, and that in his own case; and he that
has right on his side, having ordinarily but his own single
strength, hath not force enough to defend himself from injuries or to punish delinquents. To avoid these inconveniencies which disorder men's properties in the state of nature,
men unite into societies that they may have the united
strength of the whole society to secure and defend their
properties, and may have standing rules to bound it by which
everyone may know what is his. To this end it is that men
give up all their natural power to the society they enter into,
and the community put the legislative power into such hands
as they think fit, with this trust, that they shall be governed
by declared laws, or else their peace, quiet, and property will
still be at the same uncertainty as it was in the state of Nature.

137. Absolute arbitrary power, or governing without
settled standing laws, can neither of them consist with the
ends of society and government, which men would not quit
the freedom of the state of nature for, and tie themselves up
under, were it not to preserve their lives, liberties, and fortunes, and by stated rules of right and property to secure
their peace and quiet. It cannot be supposed that they
should intend, had they a power so to do, to give to any one

10. 'Human laws are measures in respect of men whose actions they must direct,
    howbeit such measures they are as have also their higher rules to be measured
    by, which rules are two — the law of God and the law of Nature; so that laws
    human must be made according to the general laws of Nature, and without
    contradiction to any positive law of Scripture, otherwise they are ill made.' —
    Hooker's *Eccl. Pol.*, lib. iii, sect. 9.
    'To constrain men to anything inconvenient doth seem unreasonable.' —
    Ibid., lib. i, sect. 10.

or more an absolute arbitrary power over their persons and estates, and put a force into the magistrate's hand to execute his unlimited will arbitrarily upon them; this were to put themselves into a worse condition than the state of nature, wherein they had a liberty to defend their right against the injuries of others, and were upon equal terms of force to maintain it, whether invaded by a single man or many in combination. Whereas by supposing they have given up themselves to the absolute arbitrary power and will of a legislator, they have disarmed themselves, and armed him to make a prey of them when he pleases; he being in a much worse condition that is exposed to the arbitrary power of one man who has the command of a hundred thousand than he that is exposed to the arbitrary power of a hundred thousand single men, nobody being secure, that his will who has such a command is better than that of other men, though his force be a hundred thousand times stronger. And, therefore, whatever form the commonwealth is under, the ruling power ought to govern by declared and received laws, and not by extemporary dictates and undetermined resolutions, for then mankind will be in a far worse condition than in the state of nature if they shall have armed one or a few men with the joint power of a multitude, to force them to obey at pleasure the exorbitant and unlimited decrees of their sudden thoughts, or unrestrained, and till that moment, unknown wills, without having any measure set down which may guide and justify their actions. For all the power the government has, being only for the good of the society, as it ought not to be arbitrary and at pleasure, so it ought to be exercised by established and promulgated laws, that both the people may know their duty, and be safe and secure within the limits of the law, and the rulers, too, kept within their due bounds, and not to be tempted by the power they have in their hands to employ it to purposes, and by such measures as they would not have known, and own not willingly.

138. *Thirdly*, The supreme power cannot take from any man any part of his property without his own consent. For

the preservation of property being the end of government, and that for which men enter into society, it necessarily supposes and requires that the people should have property, without which they must be supposed to lose that by entering into society which was the end for which they entered into it; too gross an absurdity for any man to own. Men therefore in society having property, they have such a right to the goods, which by the law of the community are theirs, that nobody hath a right to their substance, or any part of it, from them without their own consent; without this they have no property at all. For I have truly no property in that which another can by right take from me when he pleases against my consent. Hence it is a mistake to think that the supreme or legislative power of any commonwealth can do what it will, and dispose of the estates of the subject arbitrarily, or take any part of them at pleasure. This is not much to be feared in governments where the legislative consists wholly or in part in assemblies which are variable, whose members upon the dissolution of the assembly are subjects under the common laws of their country, equally with the rest. But in governments where the legislative is in one lasting assembly, always in being, or in one man as in absolute monarchies, there is danger still, that they will think themselves to have a distinct interest from the rest of the community, and so will be apt to increase their own riches and power by taking what they think fit from the people. For a man's property is not at all secure, though there be good and equitable laws to set the bounds of it between him and his fellow-subjects, if he who commands those subjects have power to take from any private man what part he pleases of his property, and use and dispose of it as he thinks good.

139. But government, into whatsoever hands it is put, being as I have before showed, entrusted with this condition, and for this end, that men might have and secure their properties, the prince or senate, however it may have power to make laws for the regulating of property between the subjects one amongst another, yet can never have a power to take

to themselves the whole, or any part of the subjects' property, without their own consent; for this would be in effect to leave them no property at all. And to let us see that even absolute power, where it is necessary, is not arbitrary by being absolute, but is still limited by that reason, and confined to those ends which required it in some cases to be absolute, we need look no farther than the common practice of martial discipline. For the preservation of the army, and in it of the whole commonwealth, requires an absolute obedience to the command of every superior officer, and it is justly death to disobey or dispute the most dangerous or unreasonable of them; but yet we see that neither the sergeant that could command a soldier to march up to the mouth of a cannon, or stand in a breach where he is almost sure to perish, can command that soldier to give him one penny of his money; nor the general that can condemn him to death for deserting his post, or not obeying the most desperate orders, cannot yet with all his absolute power of life and death dispose of one farthing of that soldier's estate, or seize one jot of his goods; whom yet he can command anything, and hang for the least disobedience. Because such a blind obedience is necessary to that end for which the commander has his power, *viz.* the preservation of the rest, but the disposing of his goods has nothing to do with it.

140. 'Tis true, governments cannot be supported without great charge, and 'tis fit everyone who enjoys his share of the protection should pay out of his estate his proportion for the maintenance of it. But still it must be with his own consent, i.e. the consent of the majority, giving it either by themselves or their representatives chosen by them; for if anyone shall claim a power to lay and levy taxes on the people by his own authority, and without such consent of the people, he thereby invades the fundamental law of property, and subverts the end of government. For what property have I in that which another may by right take when he pleases himself?

141. *Fourthly*, The legislative cannot transfer the power

of making laws to any other hands, for it being but a delegated power from the people, they who have it cannot pass it over to others. The people alone can appoint the form of the commonwealth, which is by constituting the legislative, and appointing in whose hands that shall be. And when the people have said, We will submit, and be governed by laws made by such men, and in such forms, nobody else can say other men shall make laws for them; nor can they be bound by any laws but such as are enacted by those whom they have chosen and authorized to make laws for them. The power of the legislative being derived from the people by a positive voluntary grant and institution, can be no other than what that positive grant conveyed, which being only to make laws, and not to make legislators, the legislative can have no power to transfer their authority of making laws, and place it in other hands.

142. These are the bounds which the trust that is put in them by the society and the law of God and nature have set to the legislative power of every commonwealth, in all forms of government.

First, They are to govern by promulgated established laws, not to be varied in particular cases, but to have one rule for rich and poor, for the favourite at Court, and the countryman at plough.

Secondly, These laws also ought to be designed for no other end ultimately but the good of the people.

Thirdly, They must not raise taxes on the property of the people without the consent of the people given by themselves or their deputies. And this properly concerns only such governments where the legislative is always in being, or at least where the people have not reserved any part of the legislative to deputies, to be from time to time chosen by themselves.

Fourthly, The legislative neither must nor can transfer the power of making laws to anybody else, or place it anywhere but where the people have.

(((XII)))

OF THE LEGISLATIVE, EXECUTIVE, AND FEDERATIVE POWER OF THE COMMONWEALTH

143. The legislative power is that which has a right to direct how the force of the commonwealth shall be employed for preserving the community and the members of it. But because those laws which are constantly to be executed, and whose force is always to continue, may be made in a little time; therefore there is no need that the legislative should be always in being, not having always business to do. And because it may be too great temptation to human frailty, apt to grasp at power, for the same persons who have the power of making laws, to have also in their hands the power to execute them, whereby they may exempt themselves from obedience to the laws they make, and suit the law, both in its making and execution, to their own private advantage, and thereby come to have a distinct interest from the rest of the community, contrary to the end of society and government. Therefore in well-ordered commonwealths, where the good of the whole is so considered as it ought, the legislative power is put into the hands of divers persons who, duly assembled, have by themselves, or jointly with others, a power to make laws, which when they have done, being separated again, they are themselves subject to the laws they have made; which is a new and near tie upon them to take care that they make them for the public good.

144. But because the laws that are at once, and in a short time made, have a constant and lasting force, and need a perpetual execution, or an attendance thereunto, therefore 'tis necessary there should be a power always in being, which should see to the execution of the laws that are made, and remain in force. And thus the legislative and executive power come often to be separated.

145. There is another power in every commonwealth which one may call natural, because it is that which answers

to the power every man naturally had before he entered into society. For though in a commonwealth the members of it are distinct persons, still, in reference to one another, and, as such, are governed by the laws of the society; yet, in reference to the rest of mankind, they make one body, which is, as every member of it before was, still in the state of Nature with the rest of mankind. Hence it is that the controversies that happen between any man of the society with those that are out of it are managed by the public, and an injury done to a member of their body engages the whole in the reparation of it. So that under this consideration the whole community is one body in the state of Nature in respect of all other states or persons out of its community.

146. This, therefore, contains the power of war and peace, leagues and alliances, and all the transactions with all persons and communities without the commonwealth, and may be called federative if any one pleases. So the thing be understood, I am indifferent as to the name.

147. These two powers, executive and federative, though they be really distinct in themselves, yet one comprehending the execution of the municipal laws of the society within its self upon all that are parts of it; the other the management of the security and interest of the public without, with all those that it may receive benefit or damage from, yet they are always almost united. And though this federative power in the well or ill management of it be of great moment to the commonwealth, yet it is much less capable to be directed by antecedent, standing, positive laws than the executive, and so must necessarily be left to the prudence and wisdom of those whose hands it is in, to be managed for the public good. For the laws that concern subjects one amongst another, being to direct their actions, may well enough precede them. But what is to be done in reference to foreigners, depending much upon their actions, and the variation of designs and interests, must be left in great part to the prudence of those who have this power committed to them, to be managed by the best of their skill for the advantage of the commonwealth.

148. Though, as I said, the executive and federative power of every community be really distinct in themselves, yet they are hardly to be separated and placed at the same time in the hands of distinct persons. For both of them requiring the force of the society for their exercise, it is almost impracticable to place the force of the commonwealth in distinct and not subordinate hands; or that the executive and federative power should be placed in persons that might act separately, whereby the force of the public would be under different commands, which would be apt sometime or other to cause disorder and ruin.

(((XIII)))

OF THE SUBORDINATION OF THE POWERS OF THE COMMONWEALTH

149. Though in a constituted commonwealth, standing upon its own basis and acting according to its own nature, that is, acting for the preservation of the community, there can be but one supreme power, which is the legislative, to which all the rest are and must be subordinate, yet the legislative being only a fiduciary power to act for certain ends, there remains still in the people a supreme power to remove or alter the legislative, when they find the legislative act contrary to the trust reposed in them. For all power given with trust for the attaining an end being limited by that end, whenever that end is manifestly neglected or opposed, the trust must necessarily be forfeited, and the power devolve into the hands of those that gave it, who may place it anew where they shall think best for their safety and security. And thus the community perpetually retains a supreme power of saving themselves from the attempts and designs of any body, even of their legislators, whenever they shall be so foolish or so wicked as to lay and carry on designs against the liberties and properties of the subject. For no man or society of men having a power to deliver up their preservation, or consequently

the means of it, to the absolute will and arbitrary dominion of another, whenever any one shall go about to bring them into such a slavish condition, they will always have a right to preserve what they have not a power to part with, and to rid themselves of those who invade this fundamental, sacred, and unalterable law of self-preservation, for which they entered into society. And thus the community may be said in this respect to be always the supreme power, but not as considered under any form of government, because this power of the people can never take place till the government be dissolved.

150. In all cases, whilst the government subsists, the legislative is the supreme power. For what can give laws to another must needs be superior to him; and since the legislative is no otherwise legislative of the society, but by the right it has to make laws for all the parts, and for every member of the society prescribing rules to their actions, and giving power of execution where they are transgressed, the legislative must needs be the supreme, and all other powers in any members or parts of the society, derived from and subordinate to it.

151. In some commonwealths where the legislative is not always in being, and the executive is vested in a single person who has also a share in the legislative, there that single person, in a very tolerable sense, may also be called supreme; not that he has in himself all the supreme power, which is that of law-making, but because he has in him the supreme execution from whom all inferior magistrates derive all their several subordinate powers, or at least the greatest part of them; having also no legislative superior to him, there being no law to be made without his consent, which cannot be expected should ever subject him to the other part of the legislative, he is properly enough in this sense supreme. But yet it is to be observed that though oaths of allegiance and fealty are taken to him, 'tis not to him as supreme legislator, but as supreme executor of the law made by a joint power of him with others; allegiance being nothing but an obedience ac-

cording to law, which, when he violates, he has no right to
obedience, nor can claim it otherwise than as the public
person vested with the power of the law, and so is to be considered as the image, phantom, or representative of the commonwealth, acted by the will of the society declared in its
laws; and thus he has no will, no power, but that of the law.
But when he quits this representation, this public will, and
acts by his own private will, he degrades himself, and is but
a single private person without power and without will, that
has any right to obedience; the members owing no obedience
but to the public will of the society.

152. The executive power placed any where but in a person that has also a share in the legislative, is visibly subordinate and accountable to it, and may be at pleasure changed
and displaced; so that it is not the supreme executive power
that is exempt from subordination, but the supreme executive power vested in one, who having a share in the legislative, has no distinct superior legislative to be subordinate
and accountable to, farther than he himself shall join and
consent, so that he is no more subordinate than he himself
shall think fit, which one may certainly conclude will be but
very little. Of other ministerial and subordinate powers in a
commonwealth we need not speak, they being so multiplied
with infinite variety in the different customs and constitutions of distinct commonwealths, that it is impossible to give
a particular account of them all. Only thus much which is
necessary to our present purpose we may take notice of concerning them, that they have no manner of authority, any
of them, beyond what is by positive grant and commission
delegated to them, and are all of them accountable to some
other power in the commonwealth.

153. It is not necessary — no, nor so much as convenient
— that the legislative should be always in being. But absolutely necessary that the executive power should, because
there is not always need of new laws to be made, but always
need of execution of the laws that are made. When the legislative hath put the execution of the laws they make into other

hands, they have a power still to resume it out of those hands
when they find cause, and to punish for any maladministra-
tion against the laws. The same holds also in regard of the
federative power, that and the executive being both ministerial and subordinate to the legislative, which, as has been
shewed, in a constituted commonwealth is the supreme, the
legislative also in this case being supposed to consist of several persons; (for if it be a single person it cannot but be always in being, and so will, as supreme, naturally have the
supreme executive power, together with the legislative), may
assemble and exercise their legislative at the times that either
their original constitution or their own adjournment appoints,
or when they please; if neither of these hath appointed any
time, or there be no other way prescribed to convoke them.
For the supreme power being placed in them by the people,
'tis always in them, and they may exercise it when they please,
unless by their original constitution they are limited to certain seasons, or by an act of their supreme power they have
adjourned to a certain time, and when that time comes they
have a right to assemble and act again.

154. If the legislative, or any part of it, be made up of
representatives chosen for that time by the people, which
afterwards return into the ordinary state of subjects, and
have no share in the legislature but upon a new choice, this
power of choosing must also be exercised by the people,
either at certain appointed seasons, or else when they are
summoned to it; and in this latter case, the power of convoking the legislative is ordinarily placed in the executive, and
has one of these two limitations in respect of time:— that
either the original constitution requires their assembling and
acting at certain intervals, and then the executive power does
nothing but ministerially issue directions for their electing
and assembling according to due forms; or else it is left to
his prudence to call them by new elections, when the occasions or exigencies of the public require the amendment of
old or making of new laws, or the redress or prevention of
any inconveniencies that lie on or threaten the people.

155. It may be demanded here, what if the executive power, being possessed of the force of the commonwealth, shall make use of that force to hinder the meeting and acting of the legislative, when the original constitution or the public exigencies require it? I say using force upon the people without authority, and contrary to the trust put in him that does so, is a state of war with the people, who have a right to reinstate their legislative in the exercise of their power. For having erected a legislative with an intent they should exercise the power of making laws, either at certain set times, or when there is need of it, when they are hindered by any force from what is so necessary to the society, and wherein the safety and preservation of the people consists, the people have a right to remove it by force. In all states and conditions the true remedy of force without authority is to oppose force to it. The use of force without authority always puts him that uses it into a state of war as the aggressor, and renders him liable to be treated accordingly.

156. The power of assembling and dismissing the legislative, placed in the executive, gives not the executive a superiority over it, but is a fiduciary trust placed in him for the safety of the people in a case where the uncertainty and variableness of human affairs could not bear a steady fixed rule. For it not being possible that the first framers of the government should by any foresight be so much masters of future events as to be able to prefix so just periods of return and duration to the assemblies of the legislative, in all times to come, that might exactly answer all the exigencies of the commonwealth; the best remedy could be found for this defect was to trust this to the prudence of one who was always to be present, and whose business it was to watch over the public good. Constant frequent meetings of the legislative, and long continuations of their assemblies, without necessary occasion, could not but be burthensome to the people, and must necessarily in time produce more dangerous inconveniencies, and yet the quick turn of affairs might be sometimes such as to need their present help; any

delay of their convening might endanger the public; and
sometimes, too, their business might be so great that the
limited time of their sitting might be too short for their work,
and rob the public of that benefit which could be had only
from their mature deliberation. What, then, could be done
in this case to prevent the community from being exposed
sometime or other to eminent hazard on one side or the
other, by fixed intervals and periods set to the meeting and
acting of the legislative, but to entrust it to the prudence of
some who, being present and acquainted with the state of
public affairs, might make use of this prerogative for the
public good? And where else could this be so well placed as
in his hands who was entrusted with the execution of the
laws for the same end? Thus, supposing the regulation of
times for the assembling and sitting of the legislative not
settled by the original constitution, it naturally fell into the
hands of the executive; not as an arbitrary power depending
on his good pleasure, but with this trust always to have it
exercised only for the public weal, as the occurrences of
times and change of affairs might require. Whether settled
periods of their convening, or a liberty left to the prince for
convoking the legislative, or perhaps a mixture of both, hath
the least inconvenience attending it, 'tis not my business here
to inquire, but only to shew that, though the executive
power may have the prerogative of convoking and dissolving
such conventions of the legislative, yet it is not thereby
superior to it.

157. Things of this world are in so constant a flux, that
nothing remains long in the same state. Thus people, riches,
trade, power, change their stations; flourishing mighty cities
come to ruin, and prove in time neglected desolate corners,
whilst other unfrequented places grow into populous countries filled with wealth and inhabitants. But things not always changing equally, and private interest often keeping up
customs and privileges when the reasons of them are ceased,
it often comes to pass that in governments where part of the
legislative consists of representatives chosen by the people,

that in tract of time this representation becomes very un-equal and disproportionate to the reasons it was at first established upon. To what gross absurdities the following of custom when reason has left it may lead, we may be satisfied when we see the bare name of a town, of which there remains not so much as the ruins, where scarce so much housing as a sheep-cote, or more inhabitants than a shepherd is to be found, sends as many representatives to the grand assembly of law-makers as a whole county numerous in people and powerful in riches. This strangers stand amazed at, and every one must confess needs a remedy. Though most think it hard to find one, because the constitution of the legislative being the original and supreme act of the society, antecedent to all positive laws in it, and depending wholly on the people, no inferior power can alter it. And therefore the people, when the legislative is once constituted, having in such a government as we have been speaking of, no power to act as long as the government stands, this inconvenience is thought incapable of a remedy.

158. *Salus populi suprema lex* is certainly so just and fun-damental a rule, that he who sincerely follows it cannot dan-gerously err. If therefore the executive, who has the power of convoking the legislative, observing rather the true propor-tion than fashion of representation, regulates not by old custom, but true reason, the number of members in all places, that have a right to be distinctly represented, which no part of the people, however incorporated, can pretend to; but in proportion to the assistance which it affords to the public, it cannot be judged to have set up a new legislative, but to have restored the old and true one, and to have rec-tified the disorders which succession of time had insensibly as well as inevitably introduced; for it being the interest as well as intention of the people to have a fair and equal rep-resentative, whoever brings it nearest to that is an undoubted friend to and establisher of the government, and cannot miss the consent and approbation of the community; prerogative being nothing but a power in the hands of the prince to

provide for the public good, in such cases which, depending upon unforeseen and uncertain occurrences, certain and unalterable laws could not safely direct; whatsoever shall be done manifestly for the good of the people, and establishing the government upon its true foundations, is, and always will be, just prerogative. The power of erecting new corporations, and therewith new representatives, carries with it a supposition that in time the measures of representation might vary, and those places have a just right to be represented which before had none; and by the same reason, those cease to have a right, and be too inconsiderable for such a privilege, which before had it. 'Tis not a change from the present state which perhaps, corruption or decay has introduced, that makes an inroad upon the government, but the tendency of it to injure or oppress the people, and to set up one part or party with a distinction from and an unequal subjection of the rest. Whatsoever cannot but be acknowledged to be of advantage to the society and people in general, upon just and lasting measures, will always, when done, justify it self; and whenever the people shall choose their representatives upon just and undeniably equal measures, suitable to the original frame of the government, it cannot be doubted to be the will and act of the society, whoever permitted or proposed to them so to do.

(((XIV)))

OF PREROGATIVE

159. Where the legislative and executive power are in distinct hands, as they are in all moderated monarchies and well-framed governments, there the good of the society requires that several things should be left to the discretion of him that has the executive power. For the legislators not being able to foresee and provide by laws for all that may be useful to the community, the executor of the laws, having the power in his hands, has by the common law of Nature a right to make use of it for the good of the society, in many

cases where the municipal law has given no direction, till the legislative can conveniently be assembled to provide for it; nay, many things there are which the law can by no means provide for, and those must necessarily be left to the discretion of him that has the executive power in his hands, to be ordered by him as the public good and advantage shall require; nay, 'tis fit that the laws themselves should in some cases give way to the executive power, or rather to this fundamental law of Nature and government — *viz.*, that as much as may be, all the members of the society are to be preserved. For since many accidents may happen wherein a strict and rigid observation of the laws may do harm, as not to pull down an innocent man's house to stop the fire when the next to it is burning; and a man may come sometimes within the reach of the law, which makes no distinction of persons, by an action that may deserve reward and pardon; 'tis fit the ruler should have a power in many cases to mitigate the severity of the law, and pardon some offenders, since the end of government being the preservation of all as much as may be, even the guilty are to be spared where it can prove no prejudice to the innocent.

160. This power to act according to discretion for the public good, without the prescription of the law and sometimes even against it, is that which is called prerogative; for since in some governments the law-making power is not always in being and is usually too numerous, and so too slow for the dispatch requisite to execution, and because, also, it is impossible to foresee and so by laws to provide for all accidents and necessities that may concern the public, or make such laws as will do no harm if they are executed with an inflexible rigour on all occasions, and upon all persons that may come in their way, therefore there is a latitude left to the executive power to do many things of choice which the laws do not prescribe.

161. This power, whilst employed for the benefit of the community, and suitably to the trust and ends of the government, is undoubted prerogative, and never is questioned.

For the people are very seldom or never scrupulous or nice in the point; they are far from examining prerogative whilst it is in any tolerable degree employed for the use it was meant — that is, the good of the people, and not manifestly against it. But if there comes to be a question between the executive power and the people about a thing claimed as a prerogative, the tendency of the exercise of such prerogative, to the good or hurt of the people, will easily decide that question.

162. It is easy to conceive that in the infancy of governments, when commonwealths differed little from families in number of people, they differed from them too but little in number of laws; and the governors being as the fathers of them, watching over them for their good, the government was almost all prerogative. A few established laws served the turn, and the discretion and care of the ruler supplied the rest. But when mistake or flattery prevailed with weak princes, to make use of this power for private ends of their own and not for the public good, the people were fain, by express laws, to get prerogative determined in those points wherein they found disadvantage from it, and declared limitations of prerogative in those cases which they and their ancestors had left in the utmost latitude to the wisdom of those princes who made no other but a right use of it — that is, for the good of their people.

163. And therefore they have a very wrong notion of government who say that the people have encroached upon the prerogative when they have got any part of it to be defined by positive laws. For in so doing they have not pulled from the prince any thing that of right belonged to him, but only declared that that power which they indefinitely left in him or his ancestors' hands, to be exercised for their good, was not a thing they intended him, when he used it otherwise. For the end of government being the good of the community, whatsoever alterations are made in it tending to that end cannot be an encroachment upon any body; since no body in government can have a right tending to any other end; and those only are encroachments which prejudice or hinder

the public good. Those who say otherwise speak as if the prince had a distinct and separate interest from the good of the community, and was not made for it; the root and source from which spring almost all those evils and disorders which happen in kingly governments. And, indeed, if that be so, the people under his government are not a society of rational creatures, entered into a community for their mutual good; they are not such as have set rulers over themselves to guard and promote that good; but are to be looked on as an herd of inferior creatures under the dominion of a master, who keeps them and works them for his own pleasure or profit. If men were so void of reason and brutish as to enter into society upon such terms, prerogative might indeed be, what some men would have it, an arbitrary power to do things hurtful to the people.

164. But since a rational creature cannot be supposed, when free, to put himself into subjection to another for his own harm: (though where he finds a good and a wise ruler he may not, perhaps, think it either necessary or useful to set precise bounds to his power in all things) prerogative can be nothing but the people's permitting their rulers to do several things of their own free choice where the law was silent, and sometimes too against the direct letter of the law, for the public good and their acquiescing in it when so done. For as a good prince, who is mindful of the trust put into his hands, and careful of the good of his people, cannot have too much prerogative — that is, power to do good, so a weak and ill prince, who would claim that power his predecessors exercised, without the direction of the law, as a prerogative belonging to him by right of his office, which he may exercise at his pleasure to make or promote an interest distinct from that of the public, gives the people an occasion to claim their right and limit that power, which, whilst it was exercised for their good, they were content should be tacitly allowed.

165. And therefore he that will look into the *History of England* will find that prerogative was always largest in the hands of our wisest and best princes, because the people

observing the whole tendency of their actions to be the public good; or if any human frailty or mistake (for princes are but men made as others) appeared in some small declinations from that end; yet 'twas visible the main of their conduct tended to nothing but the care of the public. The people therefore finding reason to be satisfied with these princes, whenever they acted without or contrary to the letter of the law, acquiesced in what they did, and without the least complaint, let them enlarge their prerogative as they pleased, judging rightly that they did nothing herein to the prejudice of their laws, since they acted conformable to the foundation and end of all laws, the public good.

166. Such God-like princes, indeed, had some title to arbitrary power, by the argument that would prove absolute monarchy the best government, as that which God Himself governs the universe by, because such kings partake of His wisdom and goodness. Upon this is founded that saying, That the reigns of good princes have been always most dangerous to the liberties of their people. For when their successors, managing the government with different thoughts, would draw the actions of those good rulers into precedent and make them the standard of their prerogative, as if what had been done only for the good of the people was a right in them to do for the harm of the people, if they so pleased; it has often occasioned contest, and sometimes public disorders, before the people could recover their original right and get that to be declared not to be prerogative, which truly was never so; since it is impossible any body in the society should ever have a right to do the people harm; though it be very possible and reasonable that the people should not go about to set any bounds to the prerogative of those kings or rulers who themselves transgressed not the bounds of the public good. For *prerogative is nothing but the power of doing public good without a rule.*

167. The power of calling parliaments in England, as to precise time, place, and duration, is certainly a prerogative of the king, but still with this trust, that it shall be made use

of for the good of the nation, as the exigencies of the times and variety of occasions shall require. For it being impossible to foresee which should always be the fittest place for them to assemble in, and what the best season, the choice of these was left with the executive power, as might be most subservient to the public good, and best suit the ends of parliament.

168. The old question will be asked in this matter of prerogative, But who shall be judge when this power is made a right use of? I answer: Between an executive power in being, with such a prerogative, and a legislative that depends upon his will for their convening, there can be no judge on earth. As there can be none between the legislative and the people, should either the executive or the legislative, when they have got the power in their hands, design, or go about to enslave or destroy them. The people have no other remedy in this, as in all other cases where they have no judge on earth, but to appeal to Heaven. For the rulers in such attempts, exercising a power the people never put into their hands, who can never be supposed to consent that any body should rule over them for their harm, do that which they have not a right to do. And where the body of the people, or any single man, are deprived of their right, or are under the exercise of a power without right, having no appeal on earth, they have a liberty to appeal to Heaven whenever they judge the cause of sufficient moment. And therefore, though the people cannot be judge, so as to have, by the constitution of that society, any superior power to determine and give effective sentence in the case; yet they have reserved that ultimate determination to themselves, which belongs to all mankind, where there lies no appeal on earth, by a law antecedent and paramount to all positive laws of men, whether they have just cause to make their appeal to Heaven. And this judgment they cannot part with, it being out of a man's power so to submit himself to another as to give him a liberty to destroy him; God and Nature never allowing a man so to abandon himself as to neglect his own preservation. And since

he cannot take away his own life, neither can he give another power to take it. Nor let any one think this lays a perpetual foundation for disorder; for this operates not till the inconvenience is so great that the majority feel it, and are weary of it, and find a necessity to have it amended. And this the executive power, or wise princes, never need come in the danger of; and 'tis the thing of all others they have most need to avoid, as, of all others, the most perilous.

(((XV)))

OF PATERNAL, POLITICAL AND DESPOTICAL POWER, CONSIDERED TOGETHER

169. Though I have had occasion to speak of these separately before, yet the great mistakes of late about government, having, as I suppose, arisen from confounding these distinct powers one with another, it may not perhaps be amiss to consider them here together.

170. *First*, then, paternal or parental power is nothing but that which parents have over their children to govern them, for the children's good, till they come to the use of reason, or a state of knowledge, wherein they may be supposed capable to understand that rule, whether it be the law of Nature or the municipal law of their country, they are to govern themselves by: capable, I say, to know it, as well as several others, who live as freemen under the law. The affection and tenderness God hath planted in the breasts of parents towards their children makes it evident that this is not intended to be a severe arbitrary government, but only for the help, instruction, and preservation of their offspring. But happen as it will, there is, as I have proved, no reason why it should be thought to extend to life and death, at any time, over their children, more than over any body else, or keep the child in subjection to the will of his parents when grown to a man, and the perfect use of reason any farther than the having received life and education from his parents obliges him to

respect, honour, gratitude, assistance, and support, all his life to both father and mother. And thus, 'tis true, the paternal is a natural government, but not at all extending it self to the ends and jurisdictions of that which is political. The power of the father doth not reach at all to the property of the child, which is only in his own disposing.

171. *Secondly*, political power is that power which every man having in the state of Nature has given up into the hands of the society, and therein to the governors whom the society hath set over it self, with this express or tacit trust, that it shall be employed for their good and the preservation of their property. Now this power, which every man has in the state of Nature, and which he parts with to the society in all such cases where the society can secure him, is to use such means for the preserving of his own property as he thinks good and Nature allows him; and to punish the breach of the law of Nature in others; so as (according to the best of his reason) may most conduce to the preservation of himself and the rest of mankind. So that the end and measure of this power, when in every man's hands, in the state of Nature, being the preservation of all of his society, that is, all mankind in general; it can have no other end or measure, when in the hands of the magistrate, but to preserve the members of that society in their lives, liberties, and possessions, and so cannot be an absolute, arbitrary power over their lives and fortunes, which are as much as possible to be preserved; but a power to make laws, and annex such penalties to them as may tend to the preservation of the whole, by cutting off those parts, and those only, which are so corrupt that they threaten the sound and healthy, without which no severity is lawful. And this power has its original only from compact and agreement and the mutual consent of those who make up the community.

172. *Thirdly*, despotical power is an absolute, arbitrary power one man has over another, to take away his life whenever he pleases; and this is a power which neither Nature gives, for it has made no such distinction between one man and another, nor compact can convey. For man, not having

such an arbitrary power over his own life, cannot give another man such a power over it, but it is the effect only of
forfeiture which the aggressor makes of his own life when
he puts himself into the state of war with another. For having quitted reason, which God hath given to be the rule
betwixt man and man, and the peaceable ways which that
teaches, and made use of force to compass his unjust ends
upon another where he has no right, he renders himself liable
to be destroyed by his adversary whenever he can, as any
other noxious and brutish creature that is destructive to his
being. And thus captives, taken in a just and lawful war,
and such only, are subject to a despotical power, which, as
it arises not from compact, so neither is it capable of any,
but is the state of war continued. For what compact can be
made with a man that is not master of his own life? What
condition can he perform? And if he be once allowed to be
master of his own life, the despotical, arbitrary power of his
master ceases. He that is master of himself, and his own life,
has a right, too, to the means of preserving it; so that as soon
as compact enters, slavery ceases, and he so far quits his
absolute power and puts an end to the state of war who
enters into conditions with his captive.

173. Nature gives the first of these — *viz.*, paternal power
to parents for the benefit of their children during their minority, to supply their want of ability, and understanding how
to manage their property. (By property I must be understood here, as in other places, to mean that property which
men have in their persons as well as goods.) Voluntary agreement gives the second — *viz.*, political power to governors,
for the benefit of their subjects, to secure them in the possession and use of their properties. And forfeiture gives the
third — despotical power to lords for their own benefit over
those who are stripped of all property.

174. He that shall consider the distinct rise and extent,
and the different ends of these several powers, will plainly
see that paternal power comes as far short of that of the magistrate as despotical exceeds it; and that absolute dominion,

however placed, is so far from being one kind of civil society that it is as inconsistent with it as slavery is with property. Paternal power is only where minority makes the child incapable to manage his property; political where men have property in their own disposal; and despotical over such as have no property at all.

(((XVI)))

OF CONQUEST

175. Though governments can originally have no other rise than that before mentioned, nor polities be founded on any thing but the consent of the people; yet such has been the disorders ambition has filled the world with, that in the noise of war, which makes so great a part of the history of mankind, this consent is little taken notice of; and, therefore, many have mistaken the force of arms for the consent of the people, and reckon conquest as one of the originals of government. But conquest is as far from setting up any government as demolishing a house is from building a new one in the place. Indeed, it often makes way for a new frame of a commonwealth by destroying the former; but, without the consent of the people, can never erect a new one.

176. That the aggressor, who puts himself into the state of war with another, and unjustly invades another man's right, can, by such an unjust war, never come to have a right over the conquered, will be easily agreed by all men, who will not think that robbers and pirates have a right of empire over whomsoever they have force enough to master, or that men are bound by promises which unlawful force extorts from them. Should a robber break into my house, and, with a dagger at my throat, make me seal deeds to convey my estate to him, would this give him any title? Just such a title by his sword has an unjust conqueror who forces me into submission. The injury and the crime is equal, whether committed by the wearer of a crown or some petty villain. The

title of the offender and the number of his followers make
no difference in the offence, unless it be to aggravate it. The
only difference is, great robbers punish little ones to keep
them in their obedience, but the great ones are rewarded
with laurels and triumphs, because they are too big for the
weak hands of justice in this world, and have the power in
their own possession which should punish offenders. What
is my remedy against a robber that so broke into my house?
Appeal to the law for justice. But perhaps justice is denied,
or I am crippled and cannot stir; robbed, and have not the
means to do it. If God has taken away all means of seeking
remedy, there is nothing left but patience. But my son, when
able, may seek the relief of the law, which I am denied; he or
his son may renew his appeal till he recover his right. But
the conquered, or their children, have no court, no arbitrator
on earth to appeal to. Then they may appeal, as Jephtha did,
to Heaven, and repeat their appeal till they have recovered
the native right of their ancestors, which was to have such a
legislative over them as the majority should approve, and
freely acquiesce in. If it be objected, this would cause endless
trouble, I answer, no more than justice does, where she lies
open to all that appeal to her. He that troubles his neighbour
without a cause is punished for it by the justice of the court
he appeals to. And he that appeals to Heaven must be sure
he has right on his side; and a right, too, that is worth the
trouble and cost of the appeal, as he will answer at a tribunal that cannot be deceived, and will be sure to retribute
to every one according to the mischiefs he hath created to
his fellow-subjects — that is, any part of mankind. From
whence 'tis plain that he that conquers in an unjust war can
thereby have no title to the subjection and obedience of the
conquered.

177. But supposing victory favours the right side, let us
consider a conqueror in a lawful war, and see what power he
gets, and over whom.

First, 'tis plain he gets no power by his conquest over those
that conquered with him. They that fought on his side can-

not suffer by the conquest, but must, at least, be as much free men as they were before. And most commonly they serve upon terms, and on condition to share with their leader and enjoy a part of the spoil and other advantages that attend the conquering sword, or, at least, have a part of the subdued country bestowed upon them. And the conquering people are not, I hope, to be slaves by conquest, and wear their laurels only to shew they are sacrifices to their leader's triumph. They that found absolute monarchy upon the title of the sword make their heroes, who are the founders of such monarchies, arrant *Draw-can-Sirs*, and forget they had any officers and soldiers that fought on their side in the battles they won, or assisted them in the subduing, or shared in possessing the countries they mastered. We are told by some that the *English* monarchy is founded in the *Norman* Conquest, and that our princes have thereby a title to absolute dominion: which, if it were true (as by the history it appears otherwise), and that *William* had a right to make war on this island; yet his dominion by conquest could reach no farther than to the *Saxons* and *Britons* that were then inhabitants of this country. The *Normans* that came with him and helped to conquer, and all descended from them, are freemen and no subjects by conquest, let that give what dominion it will. And if I or any body else shall claim freedom as derived from them, it will be very hard to prove the contrary; and 'tis plain, the law that has made no distinction between the one and the other intends not there should be any difference in their freedom or privileges.

178. But supposing, which seldom happens, that the conquerors and conquered never incorporate into one people under the same laws and freedom. Let us see next what power a lawful conqueror has over the subdued, and that I say is purely despotical. He has an absolute power over the lives of those, who by an unjust war, have forfeited them; but not over the lives or fortunes of those who engaged not in the war, nor over the possessions even of those who were actually engaged in it.

179. *Secondly*, I say, then, the conqueror gets no power but only over those who have actually assisted, concurred, or consented to that unjust force that is used against him. For the people having given to their governors no power to do an unjust thing, such as is to make an unjust war (for they never had such a power in themselves), they ought not to be charged as guilty of the violence and injustice that is committed in an unjust war, any farther than they actually abet it, no more than they are to be thought guilty of any violence or oppression their governors should use upon the people themselves or any part of their fellow-subjects, they having empowered them no more to the one than to the other. Conquerors, 'tis true, seldom trouble themselves to make the distinction, but they willingly permit the confusion of war to sweep all together; but yet this alters not the right; for the conqueror's power over the lives of the conquered being only because they have used force to do or maintain an injustice, he can have that power only over those who have concurred in that force; all the rest are innocent, and he has no more title over the people of that country who have done him no injury, and so have made no forfeiture of their lives, than he has over any other who, without any injuries or provocations, have lived upon fair terms with him.

180. *Thirdly*, the power a conqueror gets over those he overcomes in a just war is perfectly despotical; he has an absolute power over the lives of those who, by putting themselves in a state of war, have forfeited them; but he has not thereby a right and title to their possessions. This I doubt not, but at first sight will seem a strange doctrine, it being so quite contrary to the practice of the world; there being nothing more familiar in speaking of the dominion of countries than to say such an one conquered it. As if conquest, without any more ado, conveyed a right of possession. But when we consider that the practice of the strong and powerful, how universal soever it may be, is seldom the rule of right, however it be one part of the subjection of the con-

quered not to argue against the conditions cut out to them by the conquering sword.

181. Though in all war there be usually a complication of force and damage, and the aggressor seldom fails to harm the estate when he uses force against the persons of those he makes war upon; yet 'tis the use of force only that puts a man into the state of war. For whether by force he begins the injury, or else having quietly and by fraud done the injury, he refuses to make reparation, and by force maintains it, which is the same thing as at first to have done it by force; 'tis the unjust use of force that makes the war. For he that breaks open my house and violently turns me out of doors, or having peaceably got in, by force keeps me out, does, in effect, the same thing; supposing we are in such a state that we have no common judge on earth whom I may appeal to, and to whom we are both obliged to submit, for of such I am now speaking. 'Tis the unjust use of force, then, that puts a man into the state of war with another, and thereby he that is guilty of it makes a forfeiture of his life. For quitting reason, which is the rule given between man and man, and using force, the way of beasts, he becomes liable to be destroyed by him he uses force against, as any savage ravenous beast that is dangerous to his being.

182. But because the miscarriages of the father are no faults of the children, and they may be rational and peaceable, notwithstanding the brutishness and injustice of the father; the father, by his miscarriages and violence, can forfeit but his own life, and involves not his children in his guilt or destruction. His goods, which Nature, that willeth the preservation of all mankind as much as is possible, hath made to belong to the children to keep them from perishing, do still continue to belong to his children. For supposing them not to have joined in the war either through infancy or choice, they have done nothing to forfeit them, nor has the conqueror any right to take them away, by the bare right of having subdued him that by force attempted his destruction,

though, perhaps, he may have some right to them to repair the damages he has sustained by the war, and the defence of his own right, which how far it reaches to the possessions of the conquered, we shall see by and by; so that he that by conquest has a right over a man's person, to destroy him if he pleases, has not thereby a right over his estate to possess and enjoy it. For it is the brutal force the aggressor has used that gives his adversary a right to take away his life and destroy him, if he pleases, as a noxious creature; but 'tis damage sustained that alone gives him title to another man's goods; for though I may kill a thief that sets on me in the highway, yet I may not (which seems less) take away his money and let him go; this would be robbery on my side. His force, and the state of war he put himself in, made him forfeit his life, but gave me no title to his goods. The right, then, of conquest extends only to the lives of those who joined in the war, but not to their estates, but only in order to make reparation for the damages received and the charges of the war, and that, too, with reservation of the right of the innocent wife and children.

183. Let the conqueror have as much justice on his side as could be supposed, he has no right to seize more than the vanquished could forfeit; his life is at the victor's mercy, and his service and goods he may appropriate to make himself reparation; but he cannot take the goods of his wife and children; they too had a title to the goods he enjoyed, and their shares in the estate he possessed. For example, I in the state of Nature (and all commonwealths are in the state of Nature one with another) have injured another man, and refusing to give satisfaction, it is come to a state of war wherein my defending by force what I had gotten unjustly makes me the aggressor. I an conquered; my life, 'tis true, as forfeit, is at mercy, but not my wife's and children's They made not the war, nor assisted in it. I could not forfeit their lives, they were not mine to forfeit. My wife had a share in my estate, that neither could I forfeit. And my children also, being born of me, had a right to be maintained out of my labour or sub-

stance. Here then is the case: The conqueror has a title to reparation for damages received, and the children have a title to their father's estate for their subsistence. For as to the wife's share, whether her own labour or compact gave her a title to it, 'tis plain her husband could not forfeit what was hers. What must be done in the case? I answer: The fundamental law of Nature being, that all, as much as may be, should be preserved, it follows that if there be not enough fully to satisfy both — viz., for the conqueror's losses and children's maintenance, he that hath and to spare, must remit something of his full satisfaction, and give way to the pressing and preferable title of those who are in danger to perish without it.

184. But supposing the charge and damages of the war are to be made up to the conqueror to the utmost farthing, and that the children of the vanquished, spoiled of all their father's goods, are to be left to starve and perish; yet the satisfying of what shall, on this score, be due to the conqueror will scarce give him a title to any country he shall conquer. For the damages of war can scarce amount to the value of any considerable tract of land in any part of the world, where all the land is possessed, and none lies waste. And if I have not taken away the conqueror's land, which, being vanquished, it is impossible I should, scarce any other spoil I have done him can amount to the value of mine, supposing it equally cultivated and of an extent any way coming near what I had over run of his. The destruction of a year's product or two (for it seldom reaches four or five), is the utmost spoil that usually can be done. For as to money, and such riches and treasure taken away, these are none of Nature's goods, they have but a phantastical imaginary value; Nature has put no such upon them. They are of no more account by her standard, than the Wampompeke of the *Americans* to an *European* prince, or the silver money of *Europe* would have been formerly to an *American*. And five year's product is not worth the perpetual inheritance of land, where all is possessed and none remains waste, to be taken

up by him that is disseised, which will be easily granted, if one do but take away the imaginary value of money, the disproportion being more than between five and five hundred. Though, at the same time, half a year's product is more worth than the inheritance where, there being more land than the inhabitants possess and make use of, any one has liberty to make use of the waste. But their conquerors take little care to possess themselves of the lands of the vanquished. No damage therefore that men in the state of Nature (as all princes and governments are in reference to one another) suffer from one another can give a conqueror power to dispossess the posterity of the vanquished, and turn them out of that inheritance which ought to be the possession of them and their descendants to all generations. The conqueror indeed will be apt to think himself master. And 'tis the very condition of the subdued not to be able to dispute their right. But, if that be all, it gives no other title than what bare force gives to the stronger over the weaker. And, by this reason, he that is strongest will have a right to whatever he pleases to seize on.

185. Over those, then, that joined with him in the war, and over those of the subdued country that opposed him not, and the posterity even of those that did, the conqueror, even in a just war, hath, by his conquest, no right of dominion. They are free from any subjection to him, and if their former government be dissolved, they are at liberty to begin and erect another to themselves.

186. The conqueror, 'tis true, usually by the force he has over them, compels them, with a sword at their breasts, to stoop to his conditions, and submit to such a government as he pleases to afford them; but the inquiry is, What right he has to do so? If it be said they submit by their own consent; then this allows their own consent to be necessary to give the conqueror a title to rule over them. It remains only to be considered whether promises, extorted by force, without right, can be thought consent, and how far they bind. To which I shall say, they bind not at all; because whatsoever

another gets from me by force, I still retain the right of, and he is obliged presently to restore. He that forces my horse from me ought presently to restore him, and I have still a right to retake him. By the same reason, he that forced a promise from me ought presently to restore it — i.e., quit me of the obligation of it; or I may resume it myself — i.e., choose whether I will perform it. For the law of Nature laying an obligation on me, only by the rules she prescribes, cannot oblige me by the violation of her rules; such is the extorting any thing from me by force. Nor does it at all alter the case, to say I gave my promise, no more than it excuses the force, and passes the right, when I put my hand in my pocket and deliver my purse my self to a thief who demands it with a pistol at my breast.

187. From all which it follows that the government of a conqueror, imposed by force on the subdued, against whom he had no right of war, or who joined not in the war against him, where he had right, has no obligation upon them.

188. But let us suppose that all the men of that community being all members of the same body politic, may be taken to have joined in that unjust war, wherein they are subdued, and so their lives are at the mercy of the conqueror.

189. I say, this concerns not their children, who are in their minority. For since a father hath not, in himself, a power over the life or liberty of his child, no act of his can possibly forfeit it; so that the children, whatever may have happened to the fathers, are freemen, and the absolute power of the conqueror reaches no farther than the persons of the men that were subdued by him, and dies with them; and should he govern them as slaves, subjected to his absolute, arbitrary power, he has no such right of dominion over their children. He can have no power over them but by their own consent, whatever he may drive them to say or do; and he has no lawful authority, whilst force, and not choice, compels them to submission.

190. Every man is born with a double right: *First*, A right of freedom to his person, which no other man has a power

over, but the free disposal of it lies in himself. *Secondly*, A right, before any other man, to inherit, with his brethren, his father's goods.

191. By the first of these, a man is naturally free from subjection to any government, though he be born in a place under its jurisdiction. But if he disclaim the lawful government of the country he was born in, he must also quit the right that belonged to him, by the laws of it, and the possessions there descending to him from his ancestors, if it were a government made by their consent.

192. By the second, the inhabitants of any country, who are descended and derive a title to their estates from those who are subdued, and had a government forced upon them against their free consents, retain a right to the possession of their ancestors, though they consent not freely to the government, whose hard conditions were by force, imposed on the possessors of that country. For the first conqueror never having had a title to the land of that country, the people, who are the descendants of, or claim under those who were forced to submit to the yoke of a government by constraint, have always a right to shake it off, and free themselves from the usurpation or tyranny the sword hath brought in upon them, till their rulers put them under such a frame of government as they willingly and of choice consent to (which they can never be supposed to do, till either they are put in a full state of liberty to choose their government and governors, or at least till they have such standing laws to which they have, by themselves or their representatives, given their free consent, and also till they are allowed their due property, which is so to be proprietors of what they have that nobody can take away any part of it without their own consent, without which, men under any government are not in the state of freemen, but are direct slaves under the force of war). And who doubts but the Grecian Christians, descendants of the ancient possessors of that country, may justly cast off the Turkish yoke they have so long groaned under, whenever they have a power to do it?

193. But granting that the conqueror in a just war has a right to the estates, as well as power over the persons of the conquered, which 'tis plain, he hath not: nothing of absolute power will follow from hence in the continuance of the government. Because the descendants of these being all freemen, if he grants them estates and possessions to inhabit his country, without which it would be worth nothing, whatsoever he grants them they have, so far as it is granted, property in. The nature whereof is, that without a man's own consent it cannot be taken from him.

194. Their persons are free by a native right, and their properties, be they more or less, are their own, and at their own dispose, and not at his; or else it is no property. Supposing the conqueror gives to one man a thousand acres, to him and his heirs for ever; to another he lets a thousand acres, for his life, under the rent of £50 or £500 *per annum*. Has not the one of these a right to his thousand acres for ever, and the other during his life, paying the said rent? And hath not the tenant for life a property in all that he gets over and above his rent, by his labour and industry, during the said term, supposing it be double the rent? Can any one say, The king, or conqueror, after his grant, may, by his power of conqueror, take away all, or part of the land, from the heirs of one, or from the other during his life, he paying the rent? Or can he take away from either the goods or money they have got upon the said land at his pleasure? If he can, then all free and voluntary contracts cease, and are void in the world; there needs nothing to dissolve them at any time but power enough; and all the grants and promises of men in power are but mockery and collusion. For can there be anything more ridiculous than to say, I give you and yours this for ever, and that in the surest and most solemn way of conveyance can be devised, and yet it is to be understood that I have right, if I please, to take it away from you again to-morrow?

195. I will not dispute now whether princes are exempt from the laws of their country, but this I am sure, they owe

subjection to the laws of God and Nature. No body, no power can exempt them from the obligations of that eternal law. Those are so great and so strong, in the case of promises, that Omnipotency itself can be tied by them. Grants, promises, and oaths are bonds that hold the Almighty, whatever some flatterers say to princes of the world, who, all together, with all their people joined to them, are, in comparison of the great God, but as a drop of the bucket, or a dust on the balance, inconsiderable, nothing!

196. The short of the case in conquest, is this: The conqueror, if he have a just cause, has a despotical right over the persons of all that actually aided and concurred in the war against him, and a right to make up his damage and cost out of their labour and estates, so he injure not the right of any other. Over the rest of the people, if there were any that consented not to the war, and over the children of the captives themselves, or the possessions of either he has no power, and so can have by virtue of conquest no lawful title himself to dominion over them, or derive it to his posterity; but is an aggressor, and puts himself in a state of war against them, and has no better a right of principality, he, nor any of his successors, than Hingar, or Hubba, the Danes, had here in England, or Spartacus, had he conquered Italy; which is to have their yoke cast off as soon as God shall give those under their subjection courage and opportunity to do it. Thus, notwithstanding whatever title the kings of Assyria had over Judah, by the sword, God assisted Hezekiah to throw off the dominion of that conquering empire. *And the Lord was with Hezekiah, and he prospered; wherefore he went forth, and he rebelled against the king of Assyria, and served him not;* 2 Kings xviii. 7. Whence it is plain that shaking off a power which force, and not right, hath set over any one, though it hath the name of rebellion, yet is no offence before God, but that which he allows and countenances, though even promises and covenants, when obtained by force, have intervened. For 'tis very probable, to any one that reads the story of Ahaz and Hezekiah attentively, that the Assyrians subdued Ahaz,

and deposed him, and made Hezekiah king in his father's lifetime, and that Hezekiah, by agreement, had done him homage, and paid him tribute all this time.

(((XVII)))

OF USURPATION

197. As conquest may be called a foreign usurpation, so usurpation is a kind of domestic conquest, with this difference, that an usurper can never have right on his side, it being no usurpation but where one is got into the possession of what another has right to. This, so far as it is usurpation, is a change only of persons, but not of the forms and rules of the government; for if the usurper extend his power beyond what of right belonged to the lawful princes or governors of the commonwealth, 'tis tyranny added to usurpation.

198. In all lawful governments the designation of the persons who are to bear rule, being as natural and necessary a part as the form of the government it self, and that which had its establishment originally from the people — the anarchy being much alike, to have no form of government at all, or to agree that it shall be monarchical, but to appoint no way to design the person that shall have the power and be the monarch — all commonwealths, therefore, with the form of government established, have rules also of appointing and conveying the right to those who are to have any share in the public authority; and whoever gets into the exercise of any part of the power by other ways than what the laws of the community have prescribed, hath no right to be obeyed, though the form of the commonwealth be still preserved, since he is not the person the laws have appointed, and consequently not the person the people have consented to. Nor can such an usurper, or any deriving from him, ever have a title till the people are both at liberty to consent, and have actually consented, to allow and confirm in him the power he hath till then usurped.

(((XVIII)))

OF TYRANNY

199. As usurpation is the exercise of power which another hath a right to, so tyranny is the exercise of power beyond right, which no body can have a right to; and this is making use of the power any one has in his hands, not for the good of those who are under it, but for his own private separate advantage. When the governor, however entituled, makes not the law, but his will, the rule, and his commands and actions are not directed to the preservation of the properties of his people, but the satisfaction of his own ambition, revenge, covetousness, or any other irregular passion.

200. If one can doubt this to be truth or reason because it comes from the obscure hand of a subject, I hope the authority of a king will make it pass with him. King James the first, in his speech to the Parliament, 1603, tells them thus: *I will ever prefer the weal of the public, and of the whole commonwealth, in making of good laws and constitutions, to any particular and private ends of mine, thinking ever the wealth and weal of the commonwealth to be my greatest weal and worldly felicity; a point wherein a lawful king doth·directly differ from a tyrant. For I do acknowledge that the special and greatest point of difference that is between a rightful king and an usurping tyrant is this, That whereas the proud and ambitious tyrant doth think his kingdom and people are only ordained for satisfaction of his desires and unreasonbale appetites, the righteous and just king doth by the contrary acknowledge himself to be ordained for the procuring of the wealth and property of his people.* And again, in his speech to the Parliament, 1609, he hath these words: *The king binds himself by a double oath, to the observation of the fundamental laws of his kingdom — tacitly, as by being a king, and so bound to protect as well the people as the laws of his kingdom, and expressly by his oath at his coronation; so as every just king, in a settled kingdom, is bound to observe that paction made to his people, by his laws, in framing*

his government agreeable thereunto, according to that paction which God made with Noah after the deluge: 'Hereafter, seed-time and harvest, and cold and heat and summer and winter, and day and night, shall not cease while the earth remaineth.' And therefore a king, governing in a settled kingdom, leaves to be a king, and degenerates into a tyrant, as soon as he leaves off to rule according to his laws. And a little after: *Therefore, all kings that are not tyrants, or perjured, will be glad to bound themselves within the limits of their laws, and they that persuade them the contrary are vipers, pests both against them and the commonwealth.* Thus that learned king who well understood the notions of things, makes the difference betwixt a king and a tyrant to consist only in this, That one makes the laws the bounds of his power and the good of the public the end of his government; the other makes all give way to his own will and appetite.

201. 'Tis a mistake to think this fault is proper only to monarchies. Other forms of government are liable to it as well as that. For wherever the power that is put in any hands of the government of the people and the preservation of their properties is applied to other ends, and made use of to impoverish, harass, or subdue them to the arbitrary and irregular commands of those that have it, there it presently becomes tyranny, whether those that thus use it are one or many. Thus we read of the thirty tyrants at Athens, as well as one at Syracuse; and the intolerable dominion of the Decemviri at Rome was nothing better.

202. Wherever law ends, tyranny begins, if the law be transgressed to another's harm. And whosoever in authority exceeds the power given him by the law, and makes use of the force he has under his command to compass that upon the subject which the law allows not, ceases in that to be a magistrate, and acting without authority may be opposed, as any other man who by force invades the right of another. This is acknowledged in subordinate magistrates. He that hath authority to seize my person in the street may be opposed as a thief and a robber if he endeavours to break into my house

to execute a writ, notwithstanding that I know he has such a warrant and such a legal authority as will empower him to arrest me abroad. And why this should not hold in the highest, as well as in the most inferior magistrate, I would gladly be informed. Is it reasonable that the eldest brother, because he has the greatest part of his father's estate, should thereby have a right to take away any of his younger brother's portions? Or that a rich man, who possessed a whole country, should from thence have a right to seize, when he pleased, the cottage and garden of his poor neighbour? The being rightfully possessed of great power and riches exceedingly beyond the greatest part of the sons of Adam, is so far from being an excuse, much less a reason for rapine and oppression, which the endamaging another without authority is, that it is a great aggravation of it. For exceeding the bounds of authority is no more a right in a great than a petty officer; no more justifiable in a king than a constable. But so much the worse in him as that he has more trust put in him, is supposed from the advantage of education and counsellors to have better knowledge and less reason to do it, having already a greater share than the rest of his brethren.

203. May the commands, then, of a prince be opposed? May he be resisted as often as any one shall find himself aggrieved, and but imagine he has not right done him? This will unhinge and overturn all polities, and instead of government and order, leave nothing but anarchy and confusion.

204. To this I answer: That force is to be opposed to nothing but to unjust and unlawful force; whoever makes any opposition in any other case draws on himself a just condemnation both from God and man; and so no such danger or confusion will follow, as is often suggested. For,

205. *First*, As in some countries the person of the prince by the law is sacred, and so whatever he commands or does, his person is still free from all question or violence, not liable to force, or any judicial censure or condemnation. But yet opposition may be made to the illegal acts of any inferior officer or other commissioned by him, unless he will, by

actually putting himself into a state of war with his people
dissolve the government, and leave them to that defence,
which belongs to every one in the state of Nature. For of
such things who can tell what the end will be? And a neighbour kingdom has shewed the world an odd example. In all
other cases the sacredness of the person exempts him from
all inconveniences, whereby he is secure, whilst the government stands, from all violence and harm whatsoever. Than
which there cannot be a wiser constitution. For the harm he
can do in his own person, not being likely to happen often,
nor to extend itself far, nor being able by his single strength
to subvert the laws nor oppress the body of the people,
should any prince have so much weakness and ill-nature as
to be willing to do it, the inconveniency of some particular
mischiefs that may happen sometimes when a heady prince
comes to the throne are well recompensed by the peace of the
public and security of the government, in the person of the
chief magistrate, thus set out of the reach of danger. It being
safer for the body that some few private men should be sometimes in danger to suffer, than that the head of the republic
should be easily and upon slight occasions exposed.

206. *Secondly*, But this privilege, belonging only to the
king's person, hinders not but they may be questioned, opposed, and resisted, who use unjust force, though they pretend a commission from him which the law authorizes not.
As is plain in the case of him that has the king's writ to arrest
a man, which is a full commission from the king; and yet he
that has it cannot break open a man's house to do it, nor
execute this command of the king upon certain days nor in
certain places, though this commission have no such exception in it; but they are the limitations of the law, which, if any
one transgress, the king's commission excuses him not. For
the king's authority being given him only by the law, he
cannot empower any one to act against the law, or justify
him by his commission in so doing. The commission or
command of any magistrate, where he has no authority, being as void and insignificant as that of any private man, the

difference between the one and the other being that the magistrate has some authority so far, and to such ends, and the private man has none at all. For 'tis not the commission but the authority that gives the right of acting; and against the laws there can be no authority. But notwithstanding such resistance, the king's person and authority are still both secured, and so no danger to governor or government.

207. *Thirdly,* Supposing a government wherein the person of the chief magistrate is not thus sacred, yet this doctrine of the lawfulness of resisting all unlawful exercises of his power will not upon every slight occasion endanger him or embroil the government; for where the injured party may be relieved and his damages repaired by appeal to the law, there can be no pretence for force, which is only to be used where a man is intercepted from appealing to the law. For nothing is to be accounted hostile force but where it leaves not the remedy of such an appeal. And 'tis such force alone that puts him that uses it into a state of war, and makes it lawful to resist him. A man with a sword in his hand demands my purse in the highway, when perhaps I have not 12d. in my pocket; this man I may lawfully kill. To another I deliver £100 to hold only whilst I alight, which he refuses to restore me when I am got up again, but draws his sword to defend the possession of it by force, if I endeavour to retake it. The mischief this man does me is a hundred, or possibly a thousand times more than the other perhaps intended me (whom I killed before he really did me any); and yet I might lawfully kill the one and cannot so much as hurt the other lawfully. The reason whereof is plain; because the one using force which threatened my life, I could not have time to appeal to the law to secure it, and when it was gone 'twas too late to appeal. The law could not restore life to my dead carcass. The loss was irreparable; which to prevent, the law of Nature gave me a right to destroy him who had put himself into a state of war with me and threatened my destruction. But in the other case, my life not being in danger, I might have the

benefit of appealing to the law, and have reparation for my £100 that way.

208. *Fourthly*, But if the unlawful acts done by the magistrate be maintained (by the power he has got), and the remedy which is due by law, be by the same power obstructed, yet the right of resisting, even in such manifest acts of tyranny, will not suddenly, or on slight occasions, disturb the government. For if it reach no farther than some private men's cases, though they have a right to defend themselves, and to recover by force what by unlawful force is taken from them, yet the right to do so will not easily engage them in a contest wherein they are sure to perish; it being as impossible for one or a few oppressed men to disturb the government where the body of the people do not think themselves concerned in it, as for a raving madman or heady malcontent to overturn a well-settled state, the people being as little apt to follow the one as the other.

209. But if either these illegal acts have extended to the majority of the people, or if the mischief and oppression has light only on some few, but in such cases as the precedent and consequences seem to threaten all, and they are persuaded in their consciences that their laws, and with them, their estates, liberties, and lives are in danger, and perhaps their religion too, how they will be hindered from resisting illegal force used against them I cannot tell. This is an inconvenience, I confess, that attends all governments whatsoever, when the governors have brought it to this pass, to be generally suspected of their people, the most dangerous state they can possibly put themselves in; wherein they are the less to be pitied, because it is so easy to be avoided. It being as impossible for a governor, if he really means the good of his people, and the preservation of them and their laws together, not to make them see and feel it, as it is for the father of a family not to let his children see he loves and takes care of them.

210. But if all the world shall observe pretences of one

kind, and actions of another, arts used to elude the law, and
the trust of prerogative (which is an arbitrary power in some
things left in the prince's hand to do good, not harm, to the
people) employed contrary to the end for which it was given;
if the people shall find the ministers and subordinate magistrates chosen, suitable to such ends, and favoured or laid by
proportionably as they promote or oppose them: If they see
several experiments made of arbitrary power, and that religion underhand favoured, though publicly proclaimed
against, which is readiest to introduce it, and the operators
in it supported as much as may be; and when that cannot be
done, yet approved still, and liked the better, and a long
train of acting show the councils all tending that way, how
can a man any more hinder himself from being persuaded in
his own mind which way things are going; or from casting
about how to save himself, than he could from believing the
captain of a ship he was in was carrying him and the rest of
the company to Algiers, when he found him always steering
that course, though cross winds, leaks in his ship, and want of
men and provisions did often force him to turn his course
another way for some time, which he steadily returned to
again as soon as the wind, weather, and other circumstances
would let him?

(((XIX)))

OF THE DISSOLUTION OF GOVERNMENT

211. He that will with any clearness speak of the dissolution
of government, ought in the first place to distinguish between the dissolution of the society and the dissolution of
the government. That which makes the community, and
brings men out of the loose state of nature into one politic
society, is the agreement which every one has with the rest
to incorporate and act as one body, and so be one distinct
commonwealth. The usual, and almost only way whereby
this union is dissolved, is the inroad of foreign force making
a conquest upon them. For in that case (not being able to

maintain and support themselves as one entire and independent body) the union belonging to that body which consisted therein, must necessarily cease, and so every one return to the state he was in before, with a liberty to shift for himself and provide for his own safety, as he thinks fit, in some other society. Whenever the society is dissolved, 'tis certain the government of that society cannot remain. Thus conquerors' swords often cut up governments by the roots, and mangle societies to pieces, separating the subdued or scattered multitude from the protection of and dependence on that society which ought to have preserved them from violence. The world is too well instructed in, and too forward to allow of this way of dissolving of governments, to need any more to be said of it; and there wants not much argument to prove that where the society is dissolved, the government cannot remain; that being as impossible as for the frame of an house to subsist when the materials of it are scattered and dissipated by a whirlwind, or jumbled into a confused heap by an earthquake.

212. Besides this overturning from without, governments are dissolved from within,

First, When the legislative is altered, civil society being a state of peace amongst those who are of it, from whom the state of war is excluded by the umpirage which they have provided in their legislative for the ending all differences that may arise amongst any of them. 'Tis in their legislative that the members of a commonwealth are united and combined together into one coherent living body. This is the soul that gives form, life, and unity to the commonwealth. From hence the several members have their mutual influence, sympathy, and connexion. And therefore when the legislative is broken, or dissolved, dissolution and death follows. For the essence and union of the society consisting in having one will, the legislative, when once established by the majority has the declaring and, as it were, keeping of that will. The constitution of the legislative is the first and fundamental act of society, whereby provision is made for the con-

tinuation of their union under the direction of persons and
bonds of laws, made by persons authorized thereunto, by
the consent and appointment of the people, without which
no one man, or number of men, amongst them can have
authority of making laws that shall be binding to the rest.
When any one, or more, shall take upon them to make laws
whom the people have not appointed so to do, they make
laws without authority, which the people are not therefore
bound to obey; by which means they come again to be out
of subjection, and may constitute to themselves a new legislative, as they think best, being in full liberty to resist the
force of those who, without authority, would impose any
thing upon them. Every one is at the disposure of his own
will, when those who had, by the delegation of the society,
the declaring of the public will, are excluded from it, and
others usurp the place who have no such authority or delegation.

213. This being usually brought about by such in the
commonwealth who misuse the power they have, it is hard
to consider it aright, and know at whose door to lay it, without knowing the form of government in which it happens.
Let us suppose then the legislative placed in the concurrence
of three distinct persons.

1. A single hereditary person having the constant, supreme, executive power, and with it the power of convoking
and dissolving the other two within certain periods of time.

2. An assembly of hereditary nobility.

3. An assembly of representatives chosen *pro tempore*, by
the people. Such a form of government supposed, it is evident:

214. *First*, That when such a single person or prince sets
up his own arbitrary will in place of the laws, which are the
will of the society, declared by the legislative, then the legislative is changed. For that being in effect the legislative whose
rules and laws are put in execution, and required to be obeyed,
when other laws are set up, and other rules pretended and
enforced than what the legislative constituted by the society

have enacted, it is plain that the legislative is changed. Whoever introduces new laws, not being thereunto authorized by the fundamental appointment of the society, or subverts the old, disowns and overturns the power by which they were made, and so sets up a new legislative.

215. *Secondly*, When the prince hinders the legislative from assembling in its due time, or from acting freely, pursuant to those ends for which it was constituted, the legislative is altered. For 'tis not a certain number of men, no, nor their meeting, unless they have also freedom of debating and leisure of perfecting what is for the good of the society, wherein the legislative consists; when these are taken away, or altered, so as to deprive the society of the due exercise of their power, the legislative is truly altered. For it is not names that constitute governments, but the use and exercise of those powers that were intended to accompany them; so that he who takes away the freedom, or hinders the acting of the legislative in its due seasons, in effect takes away the legislative, and puts an end to the government.

216. *Thirdly*, When, by the arbitrary power of the prince, the electors or ways of election are altered, without the consent, and contrary to the common interest of the people, there also the legislative is altered. For if others than those whom the society hath authorized thereunto do choose, or in another way than what the society hath prescribed, those chosen are not the legislative appointed by the people.

217. *Fourthly*, The delivery also of the people into the subjection of a foreign power, either by the prince or by the legislative, is certainly a change of the legislative, and so a dissolution of the government. For the end why people entered into society being to be preserved one entire, free, independent society, to be governed by its own laws, this is lost whenever they are given up into the power of another.

218. Why, in such a constitution as this, the dissolution of the government in these cases is to be imputed to the prince is evident, because he, having the force, treasure, and offices of the State to employ, and often persuading himself,

or being flattered by others, that, as supreme magistrate, he
is uncapable of control; he alone is in a condition to make
great advances toward such changes under pretence of lawful authority, and has it in his hands to terrify or suppress
opposers as factious, seditious, and enemies to the government; whereas no other part of the legislative, or people, is
capable by themselves to attempt any alteration of the legislative without open and visible rebellion, apt enough to be
taken notice of; which, when it prevails, produces effects very
little different from foreign conquest. Besides, the prince, in
such a form of government, having the power of dissolving
the other parts of the legislative, and thereby rendering them
private persons, they can never, in opposition to him, or
without his concurrence, alter the legislative by a law, his
consent being necessary to give any of their decrees that
sanction. But yet so far as the other parts of the legislative
any way contribute to any attempt upon the government, and
do either promote, or not, what lies in them hinder such
designs, they are guilty, and partake in this, which is certainly the greatest crime men can be guilty of one towards
another.

219. There is one way more whereby such a government
may be dissolved, and that is: When he who has the supreme
executive power neglects and abandons that charge, so that
the laws already made can no longer be put in execution.
This is demonstratively to reduce all to anarchy, and so effectively to dissolve the government. For laws not being made
for themselves, but to be, by their execution, the bonds of the
society to keep every part of the body politic in its due place
and function, when that totally ceases, the government visibly
ceases, and the people become a confused multitude without
order or connexion. Where there is no longer the administration of justice for the securing of men's rights, nor any
remaining power within the community to direct the force,
or provide for the necessities of the public, there certainly
is no government left. Where the laws cannot be executed it
is all one as if there were no laws, and a government without

laws is, I suppose, a mystery in politics unconceivable to human capacity, and inconsistent with human society.

220. In these, and the like cases, when the government is dissolved, the people are at liberty to provide for themselves by erecting a new legislative, differing from the other by the change of persons, or form, or both, as they shall find it most for their safety and good. For the society can never, by the fault of another, lose the native and original right it has to preserve itself, which can only be done by a settled legislative and a fair impartial execution of the laws made by it. But the state of mankind is not so miserable that they are not capable of using this remedy till it be too late to look for any. To tell people they may provide for themselves by erecting a new legislative, when, by oppression, artifice, or being delivered over to a foreign power, their old one is gone, is only to tell them they may expect relief when it is too late, and the evil is past cure. This is in effect no more than to bid them first be slaves, and then to take care of their liberty, and, when their chains are on, tell them they may act like freemen. This, if barely so, is rather mockery than relief, and men can never be secure from tyranny if there be no means to escape it till they are perfectly under it. And therefore it is, that they have not only a right to get out of it, but to prevent it.

221. There is therefore Secondly another way whereby governments are dissolved, and that is, when the legislative, or the prince, either of them act contrary to their trust.

First, The legislative acts against the trust reposed in them when they endeavour to invade the property of the subject, and to make themselves, or any part of the community, masters or arbitrary disposers of the lives, liberties, or fortunes of the people.

222. The reason why men enter into society is the preservation of their property; and the end why they choose and authorize a legislative is that there may be laws made, and rules set, as guards and fences to the properties of all the members of the society, to limit the power and moderate the dominion of every part and member of the society. For since

it can never be supposed to be the will of the society that the legislative should have a power to destroy that which every one designs to secure by entering into society, and for which the people submitted themselves to legislators of their own making: whenever the legislators endeavour to take away and destroy the property of the people, or to reduce them to slavery under arbitrary power, they put themselves into a state of war with the people, who are thereupon absolved from any farther obedience, and are left to the common refuge which God hath provided for all men against force and violence. Whensoever therefore the legislative shall transgress this fundamental rule of society, and either by ambition, fear, folly, or corruption, endeavour to grasp themselves, or put into the hands of any other, an absolute power over the lives, liberties, and estates of the people, by this breach of trust they forfeit the power the people had put into their hands for quite contrary ends, and it devolves to the people; who have a right to resume their original liberty, and by the establishment of a new legislative (such as they shall think fit), provide for their own safety and security, which is the end for which they are in society. What I have said here concerning the legislative in general holds true also concerning the supreme executor, who having a double trust put in him, both to have a part in the legislative and the supreme execution of the law, acts against both, when he goes about to set up his own arbitrary will as the law of the society. He acts also contrary to his trust when he employs the force, treasure, and offices of the society to corrupt the representatives and gain them to his purposes, when he openly pre-engages the electors, and prescribes, to their choice, such whom he has, by solicitations, threats, promises, or otherwise, won to his designs, and employs them to bring in such who have promised beforehand what to vote and what to enact. Thus to regulate candidates and electors, and new model the ways of election, what is it but to cut up the government by the roots, and poison the very fountain of public security? For the people having reserved to themselves the choice of their representatives as the fence to their properties, could do it for no other end but that they might always be freely chosen, and so chosen, freely act and advise as the necessity of the commonwealth and the public good should, upon examination and mature debate, be judged to require. This, those who give their votes before they hear the debate, and have weighed the reasons on all sides, are not capable of doing. To prepare such an assembly as this, and endeavour to set up the declared abettors of his own will, for the true representatives of the people, and the law-makers of the society, is certainly as great a breach of trust, and as perfect a declaration of a design to subvert the government, as is possible to be met with. To which, if one shall add rewards and punishments visibly employed to the same end, and all the arts of perverted law made use of to take off and destroy all that stand in the way of such a design, and will not comply and consent to betray the liberties of their country, 'twill be past doubt what is doing. What power they ought to have in the society who thus employ it contrary to the trust went along with it in its first institution, is easy to determine; and one cannot but see that he who has once attempted any such thing as this cannot any longer be trusted.

223. To this, perhaps, it will be said, that the people being ignorant and always discontented, to lay the foundation of government in the unsteady opinion and uncertain humour of the people, is to expose it to certain ruin; and no government will be able long to subsist if the people may set up a .ew legislative whenever they take offence at the old one. To this I answer, quite the contrary. People are not so easily got out of their old forms as some are apt to suggest. They are hardly to be prevailed with to amend the acknowledged faults in the frame they have been accustomed to. And if there be any original defects, or adventitious ones introduced by time or corruption, 'tis not an easy thing to get them changed, even when all the world sees there is an opportunity for it. This slowness and aversion in the people to quit their old constitutions has in the many revolutions [that] have

been seen in this kingdom, in this and former ages, still kept us to, or after some interval of fruitless attempts, still brought us back again to our old legislative of king, lords and commons; and whatever provocations have made the crown be taken from some of our princes' heads, they never carried the people so far as to place it in another line.

224. But 'twill be said, this hypothesis lays a ferment for frequent rebellion. To which I answer:

First, No more than any other hypothesis. For when the people are made miserable, and find themselves exposed to the ill usage of arbitrary power; cry up their governors as much as you will for sons of *Jupiter*, let them be sacred and divine, descended or authorized from Heaven; give them out for whom or what you please, the same will happen. The people generally ill treated, and contrary to right, will be ready upon any occasion to ease themselves of a burden that sits heavy upon them. They will wish and seek for the opportunity, which in the change, weakness, and accidents of humane affairs, seldom delays long to offer it self. He must have lived but a little while in the world, who has not seen examples of this in his time; and he must have read very little who cannot produce examples of it in all sorts of governments in the world.

225. Secondly, I answer, such revolutions happen not upon every little mismanagement in public affairs. Great mistakes in the ruling part, many wrong and inconvenient laws, and all the slips of human frailty will be borne by the people without mutiny or murmur. But if a long train of abuses, prevarications, and artifices, all tending the same way, make the design visible to the people, and they cannot but feel what they lie under, and see whither they are going, 'tis not to be wondered that they should then rouse themselves, and endeavour to put the rule into such hands which may secure to them the ends for which government was at first erected, and without which, ancient names and specious forms are so far from being better, that they are much worse than the state of Nature or pure anarchy; the inconveniences

being all as great and as near, but the remedy farther off and
more difficult.

226. Thirdly, I answer, That this power in the people of
providing for their safety anew by a new legislative when
their legislators have acted contrary to their trust by invading their property, is the best fence against rebellion, and the
probablest means to hinder it. For rebellion being an opposition, not to persons, but authority, which is founded only in
the constitutions and laws of the government; those, whoever they be, who by force break through, and by force
justify their violation of them, are truly and properly rebels.
For when men, by entering into society and civil government, have excluded force, and introduced laws for the
preservation of property, peace, and unity amongst themselves; those who set up force again in opposition to the laws,
do *rebellare* — that is, bring back again the state of war, and
are properly rebels, which they who are in power, by the
pretence they have to authority, the temptation of force they
have in their hands, and the flattery of those about them
being likeliest to do, the properest way to prevent the evil is
to shew them the danger and injustice of it who are under the
greatest temptation to run into it.

227. In both the forementioned cases, when either the legislative is changed, or the legislators act contrary to the end for
which they were constituted, those who are guilty are guilty of
rebellion. For if any one by force takes away the established
legislative of any society, and the laws by them made, pursuant to their trust, he thereby takes away the umpirage
which every one had consented to for a peaceable decision of
all their controversies, and a bar to the state of war amongst
them. They who remove or change the legislative take away
this decisive power, which no body can have but by the appointment and consent of the people; and so destroying the
authority which the people did, and no body else can set up,
and introducing a power which the people hath not authorized, actually introduce a state of war, which is that of force
without authority; and thus by removing the legislative

established by the society, in whose decisions the people acquiesced and united as to that of their own will, they untie
the knot, and expose the people anew to the state of war.
And if those, who by force take away the legislative, are
rebels, the legislators themselves, as has been shewn, can
be no less esteemed so, when they who were set up for the
protection and preservation of the people, their liberties and
properties shall be force invade and endeavour to take them
away; and so they putting themselves into a state of war with
those who made them the protectors and guardians of their
peace, are properly, and with the greatest aggravation, *rebel-
lantes*, rebels.

228.´ But if they who say it lays a foundation for rebellion
mean that it may occasion civil wars or intestine broils to tell
the people they are absolved from obedience when illegal
attempts are made upon their liberties or properties, and may
oppose the unlawful violence of those who were their magistrates when they invade their properties, contrary to the
trust put in them; and that, therefore, this doctrine is not to
be allowed, being so destructive to the peace of the world;
they may as well say, upon the same ground, that honest men
may not oppose robbers or pirates, because this may occasion disorder or bloodshed. If any mischief come in such
cases, it is not to be charged upon him who defends his own
right, but on him that invades his neighbour's. If the innocent honest man must quietly quit all he has for peace sake
to him who will lay violent hands upon it, I desire it may be
considered what a kind of peace there will be in the world
which consists only in violence and rapine, and which is to
be maintained only for the benefit of robbers and oppressors.
Who would not think it an admirable peace betwixt the
mighty and the mean, when the lamb, without resistance,
yielded his throat to be torn by the imperious wolf? *Polyphemus*'s den gives us a perfect pattern of such a peace. Such
a government wherein *Ulysses* and his companions had nothing to do but quietly to suffer themselves to be devoured. And
no doubt, *Ulysses*, who was a prudent man, preached up pas-

sive obedience, and exhorted them to a quiet submission by representing to them of what concernment peace was to mankind, and by shewing the inconveniences might happen if they should offer to resist *Polyphemus*, who had now the power over them.

229. The end of government is the good of mankind; and which is best for mankind, that the people should be always exposed to the boundless will of tyranny, or that the rulers should be sometimes liable to be opposed when they grow exorbitant in the use of their power, and employ it for the destruction, and not the preservation, of the properties of their people?

230. Nor let any one say that mischief can arise from hence as often as it shall please a busy head or turbulent spirit to desire the alteration of the government. 'Tis true such men may stir whenever they please, but it will be only to their own just ruin and perdition. For till the mischief be grown general, and the ill designs of the rulers become visible, or their attempts sensible to the greater part, the people, who are more disposed to suffer than right themselves by resistance, are not apt to stir. The examples of particular injustice or oppression of here and there an unfortunate man moves them not. But if they universally have a persuasion grounded upon manifest evidence that designs are carrying on against their liberties, and the general course and tendency of things cannot but give them strong suspicions of the evil intention of their governors, who is to be blamed for it? Who can help it if they, who might avoid it, bring themselves into this suspicion? Are the people to be blamed if they have the sense of rational creatures, and can think of things no otherwise than as they find and feel them? And is it not rather their fault who put things in such a posture that they would not have them thought as they are? I grant that the pride, ambition, and turbulency of private men have sometimes caused great disorders in commonwealths, and factions have been fatal to states and kingdoms. But whether the mischief hath oftener begun in the people's wantonness, and a desire

to cast off the lawful authority of their rulers, or in the rulers' insolence and endeavours to get and exercise an arbitrary power over their people, whether oppression or disobedience gave the first rise to the disorder, I leave it to impartial history to determine. This I am sure, whoever, either ruler or subject, by force goes about to invade the rights of either prince or people, and lays the foundation for overturning the constitution and frame of any just government, he is guilty of the greatest crime I think a man is capable of, being to answer for all those mischiefs of blood, rapine, and desolation, which the breaking to pieces of governments bring on a country; and he who does it is justly to be esteemed the common enemy and pest of mankind, and is to be treated accordingly.

231. That subjects or foreigners attempting by force on the properties of any people may be resisted with force is agreed on all hands; but that magistrates doing the same thing may be resisted, hath of late been denied; as if those who had the greatest privileges and advantages by the law had thereby a power to break those laws by which alone they were set in a better place than their brethren; whereas their offence is thereby the greater, both as being ungrateful for the greater share they have by the law, and breaking also that trust which is put into their hands by their brethren.

232. Whosoever uses force without right, as every one does in society who does it without law, puts himself into a state of war with those against whom he so uses it, and in that state all former ties are cancelled, all other rights cease, and every one has a right to defend himself, and to resist the aggressor. This is so evident, that Barclay himself, that great assertor of the power and sacredness of kings, is forced to confess that it is lawful for the people, in some cases, to resist their king; and that, too, in a chapter wherein he pretends to shew that the Divine law shuts up the people from all manner of rebellion. Whereby it is evident, even by his own doctrine, that since they may, in some cases, resist, all resisting of *princes* is not rebellion. His words are these: *Quod si quis*

*dicat, Ergone populus tyrannicæ crudelitati et furori jugulum
semper præbebit? Ergone multitudo civitates suas fame, ferro,
et flammâ vastari, seque, conjuges, ac liberos, fortunæ ludibrio et
tyranni libidini exponi, inque omnia vitæ pericula, omnesque mis-
erias et molestias á rege deduci patientur? Num illis, quod omni
animantium generi est á naturâ tributum, denegari debet? ut sc.
vim vi repellant, seseque ab injuriâ tueantur? Huic breviter re-
sponsum sit: populo universo ne negari defensionem, quæ juris
naturalis est, neque ultionem, quæ præter naturum est, adversus
regem concedi debere. Quapropter si rex non in singulares tantum personas aliquot privatum odium exerceat, sed corpus
etiam reipublicæ, cujus ipse caput est — i.e., totum populum,
vel insignem aliquam ejus partem, immani et intolerandâ sævitiâ
seu tyrannide divexet; populo, quidem hoc casu resistendi ac
tuendi se ab injuriâ potestas competit: sed tuendi se tantum, non
enim in principem invadendi: et restituendæ injuriæ illatæ, non
recedendi à debitâ reverentiâ propter acceptam injuriam. Præ-
sentem denique impetum propulsandi, non vim præteritam ul-
ciscendi jus habet. Horum enim alterum à naturâ est, ut vitam
scilicet corpusque tueamur. Alterum vero contra naturam, ut
inferior de superiore supplicium sumat. Quod itaque populus
malum, antequam factum sit, impedire potest, ne fiat, id post-
quam factum est, in regem authorem sceleris vindicare non
potest: populus igitur hoc ampliùs quam privatus quisquam
habet: Quod huic, vel ipsis adversariis judicibus, excepto Buch-
anano, nullum nisi in patientia remedium superest. Cum ille si
intolerabilis tyrannis est (modicum enim ferre omnino debet)
resistere cum reverentiâ possit. — Barclay, Contra Monarchom.
l. 3, c. 8.*

In *English* thus: —

233. *But if any one should ask: Must the people, then, always lay themselves open to the cruelty and rage of tyranny —
must they see their cities pillaged and laid in ashes, their wives
and children exposed to the tyrant's lust and fury, and themselves and families reduced by their king to ruin and all the
miseries of want and oppression, and yet sit still? Must men
alone be debarred the common privilege of opposing force with*

*force, which Nature allows so freely to all other creatures for
their preservation from injury? I answer: Self-defence is a part
of the law of Nature; nor can it be denied the community, even
against the king himself; but to revenge themselves upon him,
must by no means be allowed them, it being not agreeable to that
law. Wherefore, if the king shall shew an hatred, not only to
some particular persons, but sets himself against the body of the
commonwealth, whereof he is the head, and shall, with intolerable ill usage, cruelly tyrannize over the whole, or a considerable
part of the people; in this case the people have a right to resist
and defend themselves from injury; but it must be with this caution, that they only defend themselves, but do not attack their
prince. They may repair the damages received, but must not, for
any provocation, exceed the bounds of due reverence and respect.
They may repulse the present attempt, but must not revenge
past violences. For it is natural for us to defend life and limb,
but that an inferior should punish a superior is against nature.
The mischief which is designed them, the people may prevent before it be done, but, when it is done, they must not revenge it on
the king, though author of the villany. This, therefore, is the
privilege of the people in general, above what any private person
hath: That particular men are allowed by our adversaries themselves* (Buchanan *only excepted), to have no other remedy but
patience; but the body of the people may, with respect, resist intolerable tyranny, for when it is but moderate they ought to endure it.*

234. Thus far that great advocate of monarchical power
allows of resistance.

235. 'Tis true, he has annexed two limitations to it, to no
purpose:

First. He says it must be with reverence.

Secondly. It must be without retribution or punishment;
and the reason he gives is, *Because an inferior cannot punish
a superior.*

First, How to resist force without striking again, or how
to strike with reverence, will need some skill to make intelligible. He that shall oppose an assault only with a shield to

receive the blows, or in any more respectful posture, without a sword in his hand to abate the confidence and force of the assailant, will quickly be at an end of his resistance, and will find such a defence serve only to draw on himself the worse usage. This is as ridiculous a way of resisting as *Juvenal* thought it of fighting: *Ubi tu pulsas, ego vapulo tantum.* And the success of the combat will be unavoidably the same he there describes it:

> *Libertas pauperis hæc est;*
> *Pulsatus rogat, et pugnis concisus, adorat,*
> *Ut liceat paucis cum dentibus inde reverti.*

This will always be the event of such an imaginary resistance, where men may not strike again. He, therefore, who may resist must be allowed to strike. And then let our author, or any body else, join a knock on the head or a cut on the face with as much reverence and respect as he thinks fit. He that can reconcile blows and reverence may, for aught I know, deserve for his pains a civil, respectful cudgelling wherever he can meet with it.

Secondly, As to his second — *An inferior cannot punish a superior* — that is true, generally speaking, whilst he is his superior. But to resist force with force, being the state of war that levels the parties, cancels all former relation of reverence, respect, and superiority; and then the odds that remains is — that he who opposes the unjust aggressor has this superiority over him, that he has a right, when he prevails, to punish the offender, both for the breach of the peace and all the evils that followed upon it. *Barclay*, therefore, in another place, more coherently to himself, denies it to be lawful to resist a king in any case. But he there assigns two cases whereby a king may unking himself. His words are:

Quid ergo, nulline casus incidere possunt quibus populo sese erigere atque in regem impotentius dominantem arma capere et invadere jure suo suâque authoritate liceat? Nulli certe quamdiu rex manet. Semper enim ex divinis id obstat, Regem honorificato, *et qui potestati resistit, Dei ordinationi resistit;* non aliàs igitur in eum populo potestas est quam si id committat

propter quod ipso jure rex esse desinat. Tunc enim se ipse princi-
patu exuit atque in privatis constituit liber; hoc modo populus et
superior efficitur, reverso ad eum scilicet jure illo quod ante re-
gem inauguratum in interregno habuit. At sunt paucorum gen-
erum commissa ejusmodi quæ hunc effectum pariunt. At ego cum
plurima animo perlustrem, duo tantum invenio, duos, inquam,
casus quibus rex ipso facto ex rege non regem se facit et omni
honore et dignitate regali atque in subditos potestate destituit;
quorum etiam meminit Winzerus. *Horum unus est, si regnum*
disperdat, quemadmodum de Nerone fertur, quod is nempe sena-
tum populumque Romanum atque adeo urbem ipsam ferro
flammaque vastare, ac novas sibi sedes quærere decrevisset. Et
de Caligula, quod palam denunciarit se neque civem neque prin-
cipem senatui amplius fore, inque animo habuerit, interempto
utriusque ordinis electissimo, quoque Alexandriam *commigrare,*
ac ut populum uno ictu interimeret, unam ei cervicem optavit.
Talia cum rex aliquis meditatur et molitur serio, omnem reg-
nandi curam et animum ilico abjiqit, ac proinde imperium in
subditos amittit, ut dominus servi pro derelicto habiti, dominium.

236. *Alter casus est, si rex in alicujus clientelam se contulit,*
ac regnum quod liberum à majoribus et populo traditum accepit,
alienæ ditioni mancipavit. Nam tunc quamvis forte non eâ
mente id agit populo plane ut incommodet; tamen quia quod
præcipuum est regiæ dignitatis amisit, ut summus scilicet in
regno secundum Deum sit, et solo Deo inferior, atque populum
etiam totum ignorantem vel invitum, cujus libertatem sartam et
tectam conservare debuit, in alterius gentis ditionem et potesta-
tem dedidit; hâc velut quadam regni abalienatione effecit, ut nec
quod ipse in regno imperium habuit retineat, nec in eum cui col-
latum voluit, juris quicquam transferat, atque ita eo facto li-
berum jam et suæ potestatis populum relinquit, cujus rei exem-
plum unum annales Scotici *suppeditant.* — Barclay, Contra
Monarchom.

Which in *English* runs thus: —

237. *What, then, can there no case happen wherein the*
people may of right, and by their own authority, help themselves,
take arms, and set upon their king, imperiously domineering

over them? None at all whilst he remains a king. Honour the king, *and* he that resists the power, resists the ordinance of God, *are Divine oracles that will never permit it. The people, therefore, can never come by a power over him unless he does something that makes him cease to be a king. For then he divests himself of his crown and dignity, and returns to the state of a private man, and the people become free and superior; the power which they had in the* interregnum, *before they crowned him king, devolving to them again. But there are but few miscarriages which bring the matter to this state. After considering it well on all sides, I can find but two. Two cases there are, I say, whereby a king,* ipso facto, *becomes no king, and loses all power and regal authority over his people, which are also taken notice of by* Winzerus. *The first is, if he endeavour to overturn the government, that is, if he have a purpose and design to ruin the kingdom and commonwealth, as it is recorded of* Nero *that he resolved to cut off the senate and people of* Rome, *lay the city waste with fire and sword, and then remove to some other place; and of* Caligula, *that he openly declared that he would be no longer a head to the people or senate, and that he had it in his thoughts to cut off the worthiest men of both ranks, and then retire to* Alexandria; *and he wished that the people had but one neck, that he might dispatch them all at a blow. Such designs as these, when any king harbours in his thoughts and seriously promotes, he immediately gives up all care and thought of the commonwealth; and, consequently, forfeits the power of governing his subjects, as a master does the dominion over his slaves whom he hath abandoned.*

238. *The other case is, when a king makes himself the dependent of another, and subjects his kingdom, which his ancestors left him, and the people put free into his hands, to the dominion of another. For however, perhaps, it may not be his intention to prejudice the people; yet because he has hereby lost the principal part of regal dignity — viz., to be next and immediately under God, supreme in his kingdom; and also because he betrayed or forced his people, whose liberty he ought to have carefully preserved, into the power and dominion of a foreign nation. By this,*

*as it were, alienation of his kingdom, he himself loses the power
he had in it before, without transferring any the least right to
those on whom he would have bestowed it; and so by this act sets
the people free, and leaves them at their own disposal. One example of this is to be found in the* Scotch *annals.*

239. In these cases *Barclay,* the great champion of absolute monarchy, is forced to allow, That a king may be resisted, and ceases to be a king. That is in short, not to multiply cases: in whatsoever he has no authority, there he is no
king, and may be resisted: for wheresoever the authority
ceases, the king ceases too, and becomes like other men who
have no authority. And these two cases he instances in,
differ little from those above mentioned, to be destructive
to governments, only that he has omitted the principle from
which his doctrine flows; and that is the breach of trust in
not preserving the form of government agreed on, and in not
intending the end of government it self, which is the public
good and preservation of property. When a king has de-
throned himself, and put himself in a state of war with his
people, what shall hinder them from prosecuting him who
is no king, as they would any other man, who has put himself into a state of war with them. *Barclay, and those of his
opinion, would do well to tell us.* This farther I desire may be
taken notice of out of *Barclay,* that he says, *The mischief that
is designed them, the People may prevent before it be done,*
whereby he allows resistance when tyranny is but in design.
Such designs as these (says he) *when any king harbours in his
thoughts and seriously promotes, he immediately gives up all
care and thought of the commonwealth;* so that according to
him the neglect of the public good is to be taken as an evidence of design, or at least for a sufficient cause of resistance.
And the reason of all he gives in these words, *because he betrayed or forced his people whose liberty he ought carefully to
have preserved.* What he adds *into the power and dominion of
a foreign nation,* signifies nothing, the fault and forefeiture
lying in the loss of their *liberty* which he *ought to have preserved,* and not in any distinction of the person to whose

dominion they were subjected. The people's right is equally invaded and their liberty lost, whether they are made slaves to any of their own, or a *foreign nation*; and in this lies the injury, and against this only have they the right of defence. And there are instances to be found in all countries, which shew that 'tis not the change of nations in the persons of their governors, but the change of government that gives the offence. *Bilson*, a bishop of our Church, and a great stickler for the power and prerogative of princes, does, if I mistake not, in his treatise of *Christian Subjection*, acknowledge that princes may forfeit their power and their title to the obedience of their subjects; and if there needed authority in a case where reason is so plain, I could send my reader to *Bracton*, *Fortescue*, and the author of the 'Mirror,' and others, writers that cannot be suspected to be ignorant of our government, or enemies to it. But I thought *Hooker* alone might be enough to satisfy those men who, relying on him for their ecclesiastical polity, are by a strange fate carried to deny those principles upon which he builds it. Whether they are herein made the tools of cunninger workmen, to pull down their own fabric, they were best look. This I am sure, their civil policy is so new, so dangerous, and so destructive to both rulers and people, that as former ages never could bear the broaching of it, so it may be hoped those to come, redeemed from the impositions of these *Egyptian* under-taskmasters, will abhor the memory of such servile flatterers, who, whilst it seemed to serve their turn, resolved all government into absolute tyranny, and would have all men born to what their mean souls fitted them, slavery.

240. Here 'tis like the common question will be made, Who shall be judge whether the prince or legislative act contrary to their trust? This, perhaps, ill-affected and factious men may spread amongst the people, when the prince only makes use of his due prerogative. To this I reply, The people shall be judge; for who shall be judge whether his trustee or deputy acts well and according to the trust reposed in him, but he who deputes him and must, by having de-

puted him, have still a power to discard him when he fails in his trust? If this be reasonable in particular cases of private men, why should it be otherwise in that of the greatest moment, where the welfare of millions is concerned and also where the evil, if not prevented, is greater, and the redress very difficult, dear, and dangerous?

241. But, farther, this question, (Who shall be judge?) cannot mean that there is no judge at all. For where there is no judicature on earth to decide controversies amongst men, God in heaven is judge. He alone, 'tis true, is judge of the right. But every man is judge for himself, as in all other cases so in this, whether another hath put himself into a state of war with him, and whether he should appeal to the supreme Judge, as *Jephtha* did.

242. If a controversy arise betwixt a prince and some of the people in a matter where the law is silent or doubtful, and the thing be of great consequence, I should think the proper umpire, in such a case, should be the body of the people. For in such cases where the prince hath a trust reposed in him, and is dispensed from the common, ordinary rules of the law; there, if any men find themselves aggrieved, and think the prince acts contrary to, or beyond that trust, who so proper to judge as the body of the people (who at first lodged that trust in him) how far they meant it should extend? But if the prince, or whoever they be in the administration, decline that way of determination, the appeal then lies nowhere but to Heaven. Force between either persons, who have no known superior on earth, or which permits no appeal to a judge on earth, being properly a state of war, wherein the appeal lies only to Heaven; and in that state the injured party must judge for himself when he will think fit to make use of that appeal and put himself upon it.

243. To conclude, The power that every individual gave the society when he entered into it, can never revert to the individuals again, as long as the society lasts, but will always remain in the community; because without this there can be no community, no commonwealth, which is contrary to the

original agreement; so also when the society hath placed the legislative in any assembly of men, to continue in them and their successors, with direction and authority for providing such successors, the legislative can never revert to the people whilst that government lasts; because, having provided a legislative with power to continue for ever, they have given up their political power to the legislative, and cannot resume it. But if they have set limits to the duration of their legis-lative, and made this supreme power in any person or assem-bly only temporary; or else when, by the miscarriages of those in authority, it is forfeited; upon the forfeiture of their rulers, or at the determination of the time set, it reverts to the society, and the people have a right to act as supreme, and continue the legislative in themselves or place it in a new form, or new hands, as they think good.

David Hume

1711 – 1776

OF THE ORIGINAL CONTRACT

OF THE ORIGINAL CONTRACT

As no party, in the present age, can well support itself without a philosophical or speculative system of principles annexed to its political or practical one, we accordingly find,
that each of the factions into which this nation is divided
has reared up a fabric of the former kind, in order to protect and cover that scheme of actions which it pursues. The
people being commonly very rude builders, especially in
this speculative way, and more especially still when actuated
by party-zeal, it is natural to imagine that their workmanship
must be a little unshapely, and discover evident marks of
that violence and hurry in which it was raised. The one
party, by tracing up government to the Deity, endeavoured to
render it so sacred and inviolate, that it must be little less
than sacrilege, however, tyrannical it may become, to touch
or invade it in the smallest article. The other party, by
founding government altogether on the consent of the
people, suppose that there is a kind of *original contract*, by
which the subjects have tacitly reserved the power of resisting their sovereign, whenever they find themselves aggrieved
by that authority, with which they have, for certain purposes,
voluntarily intrusted him. These are the speculative principles of the two parties, and these, too, are the practical consequences deduced from them.

I shall venture to affirm, *That both these* systems *of speculative principles are just; though not in the sense intended by the
parties:* and, *That both the* schemes *of practical consequences
are prudent; though not in the extremes to which each party,
in opposition to the other, has commonly endeavoured to carry
them.*

That the Deity is the ultimate author of all government,
will never be denied by any, who admit a general providence, and allow, that all events in the universe are conducted by an uniform plan, and directed to wise purposes.

As it is impossible for the human race to subsist, at least in any comfortable or secure state, without the protection of government, this institution must certainly have been intended by that beneficent Being, who means the good of all his creatures: and as it has universally, in fact, taken place, in all countries, and all ages, we may conclude, with still greater certainty, that it was intended by that omniscient Being who can never be deceived by any event or operation. But since he gave rise to it, not by any particular or miraculous interposition, but by his concealed and universal efficacy, a sovereign cannot, properly speaking, be called his vicegerent in any other sense than every power or force, being derived from him, may be said to act by his commission. Whatever actually happens is comprehended in the general plan or intention of Providence; nor has the greatest and most lawful prince any more reason, upon that account, to plead a peculiar sacredness or inviolable authority, than an inferior magistrate, or even an usurper, or even a robber and a pirate. The same Divine Superintendent, who, for wise purposes, invested a Titus or a Trajan with authority, did also, for purposes no doubt equally wise, though unknown, bestow power on a Borgia or an Angria. The same causes, which gave rise to the sovereign power in every state, established likewise every petty jurisdiction in it, and every limited authority. A constable, therefore, no less than a king, acts by a divine commission, and possesses an indefeasible right.

When we consider how nearly equal all men are in their bodily force, and even in their mental powers and faculties, till cultivated by education, we must necessarily allow, that nothing but their own consent could, at first, associate them together, and subject them to any authority. The people, if we trace government to its first origin in the woods and deserts, are the source of all power and jurisdiction, and voluntarily, for the sake of peace and order, abandoned their native liberty, and received laws from their equal and companion. The conditions upon which they were willing to submit, were either expressed, or were so clear and obvious, that it might well be esteemed superfluous to express them. If this, then, be meant by the *original contract*, it cannot be denied, that all government is, at first, founded on a contract, and that the most ancient rude combinations of mankind were formed chiefly by that principle. In vain are we asked in what records this charter of our liberties is registered. It was not written on parchment, nor yet on leaves or barks of trees. It preceded the use of writing, and all the other civilized arts of life. But we trace it plainly in the nature of man, and in the equality, or something approaching equality, which we find in all the individuals of that species. The force, which now prevails, and which is founded on fleets and armies, is plainly political, and derived from authority, the effect of established government. A man's natural force consists only in the vigour of his limbs, and the firmness of his courage; which could never subject multitudes to the command of one. Nothing but their own consent, and their sense of the advantages resulting from peace and order, could have had that influence.

Yet even this consent was long very imperfect, and could not be the basis of a regular administration. The chieftain, who had probably acquired his influence during the continuance of war, ruled more by persuasion than command; and till he could employ force to reduce the refractory and disobedient, the society could scarcely be said to have attained a state of civil government. No compact or agreement, it is evident, was expressly formed for general submission; an idea far beyond the comprehension of savages: each exertion of authority in the chieftain must have been particular, and called forth by the present exigencies of the case: the sensible utility, resulting from his interposition, made these exertions become daily more frequent; and their frequency gradually produced an habitual, and, if you please to call it so, a voluntary, and therefore precarious, acquiescence in the people.

But philosophers, who have embraced a party (if that be

not a contradiction in terms), are not contented with these concessions. They assert, not only that government in its earliest infancy arose from consent, or rather the voluntary acquiescence of the people; but also that, even at present, when it has attained its full maturity, it rests on no other foundation. They affirm, that all men are still born equal, and owe allegiance to no prince or government, unless bound by the obligation and sanction of a *promise*. And as no man, without some equivalent, would forego the advantages of his native liberty, and subject himself to the will of another, this promise is always understood to be conditional, and imposes on him no obligation, unless he meet with justice and protection from his sovereign. These advantages the sovereign promises him in return; and if he fail in the execution, he has broken, on his part, the articles of engagement, and has thereby freed his subject from all obligations to allegiance. Such, according to these philosophers, is the foundation of authority in every government, and such the right of resistance possessed by every subject.

But would these reasoners look abroad into the world, they would meet with nothing that, in the least, corresponds to their ideas, or can warrant so refined and philosophical a system. On the contrary, we find every where princes who claim their subjects as their property, and assert their independent right of sovereignty, from conquest or succession. We find also every where subjects who acknowledge this right in their prince, and suppose themselves born under obligations of obedience to a certain sovereign, as much as under the ties of reverence and duty to certain parents. These connexions are always conceived to be equally independent of our consent, in Persia and China; in France and Spain; and even in Holland and England, wherever the doctrines above-mentioned have not been carefully inculcated. Obedience or subjection becomes so familiar, that most men never make any inquiry about its origin or cause, more than about the principle of gravity, resistance, or the most universal laws of nature. Or if curiosity ever move them; as soon as they learn that they themselves and their ancestors have, for several ages, or from time immemorial, been subject to such a form of government or such a family, they immediately acquiesce, and acknowledge their obligation to allegiance. Were you to preach, in most parts of the world, that political connexions are founded altogether on voluntary consent or a mutual promise, the magistrate would soon imprison you as seditious for loosening the ties of obedience; if your friends did not before shut you up as delirious, for advancing such absurdities. It is strange that an act of the mind, which every individual is supposed to have formed, and after he came to the use of reason too, otherwise it could have no authority; that this act, I say, should be so much unknown to all of them, that over the face of the whole earth, there scarcely remain any traces or memory of it.

But the contract, on which government is founded, is said to be the *original contract*; and consequently may be supposed too old to fall under the knowledge of the present generation. If the agreement, by which savage men first associated and conjoined their force, be here meant, this is acknowledged to be real; but being so ancient, and being obliterated by a thousand changes of government and princes, it cannot now be supposed to retain any authority. If we would say any thing to the purpose, we must assert that every particular government which is lawful, and which imposes any duty of allegiance on the subject, was, at first, founded on consent and a voluntary compact. But, besides that this supposes the consent of the fathers to bind the children, even to the most remote generations (which republican writers will never allow), besides this, I say, it is not justified by history or experience in any age or country of the world.

Almost all the governments which exist at present, or of which there remains any record in story, have been founded originally, either on usurpation or conquest, or both, without any pretence of a fair consent or voluntary subjection of the people. When an artful and bold man is placed at the

head of an army or faction, it is often easy for him, by employing, sometimes violence, sometimes false pretences, to
establish his dominion over a people a hundred times more
numerous than his partisans. He allows no such open communication, that his enemies can know, with certainty, their
number or force. He gives them no leisure to assemble together in a body to oppose him. Even all those who are the
instruments of his usurpation may wish his fall; but their
ignorance of each other's intention keeps them in awe, and
is the sole cause of his security. By such arts as these many
governments have been established; and this is all the *original
contract* which they have to boast of.

The face of the earth is continually changing, by the increase of small kingdoms into great empires, by the dissolution of great empires into smaller kingdoms, by the planting
of colonies, by the migration of tribes. Is there any thing
discoverable in all these events but force and violence?
Where is the mutual agreement or voluntary association so
much talked of?

Even the smoothest way by which a nation may receive a
foreign master, by marriage or a will, is not extremely honourable for the people; but supposes them to be disposed of,
like a dowry or a legacy, according to the pleasure or interest
of their rulers.

But where no force interposes, and election takes place;
what is this election so highly vaunted? It is either the combination of a few great men, who decide for the whole, and
will allow of no opposition; or it is the fury of a multitude,
that follow a seditious ringleader, who is not known, perhaps,
to a dozen among them, and who owes his advancement
merely to his own impudence, or to the momentary caprice
of his fellows.

Are these disorderly elections, which are rare too, of such
mighty authority as to be the only lawful foundation of all
government and allegiance?

In reality, there is not a more terrible event than a total

dissolution of government, which gives liberty to the multitude, and makes the determination or choice of a new establishment depend upon a number, which nearly approaches to that of the body of the people: for it never comes entirely to the whole body of them. Every wise man then wishes to see, at the head of a powerful and obedient army, a general who may speedily seize the prize, and give to the people a master which they are so unfit to choose for themselves. So little correspondent is fact and reality to those philosophical notions.

Let not the establishment at the *Revolution* deceive us, or make us so much in love with a philosophical origin to government, as to imagine all others monstrous and irregular. Even that event was far from corresponding to these refined ideas. It was only the succession, and that only in the regal part of the government, which was then changed: and it was only the majority of seven hundred, who determined that change for near ten millions. I doubt not, indeed, but the bulk of those ten millions acquiesced willingly in the determination: but was the matter left, in the least, to their choice? Was it not justly supposed to be, from that moment, decided, and every man punished, who refused to submit to the new sovereign? How otherwise could the matter have ever been brought to any issue or conclusion?

The republic of Athens was, I believe, the most extensive democracy that we read of in history: yet if we make the requisite allowances for the women, the slaves, and the strangers, we shall find, that that establishment was not at first made, nor any law ever voted, by a tenth part of those who were bound to pay obedience to it; not to mention the islands and foreign dominions, which the Athenians claimed as theirs by right of conquest. And as it is well known that popular assemblies in that city were always full of license and disorder, not withstanding the institutions and laws by which they were checked; how much more disorderly must they prove, where they form not the established constitution, but

meet tumultuously on the dissolution of the ancient government, in order to give rise to a new one? How chimerical
must it be to talk of a choice in such circumstances?

The Achæans enjoyed the freest and most perfect democracy of all antiquity; yet they employed force to oblige some
cities to enter into their league, as we learn from Polybius.

Harry the IVth and Harry the VIIth of England, had
really no title to the throne but a parliamentary election; yet
they never would acknowledge it, lest they should thereby
weaken their authority. Strange, if the only real foundation
of all authority be consent and promise?

It is in vain to say, that all governments are, or should be,
at first, founded on popular consent, as much as the necessity of human affairs will admit. This favours entirely my
pretension. I maintain, that human affairs will never admit
of this consent, seldom of the appearance of it; but that conquest or usurpation, that is, in plain terms, force, by dissolving the ancient governments, is the origin of almost all the
new ones which were ever established in the world. And
that in the few cases where consent may seem to have taken
place, it was commonly so irregular, so confined, or so much
intermixed either with fraud or violence, that it cannot have
any great authority.

My intention here is not to exclude the consent of the
people from being one just foundation of government where
it has place. It is surely the best and most sacred of any. I
only pretend, that it has very seldom had place in any degree,
and never almost in its full extent; and that, therefore, some
other foundation of government must also be admitted.

Were all men possessed of so inflexible a regard to justice,
that, of themselves, they would totally abstain from the
properties of others; they had for ever remained in a state of
absolute liberty, without subjection to any magistrate or political society: but this is a state of perfection, of which human nature is justly deemed incapable. Again, were all men
possessed of so perfect an understanding as always to know
their own interests, no form of government had ever been

submitted to but what was established on consent, and was fully canvassed by every member of the society: but this state of perfection is likewise much superior to human nature. Reason, history, and experience shew us, that all political societies have had an origin much less accurate and regular; and were one to choose a period of time when the people's consent was the least regarded in public transactions, it would be precisely on the establishment of a new government. In a settled constitution their inclinations are often consulted; but during the fury of revolutions, conquests, and public convulsions, military force or political craft usually decides the controversy.

When a new government is established, by whatever means, the people are commonly dissatisfied with it, and pay obedience more from fear and necessity, than from any idea of allegiance or of moral obligation. The prince is watchful and jealous, and must carefully guard against every beginning or appearance of insurrection. Time, by degrees, removes all these difficulties, and accustoms the nation to regard, as their lawful or native princes, that family which at first they considered as usurpers or foreign conquerors. In order to found this opinion, they have no recourse to any notion of voluntary consent or promise, which, they know, never was, in this case, either expected or demanded. The original establishment was formed by violence, and submitted to from necessity. The subsequent administration is also supported by power, and acquiesced in by the people, not as a matter of choice, but of obligation. They imagine not that their consent gives their prince a title: but they willingly consent, because they think, that, from long possession, he has acquired a title, independent of their choice or inclination.

Should it be said, that, by living under the dominion of a prince which one might leave, every individual has given a *tacit* consent to his authority, and promised him obedience; it may be answered, that such an implied consent can only have place where a man imagines that the matter depends on his choice. But where he thinks (as all mankind do who are born under established governments) that, by his birth, he owes allegiance to a certain prince or certain form of government; it would be absurd to infer a consent or choice, which he expressly, in this case, renounces and disclaims.

Can we seriously say, that a poor peasant or artisan has a free choice to leave his country, when he knows no foreign language or manners, and lives, from day to day, by the small wages which he acquires? We may as well assert that a man, by remaining in a vessel, freely consents to the dominion of the master; though he was carried on board while asleep, and must leap into the ocean and perish, the moment he leaves her.

What if the prince forbid his subjects to quit his dominions; as in Tiberius's time, it was regarded as a crime in a Roman knight that he had attempted to fly to the Parthians, in order to escape the tyranny of that emperor? [1] Or as the ancient Muscovites prohibited all travelling under pain of death? And did a prince observe, that many of his subjects were seized with the frenzy of migrating to foreign countries, he would, doubtless, with great reason and justice, restrain them, in order to prevent the depopulation of his own kingdom. Would he forfeit the allegiance of all his subjects by so wise and reasonable a law? Yet the freedom of their choice is surely, in that case, ravished from them.

A company of men, who should leave their native country, in order to people some uninhabited region, might dream of recovering their native freedom; but they would soon find, that their prince still laid claim to them, and called them his subjects, even in their new settlement. And in this he would but act conformably to the common ideas of mankind.

The truest *tacit* consent of this kind that is ever observed, is when a foreigner settles in any country, and is beforehand acquainted with the prince, and government, and laws, to which he must submit: yet is his allegiance, though more voluntary, much less expected or depended on, than that of

---

1. Tacit. *Ann.* vi. cap. 14.

a natural born subject. On the contrary, his native prince still asserts a claim to him. And if he punish not the renegade, when he seizes him in war with his new prince's commission; this clemency is not founded on the municipal law, which in all countries condemns the prisoner; but on the consent of princes, who have agreed to this indulgence, in order to prevent reprisals.

Did one generation of men go off the stage at once, and another succeed, as is the case with silkworms and butterflies, the new race, if they had sense enough to choose their government, which surely is never the case with men, might voluntarily, and by general consent, establish their own form of civil polity, without any regard to the laws or precedents which prevailed among their ancestors. But as human society is in perpetual flux, one man every hour going out of the world, another coming into it, it is necessary, in order to preserve stability in government, that the new brood should conform themselves to the established constitution, and nearly follow the path which their fathers, treading in the footsteps of theirs, had marked out to them. Some innovations must necessarily have place in every human institution; and it is happy where the enlightened genius of the age give these a direction to the side of reason, liberty, and justice: but violent innovations no individual is entitled to make: they are even dangerous to be attempted by the legislature: more ill than good is ever to be expected from them: and if history affords examples to the contrary, they are not to be drawn into precedent, and are only to be regarded as proofs, that the science of politics affords few rules, which will not admit of some exception, and which may not sometimes be controlled by fortune and accident. The violent innovations in the reign of Henry VIII. proceeded from an imperious monarch, seconded by the appearance of legislative authority: those in the reign of Charles I. were derived from faction and fanaticism; and both of them have proved happy in the issue. But even the former were long the source of many disorders, and still more dangers; and if the measures of allegiance were to be taken from the latter, a total anarchy must have place in human society, and a final period at once be put to every government.

Suppose that an usurper, after having banished his lawful prince and royal family, should establish his dominion for ten or a dozen years in any country, and should preserve so exact a discipline in his troops, and so regular a disposition in his garrisons that no insurrection had ever been raised, or even murmur heard against his administration: can it be asserted that the people, who in their hearts abhor his treason, have tacitly consented to his authority, and promised him allegiance, merely because, from necessity, they live under his dominion? Suppose again their native prince restored, by means of an army, which he levies in foreign countries: they receive him with joy and exultation, and shew plainly with what reluctance they had submitted to any other yoke. I may now ask, upon what foundation the prince's title stands? Not on popular consent surely: for though the people willingly acquiesce in his authority, they never imagine that their consent made him sovereign. They consent; because they apprehend him to be already by birth, their lawful sovereign. And as to that tacit consent, which may now be inferred from their living under his dominion, this is no more than what they formerly gave to the tyrant and usurper.

When we assert, that all lawful government arises from the consent of the people, we certainly do them a great deal more honour than they deserve, or even expect and desire from us. After the Roman dominions became too unwieldy for the republic to govern them, the people over the whole known world were extremely grateful to Augustus for that authority which, by violence, he had established over them; and they shewed an equal disposition to submit to the successor whom he left them by his last will and testament. It was afterwards their misfortune, that there never was, in one family, any long regular succession; but that their line of princes was continually broken, either by private assassinations or public rebellions. The *prætorian* bands, on the failure of every family, set up one emperor; the legions in the East a second; those in Germany, perhaps a third; and the sword alone could decide the controversy. The condition of the people in that mighty monarchy was to be lamented, not because the choice of the emperor was never left to them, for that was impracticable, but because they never fell under any succession of masters who might regularly follow each other. As to the violence, and wars, and bloodshed, occasioned by every new settlement, these were not blameable, because they were inevitable.

The house of Lancaster ruled in this island about sixty years; yet the partisans of the white rose seemed daily to multiply in England. The present establishment has taken place during a still longer period. Have all views of right in another family been utterly extinguished, even though scarce any man now alive had arrived at the years of discretion when it was expelled, or could have consented to its dominion, or have promised it allegiance? — a sufficient indication, surely, of the general sentiment of mankind on this head. For we blame not the partisans of the abdicated family merely on account of the long time during which they have preserved their imaginary loyalty. We blame them for adhering to a family which we affirm has been justly expelled, and which, from the moment the new settlement took place, had forfeited all title to authority.

But would we have a more regular, at least a more philosophical, refutation of this principle of an original contract, or popular consent, perhaps the following observations may suffice.

All *moral* duties may be divided into two kinds. The *first* are those to which men are impelled by a natural instinct or immediate propensity which operates on them, independent of all ideas of obligation, and of all views either to public or private utility. Of this nature are love of children, gratitude to benefactors, pity to the unfortunate. When we reflect on the advantage which results to society from such humane instincts, we pay them the just tribute of moral approbation and esteem: but the person actuated by them feels their power and influence antecedent to any such reflection.

The *second* kind of moral duties are such as are not supported by any original instinct of nature, but are performed entirely from a sense of obligation, when we consider the necessities of human society, and the impossibility of supporting it, if these duties were neglected. It is thus *justice*, or a regard to the property of others, *fidelity*, or the observance of promises, become obligatory, and acquire an authority over mankind. For as it is evident that every man loves himself better than any other person, he is naturally impelled to extend his acquisitions as much as possible; and nothing can restrain him in this propensity but reflection and experience, by which he learns the pernicious effects of that license, and the total dissolution of society which must ensue from it. His original inclination, therefore, or instinct, is here checked and restrained by a subsequent judgment or observation.

The case is precisely the same with the political or civil duty of *allegiance* as with the natural duties of justice and fidelity. Our primary instincts lead us either to indulge ourselves in unlimited freedom, or to seek dominion over others; and it is reflection only which engages us to sacrifice such strong passions to the interests of peace and public order. A small degree of experience and observation suffices to teach us, that society cannot possibly be maintained without the authority of magistrates, and that this authority must soon fall into contempt where exact obedience is not paid to it. The observation of these general and obvious interests is the source of all allegiance, and of that moral obligation which we attribute to it.

What necessity, therefore, is there to found the duty of *allegiance* or obedience to magistrates on that of *fidelity* or a regard to promises, and to suppose, that it is the consent of each individual which subjects him to government, when it appears that both allegiance and fidelity stand precisely on the same foundation, and are both submitted to by mankind, on account of the apparent interests and necessities of human society? We are bound to obey our sovereign, it is said, because we have given a tacit promise to that purpose. But why are we bound to observe our promise? It must here be asserted, that the commerce and intercourse of mankind, which are of such mighty advantage, can have no security where men pay no regard to their engagements. In like manner, may it be said that men could not live at all in society, at least in a civilized society, without laws, and magistrates, and judges, to prevent the encroachments of the strong upon the weak, of the violent upon the just and equitable. The obligation to allegiance being of like force and authority with the obligation to fidelity, we gain nothing by resolving the one into the other. The general interests or necessities of society are sufficient to establish both.

If the reason be asked of that obedience, which we are bound to pay to government, I readily answer, *Because society could not otherwise subsist*; and this answer is clear and intelligible to all mankind. Your answer is, *Because we should keep our word*. But besides, that no body, till trained in a philosophical system, can either comprehend or relish this answer; besides this, I say, you find yourself embarrassed when it is asked, *Why we are bound to keep our word?* Nor can you give any answer but what would, immediately, without any circuit, have accounted for our obligation to allegiance.

But *to whom is allegiance due? And who is our lawful sovereign?* This question is often the most difficult of any, and liable to infinite discussions. When people are so happy that they can answer, *Our present sovereign, who inherits, in a direct line, from ancestors that have governed us for many ages*, this answer admits of no reply, even though historians, in tracing up to the remotest antiquity the origin of that royal family, may find, as commonly happens, that its first authority was derived from usurpation and violence. It is confessed that private justice, or the abstinence from the properties of others, is a most cardinal virtue. Yet reason tells us that there is no property in durable objects, such as lands or houses, when carefully examined in passing from hand to hand, but must, in some period, have been founded on fraud and injustice. The necessities of human society, neither in private nor public life, will allow of such an accurate inquiry; and there is no virtue or moral duty but what may, with facility, be refined away, if we indulge a false philosophy in sifting and scrutinizing it, by every captious rule of logic, in every light or position in which it may be placed.

The questions with regard to private property have filled infinite volumes of law and philosophy, if in both we add the commentators to the original text; and in the end, we may safely pronounce, that many of the rules there established are uncertain, ambiguous, and arbitrary. The like opinion may be formed with regard to the succession and rights of princes, and forms of government. Several cases no doubt occur, especially in the infancy of any constitution, which admit of no determination from the laws of justice and equity; and our historian Rapin pretends, that the controversy between Edward the Third and Philip de Valois was of this nature, and could be decided only by an appeal to heaven, that is, by war and violence.

Who shall tell me, whether Germanicus or Drusus ought to have succeeded to Tiberius, had he died while they were both alive, without naming any of them for his successor? Ought the right of adoption to be received as equivalent to that of blood, in a nation where it had the same effect in private families, and had already, in two instances, taken place in the public? Ought Germanicus to be esteemed the elder son, because he was born before Drusus; or the younger, because he was adopted after the birth of his brother? Ought the right of the elder to be regarded in a nation, where he had no advantage in the succession of private families? Ought the Roman empire at that time to be deemed hereditary, because of two examples; or ought it, even so early, to be regarded as belonging to the stronger, or to the present possessor, as being founded on so recent an usurpation?

Commodus mounted the throne after a pretty long succession of excellent emperors, who had acquired their title, not by birth, or public election, but by the fictitious rite of adoption. That bloody debauchee being murdered by a conspiracy, suddenly formed between his wench and her gallant, who happened at that time to be *Prætorian Præfect*; these immediately deliberated about choosing a master to human kind, to speak in the style of those ages; and they cast their eyes on Pertinax. Before the tyrant's death was known, the *Præfect* went secretly to that senator, who, on the appearance of the soldiers, imagined that his execution had been ordered by Commodus. He was immediately saluted emperor by the officer and his attendants, cheerfully proclaimed by the populace, unwillingly submitted to by the guards, formally recognized by the senate, and passively received by the provinces and armies of the empire.

The discontent of the *Prætorian* bands broke out in a sudden sedition, which occasioned the murder of that excellent prince; and the world being now without a master, and without government, the guards thought proper to set the empire formally to sale. Julian, the purchaser, was proclaimed by the soldiers, recognized by the senate, and submitted to by the people; and must also have been submitted to by the provinces, had not the envy of the legions begotten opposition and resistance. Pescennius Niger in Syria elected himself emperor, gained the tumultuary consent of his army, and was attended with the secret good-will of the senate and people of Rome. Albinus in Britain found an equal right to set up his claim; but Severus, who governed Pannonia, prevailed in the end above both of them. That able politician and warrior, finding his own birth and dignity too much inferior to the imperial crown, professed, at first, an intention only of revenging the death of Pertinax. He marched as general into Italy, defeated Julian, and, without our being able to fix any precise commencement even of the soldiers' consent, he was from necessity acknowledged emperor by the senate and people, and fully established in his violent authority, by subduing Niger and Albinus.

Inter hæc Gordianus Cæsar (says Capitolinus, speaking of another period) *sublatus a militibus.* Imperator *est appellatus, quia non erat alius in præsenti.* It is to be remarked, that Gordian was a boy of fourteen years of age.

Frequent instances of a like nature occur in the history of the emperors; in that of Alexander's successors; and of many other countries: nor can any thing be more unhappy than a despotic government of this kind; where the succession is disjointed and irregular, and must be determined, on every vacancy, by force or election. In a free government, the matter is often unavoidable, and is also much less dangerous. The interests of liberty may there frequently lead the people, in their own defence, to alter the succession of the crown. And the constitution, being compounded of parts, may still maintain a sufficient stability, by resting on the aristocratical or democratical members, though the monarchical be altered, from time to time, in order to accommodate it to the former.

In an absolute government, when there is no legal prince who has a title to the throne, it may safely be determined to belong to the first occupant. Instances of this kind are but too frequent, especially in the eastern monarchies. When any race of princes expires, the will or destination of the last sovereign will be regarded as a title. Thus the edict of Louis the XIVth, who called the bastard princes to the succession in case of the failure of all the legitimate princes, would, in such an event, have some authority.[2] Thus the will of Charles the Second disposed of the whole Spanish monarchy. The cession of the ancient proprietor, especially when joined to conquest, is likewise deemed a good title. The general obli-

---

2. It is remarkable, that in the remonstrance of the Duke of Bourbon and the legitimate princes, against this destination of Louis the XIVth, the doctrine of the *original contract* is insisted on, even in that absolute government. The French nation, say they, choosing Hugh Capet and his posterity to rule over them and their posterity, where the former line fails, there is a tacit right reserved to choose a new royal family; and this right is invaded by calling the bastard princes to the throne, without the consent of the nation. But the Comte de Boulainvilliers, who wrote in defence of the bastard princes, ridicules this notion of an original contract, especially when applied to Hugh Capet; who

gation, which binds us to government, is the interest and necessities of society; and this obligation is very strong. The determination of it to this or that particular prince, or form of government, is frequently more uncertain and dubious. Present possession has considerable authority in these cases, and greater than in private property; because of the disorders which attend all revolutions and changes of government.

We shall only observe, before we conclude, that though an appeal to general opinion may justly, in the speculative sciences of metaphysics, natural philosophy, or astronomy, be deemed unfair and inconclusive, yet in all questions with regard to morals, as well as criticism, there is really no other standard, by which any controversy can ever be decided. And nothing is a clearer proof, that a theory of this kind is erroneous, than to find, that it leads to paradoxes repugnant to the common sentiments of mankind, and to the practice and opinion of all nations and all ages. The doctrine, which founds all lawful government on an *original contract*, or consent of the people, is plainly of this kind; nor has the most noted of its partisans, in prosecution of it, scrupled to affirm, *that absolute monarchy is inconsistent with civil society, and so can be no form of civil government at all;* [3] and *that the supreme power in a state cannot take from any man, by taxes and impositions, any part of his property, without his own consent or that of his representatives.* [4] What authority any moral reasoning can have, which leads into opinions so wide of the general practice of mankind, in every place but this single kingdom, it is easy to determine.

The only passage I meet with in antiquity, where the ob-

mounted the throne, says he, by the same arts which have ever been employed by all conquerors and usurpers. He got his title, indeed, recognized by the states after he had put himself in possession: but is this a choice or contract? The Comte de Boulainvilliers, we may observe, was a noted republican; but being a man of learning, and very conversant in history, he knew that the people were almost never consulted in these revolutions and new establishments, and that time alone bestowed right and authority on what was commonly at first founded on force and violence. See *État de la France*, vol. iii.

3. See Locke on Government, chap. vii. § 90.
4. Ibid., chap. xi. §§ 138, 139, 140.

ligation of obedience to government is ascribed to a promise, is in Plato's *Crito*; where Socrates refuses to escape from prison, because he had tacitly promised to obey the laws. Thus he builds a *Tory* consequence of passive obedience on a *Whig* foundation of the original contract.

New discoveries are not to be expected in these matters. If scarce any man, till very lately, ever imagined that government was founded on compact, it is certain that it cannot, in general, have any such foundation.

The crime of rebellion among the ancients was commonly expressed by the terms νεωτερίζειν, *novas res moliri*.

Jean-Jacques Rousseau

1712 – 1778

THE SOCIAL CONTRACT

or, Principles of Political Right

PREFACE

This short treatise has been abstracted from a more extended work, undertaken without due consideration of my powers, and long since abandoned. Of such scraps as could be salved from what was then completed, this is the most considerable, and, in my opinion, the least unworthy of being presented to the public. The rest is now no more.

BOOK I

NOTE

It is my wish to inquire whether it be possible, within the civil order, to discover a legitimate and stable basis of Government. This I shall do by considering human beings as they are and laws as they might be. I shall attempt, throughout my investigations, to maintain a constant connexion between what right permits and interest demands, in order that no separation may be made between justice and utility. I intend to begin without first proving the importance of my subject. Am I, it will be asked, either prince or legislator that I take it upon me to write of politics? My answer is — No; and it is for that very reason that I have chosen politics as the matter of my book. Were I either the one or the other I should not waste my time in laying down what has to be done. I should do it, or else hold my peace.

I was born into a free state and am a member of its sovereign body. My influence on public affairs may be small, but because I have a right to exercise my vote, it is my duty to learn their nature, and it has been for me a matter of constant delight, while meditating on problems of Government in general, to find ever fresh reasons for regarding with true affection the way in which these things are ordered in my native land.

(((I)))

THE SUBJECT OF THE FIRST BOOK

Man is born free, and everywhere he is in chains. Many a man believes himself to be the master of others who is, no less than they, a slave. How did this change take place? I do not know. What can make it legitimate? To this question I hope to be able to furnish an answer.

Were I considering only force and the effects of force, I should say: 'So long as a People is constrained to obey, and does, in fact, obey, it does well. So soon as it can shake off its yoke, and succeeds in doing so, it does better. The fact that it has recovered its liberty by virtue of that same right by which it was stolen, means either that it is entitled to resume it, or that its theft by others was, in the first place, without justification.' But the social order is a sacred right which serves as a foundation for all other rights. This right, however, since it comes not by nature, must have been built upon conventions. To discover what these conventions are is the matter of our inquiry. But, before proceeding further, I must establish the truth of what I have so far advanced.

(((II)))

OF PRIMITIVE SOCIETIES

The oldest form of society — and the only natural one — is the family. Children remain bound to their father for only just so long as they feel the need of him for their self-preservation. Once that need ceases the natural bond is dissolved. From then on, the children, freed from the obedience which they formerly owed, and the father, cleared of his debt of responsibility to them, return to a condition of equal independence. If the bond remain operative it is no longer something imposed by nature, but has become a matter of deliberate choice. The family is a family still, but by reason of convention only.

This shared liberty is a consequence of man's nature. Its first law is that of self-preservation: its first concern is for what it owes itself. As soon as a man attains the age of reason he becomes his own master, because he alone can judge of what will best assure his continued existence.

We may, therefore, if we will, regard the family as the basic model of all political associations. The ruler is the father writ large: the people are, by analogy, his children, and all, ruler and people alike, alienate their freedom only so far as it is to their advantage to do so. The only difference is that, whereas in the family the father's love for his children is sufficient reward to him for the care he has lavished on them, in the State, the pleasure of commanding others takes its place, since the ruler is not in a relation of love to his people.

Grotius denies that political power is ever exercised in the interests of the governed, and quotes the institution of slavery in support of his contention. His invariable method of arguing is to derive Right from Fact.[1] It might be possible to adopt a more logical system of reasoning, but none which would be more favourable to tyrants.

According to Grotius, therefore, it is doubtful whether the term 'human race' belongs to only a few hundred men, or whether those few hundred men belong to the human race. From the evidence of his book it seems clear that he holds by the first of these alternatives, and on this point Hobbes is in agreement with him. If this is so, then humanity is divided into herds of livestock, each with its 'guardian' who watches over his charges only that he may ultimately devour them.

Just as the shepherd is superior in kind to his sheep, so, too, the shepherds of men, or, in other words, their rulers, are superior in kind to their peoples. This, according to Philo, was the argument advanced by Caligula, the Emperor, who drew from the analogy the perfectly true conclusion that either Kings are Gods or their subjects brute beasts.

The reasoning of Caligula, of Hobbes, and of Grotius is fundamentally the same. Far earlier, Aristotle, too, had maintained that men are not by nature equal, but that some are born to be slaves, others to be masters.[2]

Aristotle was right: but he mistook the effect for the cause. Nothing is more certain than that a man born into a condi-

---

1. 'Learned researches into Public Right are, too often, but the record of ancient abuses, and it is but a waste of time to pursue such a line of inquiry . . .' (*Traité des interêts de la France avec ses voisins*, par M. le Marquis d'Argenson, published by Rey of Amsterdam). This is precisely the error of which Grotius is guilty.
2. *Politics*, Book I, ch. 5.

tion of slavery is a slave by nature. A slave in fetters loses everything — even the desire to be freed from them. He grows to love his slavery, as the companions of Ulysses grew to love their state of brutish transformation.[3]

If some men are by nature slaves, the reason is that they have been made slaves *against* nature. Force made the first slaves: cowardice has perpetuated the species.

I have made no mention of King Adam or of the Emperor Noah, the father of three great Monarchs who divided up the universe between them, as did the children of Saturn, whom some have been tempted to identify with them. I trust that I may be given credit for my moderation, since, being descended in a direct line from one of these Princes, and quite possibly belonging to the elder branch, I may, for all I know, were my claims supported in law, be even now the legitimate Sovereign of the Human Race. However that may be, all will concur in the view that Adam was King of the World, as was Robinson Crusoe of his island, only so long as he was its only inhabitant, and that the great advantage of empire held on such terms was that the Monarch, firmly seated on his throne, had no need to fear rebellions, conspiracy, or war.

(((III)))

OF THE RIGHT OF THE STRONGEST

However strong a man, he is never strong enough to remain master always, unless he transform his Might into Right, and Obedience into Duty. Hence we have come to speak of the Right of the Strongest, a right which, seemingly assumed in irony, has, in fact, become established in principle. But the meaning of the phrase has never been adequately explained. Strength is a physical attribute, and I fail to see how any moral sanction can attach to its effects. To yield to the strong is an act of necessity, not of will. At most it is the result of a dictate of prudence. How, then, can it become a duty?

3. See the short Treatise by Plutarch, entitled *That Beasts Make Use of Reason.*

Let us assume for a moment that some such Right does really exist. The only deduction from this premise is inexplicable gibberish. For to admit that Might makes Right is to reverse the process of effect and cause. The mighty man who defeats his rival becomes heir to his Right. So soon as we can disobey with impunity, disobedience becomes legitimate. And, since the Mightiest is always right, it merely remains for us to become possessed of Might. But what validity can there be in a Right which ceases to exist when Might changes hands? If a man be constrained by Might to obey, what need has he to obey by Duty? And if he is not constrained to obey, there is no further obligation on him to do so. It follows, therefore, that the word Right adds nothing to the idea of Might. It becomes, in this connexion, completely meaningless.

Obey the Powers that be. If that means Yield to Force, the precept is admirable but redundant. My reply to those who advance it is that no case will ever be found of its violation. All power comes from God. Certainly, but so do all ailments. Are we to conclude from such an argument that we are never to call in the doctor? If I am waylaid by a footpad at the corner of a wood, I am constrained by force to give him my purse. But if I can manage to keep it from him, is it my duty to hand it over? His pistol is also a symbol of Power. It must, then, be admitted that Might does not create Right, and that no man is under an obligation to obey any but the legitimate powers of the State. And so I continually come back to the question I first asked.

(((IV)))

OF SLAVERY

Since no man has natural authority over his fellows, and since Might can produce no Right, the only foundation left for legitimate authority in human societies is Agreement.

If a private citizen, says Grotius, can alienate his liberty and make himself another man's slave, why should not a whole people do the same, and subject themselves to the will of a King? The argument contains a number of ambiguous words which stand in need of explanation. But let us confine our attention to one only — *alienate*. To alienate means to give or to sell. Now a man who becomes the slave of another does not give himself. He sells himself in return for bare subsistence, if for nothing more. But why should a whole people sell themselves? So far from furnishing subsistence to his subjects, a King draws his own from them, and from them alone. According to Rabelais, it takes a lot to keep a King. Do we, then, maintain that a subject surrenders his person on condition that his property be taken too? It is difficult to see what he will have left.

It will be said that the despot guarantees civil peace to his subjects. So be it. But how are they the gainers if the wars to which his ambition may expose them, his insatiable greed, and the vexatious demands of his Ministers cause them more loss than would any outbreak of internal dissension? How do they benefit if that very condition of civil peace be one of the causes of their wretchedness? One can live peacefully enough in a dungeon, but such peace will hardly, of itself, ensure one's happiness. The Greeks imprisoned in the cave of Cyclops lived peacefully while awaiting their turn to be devoured.

To say that a man gives himself for nothing is to commit oneself to an absurd and inconceivable statement. Such an act of surrender is illegitimate, null, and void by the mere fact that he who makes it is not in his right mind. To say the same thing of a whole People is tantamount to admitting that the People in question are a nation of imbeciles. Imbecility does not produce Right.

Even if a man can alienate himself, he cannot alienate his children. They are born free, their liberty belongs to them, and no one but themselves has a right to dispose of it. Before they have attained the age of reason their father may make, on their behalf, certain rules with a view to ensuring their preservation and well-being. But any such limitation of their freedom of choice must be regarded as neither irrevocable nor unconditional, for to alienate another's liberty is contrary to the natural order, and is an abuse of the father's rights. It follows that an arbitrary government can be legitimate only on condition that each successive generation of subjects is free either to accept or to reject it, and if this is so, then the government will no longer be arbitrary.

When a man renounces his liberty he renounces his essential manhood, his rights, and even his duty as a human being. There is no compensation possible for such complete renunciation. It is incompatible with man's nature, and to deprive him of his free will is to deprive his actions of all moral sanction. The convention, in short, which sets up on one side an absolute authority, and on the other an obligation to obey without question, is vain and meaningless. Is it not obvious that where we can demand everything we owe nothing? Where there is no mutual obligation, no interchange of duties, it must, surely, be clear that the actions of the commanded cease to have any moral value? For how can it be maintained that my slave has any 'right' against me when everything that he has is my property? His right being *my* right, it is absurd to speak of it as ever operating to my disadvantage.

Grotius, and those who think like him, have found in the fact of war another justification for the so-called 'right' of slavery. They argue that since the victor has a *right* to kill his defeated enemy, the latter may, if he so wish, ransom his life at the expense of his liberty, and that this compact is the more legitimate in that it benefits both parties.

But it is evident that this alleged *right* of a man to kill his enemies is not in any way a derivative of the state of war, if only because men, in their primitive condition of independence, are not bound to one another by any relationship sufficiently stable to produce a state either of war or of peace. They are not *naturally* enemies. It is the link between *things* rather than between *men* that constitutes war, and since a state of war cannot originate in simple personal relations, but only in relations between things, private hostility between man and man cannot obtain either in a state of nature where there is no generally accepted system of private property, or in a state of society where law is the supreme authority.

Single combats, duels, personal encounters are incidents which do not constitute a 'state' of anything. As to those private wars which were authorized by the Ordinances of King Louis IX and suspended by the Peace of God, they were merely an abuse of Feudalism — that most absurd of all systems of government, so contrary was it to the principles of Natural Right and of all good polity.

War, therefore, is something that occurs not between man and man, but between States. The individuals who become involved in it are enemies only by accident. They fight not as men or even as citizens, but as soldiers: not as members of this or that national group, but as its defenders.[4] A State can have as its enemies only other States, not men at all, seeing that there can be no true relationship between things of a different nature.

This principle is in harmony with that of all periods, and with the constant practice of every civilized society. A declaration of war is a warning, not so much to Governments as to their subjects. The foreigner — whether king, private person, or nation as a whole — who steals, murders, or holds in durance the subjects of another country without first declaring war on that country's Prince, acts not as an enemy but as

4. The Romans, who, more than any other nation, had a genuine understanding of, and respect for, the legal implications of war, carried their scruples in this matter so far that a citizen was forbidden to volunteer except for a particular campaign and against a specific enemy. When the legion in which Cato the Younger performed his first period of military service under Popilius was re-formed, his father wrote to the latter explaining that if he wished to keep the young man under his command he must administer the oath over again, since the first one was now annulled, and consequently Cato could not be called upon to bear arms against the enemy. At the same time he wrote to his son telling him to be sure not to appear on parade until he had renewed his oath. I am aware that such particular instances as the siege of Clusium may be quoted against me, but my reply would be that I am concerned to cite only laws and customs. It was very seldom that the Romans transgressed their laws, and few peoples have had better ones.

a brigand. Even when war has been joined, the just Prince, though he may seize all public property in enemy territory, yet respects the property and possessions of individuals, and, in so doing, shows his concern for those rights on which his own laws are based. The object of war being the destruction of the enemy State, a commander has a perfect right to kill its defenders so long as their arms are in their hands: but once they have laid them down and have submitted, they cease to be enemies, or instruments employed by an enemy, and revert to the condition of men, pure and simple, over whose lives no one can any longer exercise a rightful claim. Sometimes it is possible to destroy a State without killing any of its subjects, and nothing in war can be claimed as a right save what may be necessary for the accomplishment of the victor's end. These principles are not those of Grotius, nor are they based on the authority of poets, but derive from the Nature of Things, and are founded upon Reason.

The Right of Conquest finds its sole sanction in the Law of the Strongest. If war does not give to the victor the right to massacre his defeated enemies, he cannot base upon a non-existent right any claim to the further one of enslaving them. We have the right to kill our enemies only when we cannot enslave them. It follows, therefore, that the right to enslave cannot be deduced from the right to kill, and that we are guilty of enforcing an iniquitous exchange if we make a vanquished foeman purchase with his liberty that life over which we have no right. Is it not obvious that once we begin basing the right of life and death on the right to enslave, and the right to enslave on the right of life and death, we are caught in a vicious circle? Even if we assume the existence of this terrible right to kill all and sundry, I still maintain that a man enslaved, or a People conquered, in war is under no obligation to obey beyond the point at which force ceases to be operative. If the victor spares the life of his defeated opponent in return for an equivalent, he cannot be said to have shown him mercy. In either case he destroys him, but in the latter case he derives value from his act, while in the former he gains nothing. His authority, however, rests on no basis but that of force. There is still a state of war between the two men, and it conditions the whole relationship in which they stand to one another. The enjoyment of the Rights of War presupposes that there has been no treaty of Peace. Conqueror and conquered have, to be sure, entered into a compact, but such a compact, far from liquidating the state of war, assumes its continuance.

Thus, in whatever way we look at the matter, the 'Right' to enslave has no existence, not only because it is without legal validity, but because the very term is absurd and meaningless. The words *Slavery* and *Right* are contradictory and mutually exclusive. Whether we be considering the relation of one man to another man, or of an individual to a whole People, it is equally idiotic to say — 'You and I have made a compact which represents nothing but loss to you and gain to me. I shall observe it so long as it pleases me to do so — and so shall you, until I cease to find it convenient.'

(((V)))

THAT WE MUST ALWAYS GO BACK TO AN ORIGINAL COMPACT

Even were I to grant all that I have so far refuted, the champions of despotism would not be one whit the better off. There will always be a vast difference between subduing a mob and governing a social group. No matter how many isolated individuals may submit to the enforced control of a single conqueror, the resulting relationship will ever be that of Master and Slave, never of People and Ruler. The body of men so controlled may be an agglomeration; it is not an association. It implies neither public welfare nor a body politic. An individual may conquer half the world, but he is still only an individual. His interests, wholly different from those of his subjects, are private to himself. When he dies his empire is left scattered and disintegrated. He is like an oak which crumbles and collapses in ashes so soon as the fire consumes it.

'A People,' says Grotius, 'may give themselves to a king.' His argument implies that the said People were already a People before this act of surrender. The very act of gift was that of a political group and presupposed public deliberation. Before, therefore, we consider the act by which a People chooses their king, it were well if we considered the act by which a People is constituted as such. For it necessarily precedes the other, and is the true foundation on which all Societies rest.

Had there been no original compact, why, unless the choice were unanimous, should the minority ever have agreed to accept the decision of the majority? What right have the hundred who desire a master to vote for the ten who do not? The institution of the franchise is, in itself, a form of compact, and assumes that, at least once in its operation, complete unanimity existed.

(((VI)))

OF THE SOCIAL PACT

I assume, for the sake of argument, that a point was reached in the history of mankind when the obstacles to continuing in a state of Nature were stronger than the forces which each individual could employ to the end of continuing in it. The original state of Nature, therefore, could no longer endure, and the human race would have perished had it not changed its manner of existence.

Now, since men can by no means engender new powers, but can only unite and control those of which they are already possessed, there is no way in which they can maintain themselves save by coming together and pooling their strength in a way that will enable them to withstand any resistance exerted upon them from without. They must develop some sort of central direction and learn to act in concert.

Such a concentration of powers can be brought about only as the consequence of an agreement reached between individuals. But the self-preservation of each single man derives primarily from his own strength and from his own freedom. How, then, can he limit these without, at the same time, doing himself an injury and neglecting that care which it is his duty to devote to his own concerns? This difficulty, in so far as it is relevant to my subject, can be expressed as follows:

'Some form of association must be found as a result of which the whole strength of the community will be enlisted for the protection of the person and property of each constituent member, in such a way that each, when united to his fellows, renders obedience to his own will, and remains as free as he was before.' That is the basic problem of which the Social Contract provides the solution.

The clauses of this Contract are determined by the Act of Association in such a way that the least modification must render them null and void. Even though they may never have been formally enunciated, they must be everywhere the same, and everywhere tacitly admitted and recognized. So completely must this be the case that, should the social compact be violated, each associated individual would at once resume all the rights which once were his, and regain his natural liberty, by the mere fact of losing the agreed liberty for which he renounced it.

It must be clearly understood that the clauses in question can be reduced, in the last analysis, to one only, to wit, the complete alienation by each associate member to the community of *all his rights*. For, in the first place, since each has made surrender of himself without reservation, the resultant conditions are the same for all: and, because they are the same for all, it is in the interest of none to make them onerous to his fellows.

Furthermore, this alienation having been made unreservedly, the union of individuals is as perfect as it well can be, none of the associated members having any claim against the community. For should there be any rights left to individuals, and no common authority be empowered to pronounce as between them and the public, then each, being in some things his own judge, would soon claim to be so in all. Were that so, a state of Nature would still remain in being, the conditions of association becoming either despotic or ineffective.

In short, whoso gives himself to all gives himself to none. And, since there is no member of the social group over whom we do not acquire precisely the same rights as those over ourselves which we have surrendered to him, it follows that we gain the exact equivalent of what we lose, as well as an added power to conserve what we already have.

If, then, we take from the social pact everything which is not essential to it, we shall find it to be reduced to the following terms: 'each of us contributes to the group his person and the powers which he wields as a person under the supreme direction of the general will, and we receive into the body politic each individual as forming an indivisible part of the whole.'

As soon as the act of association becomes a reality, it substitutes for the person of each of the contracting parties a moral and collective body made up of as many members as the constituting assembly has votes, which body receives from this very act of constitution its unity, its dispersed *self*, and its will. The public person thus formed by the union of individuals was known in the old days as a *City*, but now as the *Republic* or *Body Politic*.[5] This, when it fulfils a passive

5. The true meaning of the word 'City' has been almost entirely lost by the moderns, most of whom think that a Town and a City are identical, and that to be a Burgess is the same thing as to be a Citizen. They do not know that houses may make a town, but that only citizens can make a City. This same error cost the people of Carthage dear in the past. I have never anywhere read that the title '*cives*' could be conferred on the subject of a Prince, not even upon the Macedonians of ancient times, nor upon the English in our own day, though the latter are more nearly in the enjoyment of freedom than any other people. Only the French use *citizens* as a familiar word, the reason for this being that they have no true apprehension of its meaning, as may be seen by anyone who consults a French dictionary. Were it otherwise, they would fall, by adopting it,

role, is known by its members as *The State,* when an active
one, as *The Sovereign People,* and, in contrast to other similar
bodies, as a *Power.* In respect of the constituent associates,
it enjoys the collective name of *The People,* the individuals
who compose it being known as *Citizens* in so far as they
share in the sovereign authority, as *Subjects* in so far as they
owe obedience to the laws of the State. But these different
terms frequently overlap, and are used indiscriminately one
for the other. It is enough that we should realize the difference between them when they are employed in a precise
sense.

(((VII)))

OF THE SOVEREIGN

It is clear from the above formula that the act of association
implies a mutual undertaking between the body politic and
its constituent members. Each individual comprising the
former contracts, so to speak, with himself and has a twofold
function. As a member of the sovereign people he owes a
duty to each of his neighbours, and, as a Citizen, to the
sovereign people as a whole. But we cannot here apply that
maxim of Civil Law according to which no man can be held
to an undertaking entered into with himself, because there
is a great difference between a man's duty to himself and to a
whole of which he forms a part.

Here it should be pointed out that a public decision which
can enjoin obedience on all subjects to their Sovereign, by
reason of the double aspect under which each is seen, cannot, on the contrary, bind the sovereign in his dealings with
himself. Consequently, it is against the nature of the body

---

he commits a grave blunder in giving the same meaning to the two words. Not
so deceived is M. d'Alembert, who, in his article on GENEVA, properly distinguishes between the four Orders (five, if foreigners be counted) which go to
make up our city, of which two only constitute the Republic. No French author
known to me understands the meaning of the word 'Citizen.'

politic that the sovereign should impose upon himself a law which he cannot infringe. For, since he can regard himself under one aspect only, he is in the position of an individual entering into a contract with himself. Whence it follows that there is not, nor can be, any fundamental law which is obligatory for the whole body of the People, not even the social contract itself. This does not mean that the body politic is unable to enter into engagements with some other Power, provided always that such engagements do not derogate from the nature of the Contract; for the relation of the body politic to a foreign Power is that of a simple individual.

But the body politic, or Sovereign, in that it derives its being simply and solely from the sanctity of the said Contract, can never bind itself, even in its relations with a foreign Power, by any decision which might derogate from the validity of the original act. It may not, for instance, alienate any portion of itself, nor make submission to any other sovereign. To violate the act by reason of which it exists would be tantamount to destroying itself, and that which is nothing can produce nothing.

As soon as a mob has become united into a body politic, any attack upon one of its members is an attack upon itself. Still more important is the fact that, should any offence be committed against the body politic as a whole, the effect must be felt by each of its members. Both duty and interest, therefore, oblige the two contracting parties to render one another mutual assistance. The same individuals should seek to unite under this double aspect all the advantages which flow from it.

Now, the Sovereign People, having no existence outside that of the individuals who compose it, has, and can have, no interest at variance with theirs. Consequently, the sovereign power need give no guarantee to its subjects, since it is impossible that the body should wish to injure all its members, nor, as we shall see later, can it injure any single individual. The Sovereign, by merely existing, is always what it should be.

But the same does not hold true of the relation of subject to sovereign. In spite of common interest, there can be no guarantee that the subject will observe his duty to the sovereign unless means are found to ensure his loyalty.

Each individual, indeed, may, as a man, exercise a will at variance with, or different from, that general will to which, as citizen, he contributes. His personal interest may dictate a line of action quite other than that demanded by the interest of all. The fact that his own existence as an individual has an absolute value, and that he is, by nature, an independent being, may lead him to conclude that what he owes to the common cause is something that he renders of his own free will; and he may decide that by leaving the debt unpaid he does less harm to his fellows than he would to himself should he make the necessary surrender. Regarding the moral entity constituting the State as a rational abstraction because it is not a man, he might enjoy his rights as a citizen without, at the same time, fulfilling his duties as a subject, and the resultant injustice might grow until it brought ruin upon the whole body politic.

In order, then, that the social compact may not be but a vain formula, it must contain, though unexpressed, the single undertaking which can alone give force to the whole, namely, that whoever shall refuse to obey the general will must be constrained by the whole body of his fellow citizens to do so: which is no more than to say that it may be necessary to compel a man to be free — freedom being that condition which, by giving each citizen to his country, guarantees him from all personal dependence and is the foundation upon which the whole political machine rests, and supplies the power which works it. Only the recognition by the individual of the rights of the community can give legal force to undertakings entered into between citizens, which, otherwise, would become absurd, tyrannical, and exposed to vast abuses.

VIII

OF THE CIVIL STATE

The passage from the state of nature to the civil state produces a truly remarkable change in the individual. It substitutes justice for instinct in his behaviour, and gives to his actions a moral basis which formerly was lacking. Only when the voice of duty replaces physical impulse and when right replaces the cravings of appetite does the man who, till then, was concerned solely with himself, realize that he is under compulsion to obey quite different principles, and that he must now consult his reason and not merely respond to the promptings of desire. Although he may find himself deprived of many advantages which were his in a state of nature, he will recognize that he has gained others which are of far greater value. By dint of being exercised, his faculties will develop, his ideas take on a wider scope, his sentiments become ennobled, and his whole soul be so elevated, that, but for the fact that misuse of the new conditions still, at times, degrades him to a point below that from which he has emerged, he would unceasingly bless the day which freed him for ever from his ancient state, and turned him from a limited and stupid animal into an intelligent being and a Man.

Let us reduce all this to terms which can be easily compared. What a man loses as a result of the Social Contract is his natural liberty and his unqualified right to lay hands on all that tempts him, provided only that he can compass its possession. What he gains is civil liberty and the ownership of what belongs to him. That we may labour under no illusion concerning these compensations, it is well that we distinguish between natural liberty which the individual enjoys so long as he is strong enough to maintain it, and civil liberty which is curtailed by the general will. Between possessions which derive from physical strength and the right of the first-comer, and ownership which can be based only on a positive title.

To the benefits conferred by the status of citizenship might
be added that of Moral Freedom, which alone makes a man
his own master. For to be subject to appetite is to be a slave,
while to obey the laws laid down by society is to be free. But
I have already said enough on this point, and am not concerned here with the philosophical meaning of the word
liberty.

(((IX)))

OF REAL PROPERTY

Each individual member of the Community gives himself to
it at the moment of its formation. What he gives is the whole
man as he then is, with all his qualities of strength and
power, and everything of which he stands possessed. Not
that, as a result of this act of gift, such possessions, by changing hands and becoming the property of the Sovereign,
change their nature. Just as the resources of strength upon
which the City can draw are incomparably greater than those
at the disposition of any single individual, so, too, is public
possession when backed by a greater power. It is made more
irrevocable, though not, so far, at least, as regards foreigners,
more legitimate. For the State, by reason of the Social Contract which, within it, is the basis of all Rights, is the master
of all its members' goods, though, in its dealings with other
Powers, it is so only by virtue of its rights as first occupier,
which come to it from the individuals who make it up.

The Right of 'first occupancy,' though more real than the
'Right of the strongest,' becomes a genuine right only after
the right of property has been established. All men have a
natural right to what is necessary to them. But the positive
act which establishes a man's claim to any particular item of
property limits him to that and excludes him from all others.
His share having been determined, he must confine himself
to that, and no longer has any claim on the property of the
community. That is why the right of 'first occupancy,' however weak it be in a state of nature, is guaranteed to every

man enjoying the status of citizen. In so far as he benefits from this right, he withholds his claim, not so much from what is another's, as from what is not specifically his.

In order that the right of 'first occupancy' may be legalized, the following conditions must be present. (1) There must be no one already living on the land in question. (2) A man must occupy only so much of it as is necessary for his subsistence. (3) He must take possession of it, not by empty ceremony, but by virtue of his intention to work and to cultivate it, for that, in the absence of legal title, alone constitutes a claim which will be respected by others.

In effect, by according the right of 'first occupancy' to a man's needs and to his will to work, are we not stretching it as far as it will go? Should not some limits be set to this right? Has a man only to set foot on land belonging to the community to justify his claim to be its master? Just because he is strong enough, at one particular moment, to keep others off, can he demand that they shall never return? How can a man or a People take possession of vast territories, thereby excluding the rest of the world from their enjoyment, save by an act of criminal usurpation, since, as the result of such an act, the rest of humanity is deprived of the amenities of dwelling and subsistence which nature has provided for their common enjoyment? When Nuñez Balboa, landing upon a strip of coast, claimed the Southern Sea and the whole of South America as the property of the crown of Castille, was he thereby justified in dispossessing its former inhabitants, and in excluding from it all the other princes of the earth? Grant that, and there will be no end to such vain ceremonies. It would be open to His Catholic Majesty to claim from his Council Chamber possession of the whole Universe, only excepting those portions of it already in the ownership of other princes.

One can understand how the lands of individuals, separate but contiguous, become public territory, and how the right of sovereignty, extending from men to the land they occupy, becomes at once real and personal — a fact which makes their owners more than ever dependent, and turns their very strength into a guarantee of their fidelity. This is an advantage which does not seem to have been considered by the monarchs of the ancient world, who, claiming to be no more than kings of the Persians, the Scythians, the Macedonians, seem to have regarded themselves rather as the rulers of men than as the masters of countries. Those of our day are cleverer, for they style themselves kings of France, of Spain, of England, and so forth. Thus, by controlling the land, they can be very sure of controlling its inhabitants.

The strange thing about this act of alienation is that, far from depriving its members of their property by accepting its surrender, the Community actually establishes their claim to its legitimate ownership, and changes what was formerly mere usurpation into a right, by virtue of which they may enjoy possession. As owners they are Trustees for the Commonwealth. Their rights are respected by their fellow citizens and are maintained by the united strength of the community against any outside attack. From ceding their property to the State — and thus, to themselves — they derive nothing but advantage, since they have, so to speak, acquired all that they have surrendered. This paradox is easily explained once we realize the distinction between the rights exercised by the Sovereign and by the Owner over the same piece of property, as will be seen later.

It may so happen that a number of men begin to group themselves into a community before ever they own property at all, and that only later, when they have got possession of land sufficient to maintain them all, do they either enjoy it in common or parcel it between themselves in equal lots or in accordance with such scale of proportion as may be established by the sovereign. However this acquisition be made, the right exercised by each individual over his own particular share must always be subordinated to the overriding claim of the Community as such. Otherwise there would be no strength in the social bond, nor any real power in the exercise of sovereignty.

I will conclude this chapter, and the present Book, with a remark which should serve as basis for every social system: that, so far from destroying natural equality, the primitive compact substitutes for it a moral and legal equality which compensates for all those physical inequalities from which men suffer. However unequal they may be in bodily strength or in intellectual gifts, they become equal in the eyes of the law, and as a result of the compact into which they have entered.[6]

6. Under a bad government such equality is but apparent and illusory. It serves only to keep the poor man confined within the limits of his poverty, and to maintain the rich in their usurpation. In fact, laws are always beneficial to the 'haves' and injurious to the 'have-nots.' Whence it follows that life in a social community can thrive only when all its citizens have something, and none have too much.

BOOK II

I

THAT SOVEREIGNTY IS INALIENABLE

The first, and most important, consequence of the principles so far established is that only the general will can direct the powers of the State in such a way that the purpose for which it has been instituted, which is the good of all, will be achieved. For if the establishment of societies has been made necessary by the antagonism that exists between particular interests, it has been made possible by the conformity that exists between these same interests. The bond of society is what there is in common between these different interests, and if there were not some point in which all interests were identical, no society could exist. The bond of society is that identity of interests which all feel who compose it. In the absence of such an identity no society would be possible. Now, it is solely on the basis of this common interest that society must be governed.

I maintain, therefore, that sovereignty, being no more than the exercise of the general will, can never be alienated, and that the sovereign, who is a collective being only, can be represented by no one but himself. Power can be transmitted, but not will. And though, in fact, it is possible that the will of the individual may, on some point, accord with the general will, what is impossible is that any such agreement should be durable and constant. For the will of the individual tends naturally to privilege, the general will to equality. Still more impossible is it that there should be any guarantee of such a harmony of interests, even where it exists, since chance only, and not contrivance, is the foundation upon which it rests. It is certainly open to the sovereign to say — 'What I wish at this moment agrees with what this or that individual wishes or says that he wishes': but he cannot say, 'What he may wish to-morrow will conform in every respect to my

190

wish,' it being absurd to think that will can bind itself in respect of the future, and it being no part of the function of
will to consent to any action contrary to the will of him who
wills. If, therefore, the People undertake simply and solely
to obey, they, by that very act, dissolve the social bond, and
so lose their character as a People. Once the Master appears
upon the scene, the sovereign vanishes, and the body politic
suffers destruction.

This is not to say that orders issued by rulers may not take
on the semblance of the general will, so long as the sovereign,
free by definition to oppose them, does not do so. In such
cases, general silence may be held to imply the People's consent. This I shall explain more at length.

(((II)))

THAT SOVEREIGNTY IS INDIVISIBLE

For the same reason that sovereignty is inalienable, so, too,
is it indivisible. For either the will is general or it is not.[1]
Either it is the will of the whole body of the People, or it is
the will merely of one section. In the first case, this declared
will is an act of sovereignty, and has the force of law. In the
second, it is partial only, or, in other words, an act imposed
by Government; and then, the most that can be said of it is
that it is a decree.

But our politicians, finding it impossible to divide the
principle of sovereignty, none the less divide its objects. Act
is separated from Will, Legislative power from Executive;
the right of levying taxes from the right of administering
justice or declaring war; the administering of internal affairs
from that of treating with foreign powers. Sometimes we
find these various aspects of government intermingled,
sometimes divided. Those responsible for such division

---

1. That Will be general, it is not always necessary that it be unanimous, though
   it is necessary that every vote cast should be counted. Any deliberate exclusion
   breaks the general nature of the decision.

make of the sovereign a fantastic creature of shreds and patches. It is as though a man were to be composed of different bodies, the one having eyes, another arms, a third feet, but none furnished with more than a single set of organs. It is said that the conjurors of Japan will cut a child in pieces in full view of the audience, and then, casting the fragments into the air, bring them to earth again all duly assembled into a living infant. Such, or almost such, are the tricks performed by our modern men of politics. The body of the Commonwealth is first dismembered with an adroitness which would do credit to a country fair, and then reassembled, no one knows how.

This error arises from a mistaken notion of the nature of sovereign authority, and from treating as separable parts what, in fact, are only different manifestations. For instance, it has become customary to consider the declaration of war and the making of peace as separate acts of sovereignty. But this is not so, since neither act is a law but only an application of the law, determining the special way in which the law shall be understood; as will be abundantly clear when the idea of law shall have been accurately defined.

If we follow up similarly the other, divided functions of sovereignty, we shall see that wherever it appears to be separated that is only because we are viewing it wrongly, taking for parts of the sovereign power what, in reality, are all subordinated to it, implying a supreme act of will which such rights only exist to realize in fact.

It would be difficult to exaggerate the confusion which this lack of clear thinking has caused in the minds of those authors who have set themselves to define the different fields in which, on the basis of the general rules which they have laid down, the rights of kings and the rights of the people are separately valid. It must be obvious to any reader of the third and fourth chapters of Grotius's First Book, how hopelessly that learned writer, and his translator Barbeyrac, become bogged down and tangled in their own sophisms, fearing to deduce too much or too little from their own premises, or to set at odds those very interests which they have been at pains to conciliate. Grotius, living in France as a refugee, and out of love with his own country, was anxious to win the favour of Louis XIII to whom his book was dedicated. Consequently, he spared no pains to strip the People of all their rights, and expended much art in an attempt to transfer all of them to the king. In this he would have had the full sympathy of Barbeyrac, who dedicated his translation to George I, King of England. Unfortunately, however, as the result of the expulsion of James II (which he called his 'abdication') he found himself compelled to watch his words with the greatest care, twisting and shuffling in his efforts not to show William III in the light of a usurper. Had these two men based their work on true principles, all difficulties would have vanished, and their arguments would have been consistent. They would have found themselves, with wry faces, telling the truth and paying court only to the People. But the way of truth is not the high-road to fortune: nor are embassies, professorships, and pensions in the People's gift.

(((III)))

WHETHER THE GENERAL WILL CAN ERR

It follows from what has been said above that the general will is always right and ever tends to the public advantage. But it does not follow that the deliberations of the People are always equally beyond question. It is ever the way of men to wish their own good, but they do not at all times see where that good lies. The People are never corrupted though often deceived, and it is only when they are deceived that they appear to will what is evil.

There is often considerable difference between the will of all and the general will. The latter is concerned only with the common interest, the former with interests that are partial, being itself but the sum of individual wills. But take from the expression of these separate wills the pluses and minuses

— which cancel out, the sum of the differences is left, and
that is the general will.[2]

If the People, engaged in deliberation, were adequately informed, and if no means existed by which the citizens could
communicate one with another, from the great number of
small differences the general will would result, and the decisions reached would always be good. But when intriguing
groups and partial associations are formed to the disadvantage of the whole, then the will of each of such groups is general only in respect of its own members, but partial in respect
of the State. When such a situation arises it may be said that
there are no longer as many votes as men, but only as many
votes as there are groups. Differences of interest are fewer
in number, and the result is less general. Finally, when one of
these groups becomes so large as to swamp all the others, the
result is not the sum of small differences, but one single difference. The general will does not then come into play at all,
and the prevailing opinion has no more validity than that of
an individual man.

If, then, the general will is to be truly expressed, it is essential that there be no subsidiary groups within the State,
and that each citizen voice his own opinion and nothing but
his own opinion.[3] It was the magnificent achievement of
Lycurgus to have established the only State of this kind ever
seen. But where subsidiary groups do exist their numbers
should be made as large as possible, and none should be more
powerful than its fellows. This precaution was taken by

2. 'Every interest,' says the Marquis d'Argenson, 'has different principles. An
   identity of interests between any two given persons is established by reason
   of their opposition to the interests of a third.' He might have added that the
   identity of the interests of all is established by reason of their opposition to the
   interests of each. Did individual interests not exist, the idea of a common
   interest could scarcely be entertained, for there would be nothing to oppose it.
   Society would become automatic, and politics would cease to be an art.

3. 'Vera cosa,' says Machiavelli, 'che alcuni divisioni nuocono alle republiche e
   alcune giovano: quelle nuocono che sono dalle sette e da partigiani accom-
   pagnate: quelle giovano che senza sette, senza partigiani si mantengono. Non
   potendo adunque provedere un fundatore d'una repubblica che non siano
   nimizichie in quella, ha da proveder almeno che non vi siano sette.' (*History
   of Florence*, Book VII.)

Solon, Numa, and Servius. Only if it is present will it be possible to ascertain the general will, and to make sure that the People are not led into error.

(((IV)))

OF THE LIMITS OF THE SOVEREIGN POWER

If the State or the City is nothing but a moral person the life of which consists in the union of its members, and if the most important of its concerns is the maintenance of its own being, then it follows that it must have at its disposition a power of compulsion covering the whole field of its operations in order that it may be in a position to shift and adjust each single part in a way that shall be most beneficial to the whole. As nature gives to each man complete power over his limbs, so, too, the social compact gives to the body politic complete power over its members: and it is this power, directed by the general will, which, as I have already pointed out, bears the name of sovereignty.

But we have to consider not only the State as a public person, but those individual persons, too, who compose it, and whose lives and liberties are, in nature, independent of it. It is important, therefore, that we carefully distinguish between the rights of the citizens and the rights of the sovereign, between the duties which the former owe as subjects, and the natural rights which, as men, they are entitled to enjoy.[4]

It is agreed that what, as a result of the social compact, each man alienates of power, property, and liberty is only so much as concerns the well-being of the community. But, further, it must be admitted that the sovereign alone can determine how much, precisely, this is.

Such services as the citizen owes to the State must be rendered by him whenever the sovereign demands. But

4. I must beg the attentive reader not hurriedly to accuse me of contradiction. The terms of which I have made use might give some colour to such a charge, but that is owing to the poverty of human language. But wait.

the sovereign cannot lay upon its subjects any burden not necessitated by the well-being of the community. It cannot even wish to do so, for in the realm of reason, as of nature, nothing is ever done without cause.

The undertakings which bind us to the Commonwealth are obligatory only because they are mutual: their nature being such that we cannot labour for others without, at the same time, labouring for ourselves. For how can the general will be always right, and how can all constantly will the happiness of each, if every single individual does not include himself in that word *each*, so that in voting for the general interest he may feel that he is voting for his own? Which goes to show that the equality of rights and the idea of justice which it produces derive from the preference which each man has for his own concerns — in other words, from human nature: that the general will, if it be deserving of its name, must be general, not in its origins only, but in its objects, applicable to all as well as operated *by* all, and that it loses its natural validity as soon as it is concerned to achieve a merely individual and limited end, since, in that case, we, pronouncing judgement on something outside ourselves, cease to be possessed of that true principle of equity which is our guide.

In fact, as soon as issue is joined on some *particular* point, on some *specific* right arising out of a situation which has not previously been regulated by some form of general agreement, we are in the realm of debate. The matter becomes a trial in which certain interested individuals are ranged against the public, but where there is no certainty about what law is applicable nor about who can rightly act as judge. It would be absurd in such a case to demand an *ad hoc* decision of the general will, since the general will would then be the decision of one of the parties only. To the other it would appear in the guise of a pronouncement made by some outside power, sectarian in its nature, tending to injustice in the particular instance, and subject to error. Thus, just as the will of the individual cannot represent the general will, so, too, the general will changes its nature when called upon to pronounce upon a particular object. In so far as it is general, it cannot judge of an individual person or an isolated fact. When, for instance, the people of Athens appointed or removed their leaders, according honours to one and penalties to another: when, in other words, using the machinery supplied by a multiplicity of specific decrees, they exercised, in a muddled sort of way, all the functions of government, they ceased, strictly speaking, to have any general will at all, and behaved not as sovereign so much as magistrate. This statement may seem to be at variance with generally accepted ideas. I ask only that I may be granted time in which to develop my own. What makes the will general is not the number of citizens concerned but the common interest by which they are united. For in the sort of community with which I am dealing, each citizen necessarily submits to the conditions which he imposes on his neighbours. Whence comes that admirable identity of interest and justice which gives to the common deliberations of the People a complexion of equity. When, however, discussion turns on specific issues, this complexion vanishes, because there is no longer any common interest uniting and identifying the pronouncement of the judge with that of the interested party.

No matter by what way we return to our general principle, the conclusion must always be the same, to wit, that the social compact establishes between all the citizens of a State a degree of equality such that all undertake to observe the same obligations and to claim the same rights. Consequently, by the very nature of the pact, every act of sovereignty — that is to say, every authentic act of the general will — lays the same obligations and confers the same benefits on all. The sovereign knows only the nation as a whole and does not distinguish between the individuals who compose it.

What, then, is a true act of sovereignty? It is not a convention established between a superior and an inferior, but between the body politic and each of its members: a convention having the force of law because it is based upon the social contract: equitable, because it affects all alike: useful, because its sole object is the general good: firm, because it is backed by public force and the supreme power. So long as the subjects of a State observe only conventions of this kind, they are obeying not a single person, but the decision of their own wills. To ask what are the limits of the respective rights of sovereign and citizens is merely to ask to what extent the latter can enter into an undertaking with themselves, each in relation to all, and all in relation to each.

From which it becomes clear that the sovereign power, albeit absolute, sacrosanct, and inviolable, does not, and cannot, trespass beyond the limits laid down by general agreement, and that every man has full title to enjoy whatever of property and freedom is left to him by that agreement. The sovereign is never entitled to lay a heavier burden on any one of its subjects than on others, for, should it do so, the matter would at once become particular rather than general, and, consequently, the sovereign power would no longer be competent to deal with it.

These distinctions once admitted, it becomes abundantly clear that to say that the individual, by entering into the social contract, makes an act of renunciation is utterly false. So far from that being the case, his situation within the contract is definitely preferable to what it was before. Instead of giving anything away, he makes a profitable bargain, exchanging peril and uncertainty for security, natural independence for true liberty, the power of injuring others for his own safety, the strength of his own right arm — which others might always overcome — for a right which corporate solidity renders invincible. The life which he devotes to the State is, by the State continually protected, and, when he offers it in the State's defence, what else is he doing than giving back the very boon which he has received at its hands? What, in such circumstances, does he do that he has not done more often and more perilously in a state of nature when, inevitably involved in mortal combat, he defended at the risk of his life what served him to maintain it? All citizens, it is true, may, should the need arise, have to fight for their country, but no one of them has ever to fight singly for himself. Is it not preferable, in the interest of what makes for our security, to run some part of the risks which we should have to face in our own defence, were the boon of forming one of a society taken from us?

(((V)))

OF THE RIGHT OF LIFE AND DEATH

It will be asked how the single citizen, having no right over his own life, can transfer that same right to the sovereign. How can he give to another what is not his to give? This problem seems difficult of solution only because it is badly formulated. Every man has the right to risk his life with the object of preserving it. Has it ever been seriously argued that he who throws himself from a window to escape from fire is guilty of suicide? Or has that same crime ever been imputed to the man who perishes at sea in a storm, the danger of which he knew not when he embarked?

The social treaty has, as its aim, the safety of the contracting parties. Who wills the end wills also the means, and the means in this case are inseparable from certain risks, even from certain mortal accidents. He who would preserve his own life at other's cost is under an obligation to give his own for him should the necessity arise. Now, the citizen is no longer judge of the peril to which the law would have him expose his person; and, when the prince says to him, 'It is expedient, in the interests of the State, that you should die,' die he must, since only on that condition has he lived, till then, in safety. His life is not now, as it once was, merely nature's gift to him. It is something that he holds, on terms, from the State.

The penalty of death inflicted on criminals may be regarded in much the same way. That he may be saved from dying beneath the assassin's knife the citizen must be ready to pay with his life should he himself elect to play the assassin's part. So far from a man disposing of his own life under the terms of the compact, the sole object of that instrument is to preserve it. It is unlikely that any of the contracting parties will scheme to get himself hanged.

Furthermore, the evil-doer who attacks the fabric of social right becomes, by reason of his crime, a rebel and a traitor to his country. By violating its laws he ceases to be a member of it, and may almost be said to have made war upon it. The preservation, therefore, of the State is seen to be incompatible with his own continued existence. One of the two must perish, and, when the guilty man is put to death, it is as an enemy rather than as a citizen. His trial and sentence constitute the proof and declaration that he has broken the terms of the social treaty, and that, consequently, he is no longer a member of the State. Now, since he has always admitted that that is what he was, if only tacitly by reason of his residence, he must be separated from the body politic either by exile, as one who has infringed the compact, or by death as a public enemy. For such an enemy is not a moral person, but a man; and, in such a case, the right of war involves the killing of the vanquished.

But, it may be said, the condemnation of a criminal is an *ad hoc* act. Agreed. I would point out also that it is an act which does not pertain to the sovereign. It is a right which he can confer without exercising it himself. All my ideas are consistent, but I cannot express them all at once.

When punishments are frequent it is always a sign that the government is weak or lazy. There is no man, be he ever so bad, who cannot be made good for something. No man should be put to death, even to serve as an example, unless his continued existence is a source of danger.

As to the right of pardon, of exempting the guilty from the punishment decreed by law and pronounced by the judge, this belongs only to him who is above both law and judge — in other words, to the sovereign. But this right is not clearly defined, and its employment is very rare. In a

well-governed State there are few punishments, not because
pardons are frequent, but because criminals are few. The
great number of crimes which occur when the State is in a
condition of decadence confers immunity on the criminals.
In the days of the Roman Republic neither the Senate nor
the Consuls ever attempted to pardon the guilty. Even the
People did not do so, though they sometimes revoked their
own judgement. When pardons wax plentiful it is a sure sign
that crimes will soon have no need of them, and everyone can
see what that means. But I can hear my heart murmuring
and checking my pen. Let us leave such questions to the
Just Man who has never been at fault: who has never, in his
own person, stood in need of pardon.

(((VI)))

OF THE LAW

By the social compact we have given life and existence to the
body politic. It remains now to endow it with a will and with
a power of movement. This it can have only if it be equipped
with a body of laws. For the primal act by which the body
politic is formed and unified does not of itself determine the
steps that it must take if it is to maintain itself.

What is good and favourable to the establishment of order
is so by nature and owes nothing to human conventions. All
justice is from God: He only is its source. Did we but know
how to receive Heaven's ordinances direct, then we should
stand in need neither of government nor of law. There exists,
undoubtedly, a universal justice which is the pure product
of Reason, but if mankind is to acknowledge its claims, these
must be reciprocal. If we confine ourselves to the human aspect of the matter, we shall see at once that law and justice
is of no avail among men unless it be supported by natural
sanctions. If its operation be one-sided, then the only result
will be to make the wicked to flourish and the just man to
suffer wrong. There must be an agreed code of laws to im-

plement it in order that rights and duties be knit together, and Justice enabled to achieve its object. In a state of nature, where everything is in common, I owe nothing where I have promised nothing. I recognize the claim of my neighbour only to what I do not need myself. Such is not the case in the civil order of society where all rights are fixed by law.

But what, then, in the last analysis, is a law? So long as we are content to attach only a metaphysical meaning to the word, no amount of argument will bring understanding. We may describe adequately what is a law of nature without coming any nearer to grasping what is meant by a law of the State.

I have said already that *ad hoc* decisions are not the concern of the general will. Such decisions lie either within or without the confines of the State. If without, then a will foreign to it is not general in relation to it: if within, then it forms part of its life. A relation is set up between the whole and the part, between two terms, the part on one side, and, on the other, the whole *less* that part. But the whole *less* a part is no longer a whole. Consequently, where this relation obtains, we are dealing not with a whole but with two unequal parts. Whence it follows that the will of the one is no longer general so far as concerns the other.

But when the whole body of the people makes an enactment valid for all alike, it has in mind only itself. Whatever be the relation that emerges, the two terms are the same — the whole seen in one light, operating upon the same whole seen in another. There is no division between them. When that is so, then the matter about which the enactment is concerned is as much general as the will which produces the enactment. It is an action of this kind to which I give the name 'law.'

When I say that the matter of law is general, I mean that the law is concerned with the subjects of a State taken as a whole, and with actions considered as purely abstract. It never treats a man as an individual, nor an act as special or exceptional. Thus, while it is open to the law to enact that there shall be privileges, it is not its business to assign those privileges to actual individual men and women. The law may create various classes within the State, and may decide what qualities are to determine to which of them a citizen shall belong, but it cannot assign citizens by name to any. The law may establish a royal government and an hereditary succession, but it cannot elect a particular king, nor indicate which among all the families in the nation shall be the Royal Family. In short, it is not the function of the legislative power to concern itself with specific actions.

Once this is understood it will become immediately obvious that no longer need it be asked who has the right of making laws — seeing that they are acts of the general will; nor whether the prince stands above the law — since he is a member of the State; nor whether the law can be unjust, since no man is unjust to himself; nor how the citizen can, at one and the same time, be free, yet subject to the law, since laws are nothing but the record of what our wills have determined.

It is clear, too, that, since law combines universality of will with universality of object, that which a man, no matter who he be, orders on his own authority can never have the force of law. Even what the sovereign orders on its own authority is no law but a decree, no act of sovereignty but of administrative government. By a Republic, then, I understand any State ruled by law, quite irrespective of the form its government may take. For only then is public interest in the ascendent, only then does the word Commonwealth have any meaning. All legitimate government is, of its nature, republican. At a later stage I will explain what I understand by *government*.[5] Strictly speaking, laws are merely those conditions which determine the existence of a civil society. The People, subject to the enactments of law, must be its authors,

5. When I use the word 'republican' I do not mean necessarily either an aristocracy or a democracy, but any government guided by the general will, or, in other words, by law. Legitimacy does not mean that government is one with the sovereign, but that it acts as its minister. In this sense even a monarchy can be a republic. This will appear more clearly in the next book.

for it belongs only to those who have combined together to
order the conditions of their society. How, then, shall they
do this? Shall it be by common acclamation, by sudden inspiration? Has the body politic any specific organ which may
serve to give form to its will? Whence shall come the foresight which is necessary if its decisions are to be given shape
and published in advance of those circumstances which it is
their function to control? How shall it be sure of being able
to declare the law when need arises? How can the blind
multitude, which often does not know what it wants because
only rarely does it know what is for its own good, undertake,
of itself, an enterprise so extensive and so difficult as the
formulation of a system of law? Left to themselves, the
People always desire the good, but, left to themselves, they
do not always know where that good lies. The general will is
always right, but the judgement guiding it is not always well
informed. It must be made to see things as they are, sometimes as they ought to be. It must be shown how to attain the
good it seeks, must be protected against the temptations
inherent in particular interests; must be made to understand
places and seasons, and must learn to weigh present and
obvious advantage against remote and hidden dangers. Individuals see the good which they reject: the public desires
the good which it does not see. Both, equally, are in need of
guidance. The first must be constrained to submit their
wishes to their reason, the second to learn what it is they
want. From public vision comes union of understanding and
of will in the body of society: from which union flows the due
co-operation of parts and, finally, the strength of the whole
in its maximum manifestation. That is why a legislator is a
necessity.

(((VII)))

OF THE LEGISLATOR

In order to discover what social regulations are best suited
to nations, there is needed a superior intelligence which can
survey all the passions of mankind, though itself exposed to

none: an intelligence having no contact with our nature, yet knowing it to the full: an intelligence, the well-being of which is independent of our own, yet willing to be concerned with it: which, finally, viewing the long perspectives of time, and preparing for itself a day of glory as yet far distant, will labour in one century to reap its reward in another.[6] In short, only Gods can give laws to men.

The same argument which Caligula applied in practice Plato used in theory when, in his dialogue of *The Statesman*, he sought to define the nature of the Civil or 'Royal' man.[7] But if it be true that a great prince occurs but rarely, what shall be said of a great Law-giver? The first has but to follow the rules laid down by the latter. The Law-giver invents the machine, the prince merely operates it. 'When societies first come to birth,' says Montesquieu, 'it is the leaders who produce the institutions of the Republic. Later, it is the institutions which produce the leaders.'

Whoso would undertake to give institutions to a People must work with full consciousness that he has set himself to change, as it were, the very stuff of human nature; to transform each individual who, in isolation, is a complete but solitary whole, into a part of something greater than himself, from which, in a sense, he derives his life and his being; to substitute a communal and moral existence for the purely physical and independent life with which we are all of us endowed by nature. His task, in short, to take from a man his own proper powers, and to give him in exchange powers foreign to him as a person, which he can use only if he is helped by the rest of the community. The more complete the death and destruction of his natural powers, the greater and more durable will those be which he acquires, and the more solid and perfect will that community be of which he forms a part. So true is this that the citizen by himself is nothing,

6. A nation becomes famous only when its legislation begins to decline. We know not for how many centuries the institutions of Lycurgus gave prosperity to Sparta before she became involved in the general destinies of Greece.

7. See Plato's dialogue which, in its Latin version, is called *Politicus* or *The Citizen*. It is occasionally entitled *The Statesman*.

and can do nothing, save with the co-operation of his neighbours, and the power acquired by the whole is equal or superior to the sum of the powers possessed by its citizens regarded as natural men. When that result has been achieved, and only then, can we say that the art of legislation has reached the highest stage of perfection of which it is capable.

The Legislator must, in every way, be an extraordinary figure in the State. He is so by reason of his genius, and no less so by that of his office. He is neither magistrate nor sovereign. His function is to constitute the State, yet in its Constitution it has no part to play. It exists in isolation, and is superior to other functions, having nothing to do with the governance of men. For if it be true that he who commands men should not ordain laws, so, too, he who ordains laws should be no longer in a position to command men. Were it otherwise, the laws, mere ministers to his passions, would often do no more than perpetuate his acts of injustice, nor could he ever avoid the danger that his views as a man might detract from the sanctity of his work.

When Lycurgus gave laws to his country, he began by abdicating his royal powers. It was a custom obtaining in most of the Greek city-states, that the framing of their constitutions should be entrusted to foreigners. This practice has not seldom been copied in modern times by the republics of Italy, and was adopted by the State of Geneva, where it worked well.[8] Rome, in her greatest age, saw all the crimes of tyranny revive within her frontiers, and was near to perishing, simply because she had united in the same hands legislative authority and sovereign power.

For all that, the Decemvirs never arrogated to themselves the power to establish any law on their own authority.

---

8. Those who think of Calvin only as a theologian know very little of the full extent of his genius. Our wise edicts, in the framing of which he played a large part, do him no less honour than his *Institutes*. Whatever changes time may bring to our religious observances, so long as the love of country and of liberty is a living reality with us, the memory of that great man will be held in veneration.

'Nothing of what we propose,' they said to the People, 'can become law without your consent. Romans, be yourselves the authors of those laws which are to ensure your happiness.'

Whoso codifies the laws of a community, therefore, has not, or should not have, any legislative right, a right that is incommunicable, and one of which the People, even should they wish to do so, cannot divest themselves. For, by reason of the social compact, the general will alone can constrain the individual citizen: nor is there any other way of making sure that the will of the individual is in conformity with the general will, save by submitting it to the free votes of the People. This I have said once already; but it is well that it should be repeated.

Two things, therefore, seemingly incompatible, are to be found within the operation of law-making — it is a task beyond the capabilities of mere humans to perform: for its execution we are offered an authority which is a thing of naught.

There is another difficulty, too, that demands attention. Those wise men who, in speaking to the vulgar herd, would use not its language but their own, will never be understood. Many thousands of ideas there are which cannot be translated into popular phraseology. Excessive generalizations and long-range views are equally beyond the comprehension of the average man, who, as a rule, approves only such schemes, in matters of government, as will redound to his personal advantage. He finds it difficult to see what benefit he is likely to derive from the ceaseless privations which good laws will impose upon him. For a young people to understand fully the pondered maxims of the statesman and to follow the rules of conduct which are essential to healthy community life, would be for the effect to precede the cause. For such a thing to happen, the social spirit which can be the product only of a country's institutions would have, in fact, to be present at their birth, and, even before the laws are operative, the citizen would have to be such as those same laws would make him. Since, then, the legislator can use neither force nor argument, he must, of necessity, have recourse to authority of a different kind which can lead without violence and persuade without convincing.

That is why, in all periods, the Fathers of their country have been driven to seek the intervention of Heaven, attributing to the Gods a Wisdom that was really their own, in order that the People, subjected to the laws of the State no less than to those of nature, and recognizing in the creation of the City the same Power at work as in that of its inhabitants, might freely obey and might bear with docility the yoke of public happiness. The legislator, by putting into the mouths of the immortals that sublime reasoning which is far beyond the reach of poor mankind, will, under the banner of divine authority, lead those to whom mere mortal prudence would ever be a stumbling-block.[9] But it is not within the competence of every man to make the Gods speak, nor to get himself believed when he claims to be their interpreter. The real miracle, and the one sufficient proof of the Legislator's mission, is his own greatness of soul. Anyone can incise words on stone, bribe an oracle, claim some secret understanding with a high divinity, train a bird to whisper in his ear, or invent other ways, no less crude, for imposing on the People. He whose powers go no farther than that, may, if he be fortunate, hold the attention of a superstitious mob: but he will never found an empire, and his extravagant production will, in no long time, perish with him. Authority which has no true basis forms but a fragile bond. Only in wisdom can it find hope of permanence. The Jewish Law still lives, and the Law of the child of Ishmael which, for ten centuries, has regulated the conduct of half the world. They bear witness, even to-day, to the great men who gave them form. To the eyes of pride bred of philosophy or the blind spirit of Party, they may seem no more than fortunate im-

9. 'E veramente,' said Machiavelli, 'mai non fù alcuno ordinatore di leggi straordinarie in un popolo, che non ricorresse a Dio, perchè altrimenti non sarebbero accettate; perchè sono molti beni conosciuti da uno prudente, i quali non hanno in se ragioni evidenti da potergli persuadere ad altrui . . .' (*Discourses on Titus Livius*, Book I, ch. xi).

postors, but true political wisdom will ever admire in their institutions the great and powerful genius which watches over the birth of civilizations destined to endure.

We should not, from all this, conclude, with Warburton, that politics and religion have, in the modern world, the self-same aim, but rather that, in the forming of nations, the one serves as the other's instrument.

(((VIII)))

OF THE PEOPLE

Just as an architect, before he sets about constructing a great building, surveys and tests the site to see whether the ground is capable of bearing its weight, so, too, the wise legislator will not at once proceed to the formulating of laws, however good in themselves, but will first inquire whether the People who are to be ruled by his institutions can observe and maintain them. For that reason it was that Plato refused to make laws for the inhabitants of Arcadia and Cyrene, knowing that both communities, being rich, could endure no system of equality. So, too, Crete provided a spectacle of good laws but bad citizens, because Minos had merely imposed discipline on a people who were weighed down by their vices.

The earth has known many brilliant civilizations which could never have endured the regulation of good laws: while some, which might have borne with such have never had them save for a relatively short period of their total history. Most Peoples, like most men, are tractable only in their youth. As they grow old they become incorrigible. Once customs have become established and prejudices have taken root, any attempt at reform is a vain and dangerous enterprise. The People cannot bear that a man should lay a finger on the evils of their State, to destroy them, being, in that, like those foolish and cowardly sufferers who tremble at the mere sight of a doctor. Nevertheless, just as there are diseases which, by preying on the victim's mind, take from him all memory of the past, so, sometimes in the life of a People, there come periods of violence in which revolution works upon them as certain crises work upon the health of individuals. At such times a horror of the past takes the place of forgetfulness, and the State, inflamed by civil strife, is, so to speak, reborn in its ashes, and breaks from the very arms of death with a new sense of youth revived. This was the case in Sparta at the time of Lycurgus, in Rome after the Tarquins: in later times too, as in Holland and in Switzerland, after the expulsion of their tyrants.

But such events are rare. They are exceptions, and the reason for them is to be found always in the particular constitution of the State concerned. Nor could they happen twice in the lifetime of any one civilization. For, while it is always possible for a barbaric people to fight their way to freedom, it is no longer so when the springs of civil administration have become worn and have lost their resilience. Where that has happened a State may be destroyed by civil troubles: it will not be restored by revolution. Its fetters once struck off it falls apart and ceases to exist as a unity. What it needs thenceforward is not a liberator but a master. Free Peoples of the world remember this maxim: 'Liberty may be gained, but never recovered.'

Youth is not infancy. For all nations, as for all men, there is a time of youth, or, if the word be preferred, of maturity. For this they must wait before submitting to the governance of law. But it is not easy to determine when a nation is young; and should we anticipate the proper moment our labour will be lost. Some peoples are capable of discipline from the first: others, not till ten centuries have elapsed. The Russians will never be genuinely civilized because civilization was imposed upon them too early. Peter the Great's genius was imitative rather than genuine: and by genuine genius I mean the power to create everything from nothing. Some of the things he did were good, but most were ill timed. He saw that his subjects were barbarians: what he did not see was that they were not ready for civilization. He tried to civilize them when he should have been striving to season them. He began by endeavouring to turn them into Germans and Englishmen, when he should have been turning them into Russians. By persuading them that they were what they were not, he prevented them from ever realizing their true potentialities. Such is the way of the French tutor who spares no pains to endow his pupil with a precocious brilliance, thereby producing only a flash in the pan which is barren of results. The Russian Empire will wish to subjugate Europe, and will itself be subjugated. The Tartars, whether as subjects or as neighbours, will become its masters, and ours as well. Some such revolution seems to me to be inevitable. All the kings of Europe are working together to accelerate it.

(((IX)))

OF THE PEOPLE (*continued*)

Just as nature has set limits to the growth of a well-formed man, beyond which it produces only giants or imbeciles, so, too, there are limits of extent outside which a State cannot have the best possible constitution. It must be neither too large to make good government impossible, nor too small to defend itself unaided. In every body politic there is a maximum of force which it must not exceed, though, very often, by the mere process of becoming great it renders itself guilty of precisely that excess. The more the social bond is stretched the weaker does it become. Generally speaking, a small State is relatively stronger than a large one.

For this there are many reasons. In the first place, administration becomes increasingly difficult over long distances, just as a weight becomes heavier at the end of a long lever than a short one. It becomes, too, more oppressive when its parts are multiplied, since each city has its own administrative body which is paid for by the People, and each district, too, the expenses of which are similarly defrayed. Furthermore, there are the provincial organizations, the great outlying Governments, Satrapies, and Vice-Royalties, the cost of which always increases the higher one goes in the scale. In every case it is the poor People who pay. And at the very top comes the central government which is the last straw which breaks the camel's back. All these charges constitute a continual drain on a country's subjects. Far from being better governed by this vast hierarchy, they are a good deal less well governed than if they had but a single master. There is scarcely a penny left over with which to meet extraordinary calls, and when money has to be found, it always means that the State is faced with the prospect of complete ruin.

Nor is this all. Not only does the government act less firmly and less speedily in compelling the observance of the laws, in preventing unfairness, correcting abuses, and nipping in the bud seditious plots which abound where parts of a country are at distances far removed from the capital, but the People have less affection for their rulers, whom they never see, for their country, which is no closer to them than the world at large, and for their fellow citizens, many of whom they do not even know. It is impossible that the same laws should be suitable to so many different provinces, each with its own customs, its own climatic conditions, and its own ideas about the type of government it would like. A variety of laws, on the other hand, leads only to trouble and confusion when it obtains within the boundaries of a single State. For its subjects, living all under the same rulers, and being in constant communion with one another, visiting and intermarrying, are hard put to it, where local customs vary, to be sure that what they have inherited is ever truly theirs. When a great multitude of men, all strangers to one another, are brought together by the concentration of a central government in one place, talents lie buried, virtues are ignored, and vices tend to remain unpunished. The rulers, overburdened with work, have first-hand knowledge of nothing. The real governor of the State, in such cases, is the Civil Servant. The general effort is devoted to maintaining a governmental authority which is many scattered officials are for ever trying either to avoid or to impose. Little enough is left over for the fostering of public well-being, and barely sufficient to guarantee national defence when the need arises. Consequently, when a body politic is too large for its constitution, it tends to collapse under the weight of its own superstructure.

On the other hand, a State must have an adequate foundation if its stability is to be assured, and if it is to be in a position to withstand inevitable shocks and to take those measures necessary to its own continuance. For, in every nation there is what one may call a centrifugal tendency which becomes apparent in external relations, so that each pursues its own greatness at its neighbours' expense, much in the manner of Descartes' vortices. There is, therefore, much risk that weak nations will soon be swallowed up. It is but rarely that a nation can maintain itself save when it is in a condition of equilibrium with its neighbours, or, in other words, when the pressure over a given area is, to all intents and purposes, the same.

It must be apparent from what I have said that there are reasons both for extension and for concentration, and not the least of the statesman's gifts is to find the proportion between them which will ensure the life of the community. It may be laid down as a general rule that international relations should take second place to considerations of internal stability. The former are but relatively valuable, the latter absolutely. A strong and healthy constitution is the prime necessity, and vitality born of good government more reliable than any resources ensured by a wide territorial expansion.

There have been States so constituted that conquest becomes a necessity of their being. If they are to continue they must be for ever concerned with further extensions of their power. They may, perhaps, find matter for self-congratulation in this happy necessity, but one thing is certain: should they cease to grow, they will be faced with the prospect of inevitable collapse.

(((X)))

OF THE PEOPLE (*continued*)

A body politic may be viewed in two ways — according to
the extent of its territory, or according to the size of its population, and the proper size of any State depends upon a ratio
between these two. It is men who make a State, but it is land
that provides them with their food and sustenance. The
ideal is achieved when the land can support its population,
and when the population is of a size to absorb all the products of the land. Only where these two demands are met can
a given number of inhabitants be said to have attained its
maximum strength. For when a land is too large for its population, its defence becomes a burden; the fields are inade-
quately farmed, and there is too large a margin of natural
products. Such conditions are the immediate causes of de-
fensive wars. Where, on the other hand, a country is too
small to maintain its population, it is at the mercy of its
neighbours from whom alone it can obtain the commodities
it lacks, and this produces aggression. Every country which,
because of its situation, is forced to choose between trade
and war, is essentially weak. It depends upon its neighbours,
and it depends upon events. Its existence is bound to be
precarious and short. Either it conquers, and thereby
changes its situation, or it is conquered and ceases to exist.
It can remain free only if it is sufficiently small or sufficiently
large.

It is impossible to lay down a fixed ratio between extent of
territory and numbers of population. Not only does land
vary in quality, some being more fertile than others, but the
nature of its products is never the same, nor are the effects
of climate ever constant. So, too, there is no uniformity in
the temperament of those who inhabit different parts of the
earth. Some never get the best out of good land, while others
can show remarkable results with poor material. The fertility
of the women must, too, be taken into account, as well as the

effects of the climate on the inhabitants, and the advantages or disadvantages which may be expected from legislation. The wise ruler will never base his judgement on what, at any given moment, he *sees*, but on what he *foresees*. He should never take as his norm the size of the population when he begins his work, but should ever have before his eyes the total which it is likely to reach at some future date. Again and again it will be found that the natural peculiarities of a land make it allowable, or even necessary, to set its frontiers wider than might at first sight seem desirable. For instance, population density may be considerably thinned in a mountainous district where wood and pasture can be had with a minimum of labour, where experience shows that the women are more fruitful than in flat lands, and where the slopes of the hills provide little of that level country which is so necessary for vegetation. On the other hand, in coastal districts abounding in rock and sand which is for the most part sterile, a population may well be concentrated, because fishing can, to a large extent, make up for the non-existent products of the country-side, where a compact population is needed if pirates are to be held at bay, and where any surplus mouths can be absorbed into colonial emigration.

To these conditions which attend the founding of nations one more must be added. It cannot supply the place of any other, but without it all the others are of no avail — I refer to an assured period of peace. It is with a State in its infancy as with a newly formed regiment: it is weaker at its inception than at any other time, and more vulnerable. Resistance could be more successfully staged when all is chaos than in the early days of fermentation, when every man is busy with his duties within the community, and no one has a thought to spare for perils threatening from without. Should war, famine, or sedition occur at such a time, it will mean the inevitable overturning of the State.

Many governments, indeed, may be established during such periods of stress, but they are the very governments which destroy the State. Usurpers always choose times of domestic trouble to exploit public panic in the interests of destructive legislation which the People, in their calmer moments, would never approve. The work of the true legislator can best be distinguished from that of the tyrant by noting the precise moment of history which he has chosen for the establishment of his power.

What people, then, is the best raw material for laws? One which has a certain basic bond of common interests or agreed conventions, but has not yet borne the yoke of government: whose customs and superstitions are not deeply rooted: which is in no fear of being overwhelmed by sudden invasion. One which, without being involved in the quarrels of its neighbours, can stand alone against each one of them, or can call in the help of one to aid it in resisting another. One in which every man has personal knowledge of his fellows, and none has laid upon him a burden greater than he can bear. One which is not dependent upon other nations, nor needed by them.[10] One which is neither rich nor poor, but self-sufficient. One, finally, which combines the solidity of an ancient people with the docility of a new one. The real difficulty for the legislator lies not so much in deciding what new institutions he must establish, as which of the old ones he must destroy, and successes in this field are rare, mainly because of the impossibility of finding the simplicity of nature joined with what is necessary for social organization. It is no easy matter, admittedly, to find all these conditions present at one and the same time. That is why there are not more well-governed States.

There is still one country in Europe capable of legislation

---

10. Where, of two neighbouring nations, one is dependent upon the other, a situation arises which is very hard for the first and very dangerous for the second. At such times, a wise nation will take the quickest way to free the other from its condition of dependence. The Republic of Thlascala, which formed an enclave within the Empire of Mexico, preferred to do without salt rather than buy it from the Mexicans or to accept it from them as a gift. The Thlascalans, in their wisdom, saw the trap hiding behind the appearance of liberality. They retained their freedom and, though a small State imprisoned within the structure of a great Empire, played ultimately a part in bringing about the latter's ruin.

— the island of Corsica. The courage and determination with which its brave people have recovered and defended their liberty deserves that some wise man should teach it how it may be preserved. I have a premonition that this tiny island may one day astonish Europe.

(((XI)))

OF DIVERS SYSTEMS OF LEGISLATION

Should we inquire in what consist the greatest good of all, the ideal at which every system of legislation ought to aim, we shall find that it can be reduced to two main heads: *liberty* and *equality*: liberty, because when a subject is in a condition of dependence, by so much is the State cheated of part of his strength: equality, because without it there can be no liberty.

I have already described the nature of civil liberty: I turn now to equality. Let it be clearly understood that, in using the word, I do not mean that power and wealth must be absolutely the same for all, but only that power should need no sanction of violence but be exercised solely by virtue of rank and legality, while wealth should never be so great that a man can buy his neighbour, nor so lacking that a man is compelled to sell himself.[11] The great should be moderately endowed with goods and credit, the humble should be free of avarice and cupidity.

But such equality, it will be said, is but an airy day-dream, and cannot exist in practice. Does it, then, follow that because abuses will come, they should not at least be regulated? It is just because the pressure of events tends always to the destruction of equality that the force of legislation should always be directed to maintaining it.

But these general truths of all good statecraft have to be

11. If you would have a solid and enduring State, you must see that it contains no extremes of wealth. It must have neither millionaires nor beggars. These are inseparable from one another, and both are fatal to the common good. One produces the makers of tyrants, the other, tyrants themselves. Where they exist public liberty becomes a commodity of barter. The rich buy it, the poor sell it.

modified in each country to suit local conditions and the
character of the people. A system must be found which is
suited to these differences. It may not be the best in any
absolute sense, but it will be the best that can be found for
the country destined to make use of it. For instance, where
the soil is difficult or sterile, and the country too small for
its population, it will be well to encourage industry and the
arts, so that by exchanging manufactured products it may
obtain the foodstuffs of which it stands in need. On the other
hand, every advantage should be taken of rich plains and
fertile hill-sides. Where the soil is good but the population
thinly spread, all efforts should be concentrated on agriculture, which in itself increases the birth-rate. But the arts
should be eschewed, since they will merely aggravate the
shortage of man-power by attracting the available population to certain fixed localities.[12] Long and convenient coast-
lines should be adequately settled. Where they exist, large
fleets should be built, and commerce and navigation encouraged. The life of such maritime communities will be
brilliant though short. Should the sea be girt with rock and
the land be inaccessible, it were well to remain primitive and
to live mainly off fish. The life of those inhabiting such areas
will be tranquil, better, and, perhaps, happier than that of
many others. In short, apart from certain general maxims
which are applicable to all nations, the conditions of each
separate people inevitably induce a special way of life and
produce the sort of constitution best suited to the circumstances. Recognizing this, the Jews of old, and, more recently,
the Arabs, made of religion the chief object of their attention; Athens, literature; Tyre and Carthage, trade; Rhodes,
seafaring; and Rome, virtue. The author of *L'Esprit des Lois*
has adduced a wealth of examples to show the art by which
the legislator guides his country in the accomplishment of
each of these different ideals.

12. The advantages of foreign commerce, says Monsieur d'Argenson, are, in gen-
    eral, apparent rather than real. It may enrich individuals and even particular
    towns, but the country as a whole reaps no benefit, and the people are no
    better off because of it.

The structure of the State is truly solid and durable only when, as the result of careful adaptation, natural conditions and man-made laws are ever in agreement, so that the latter do but ratify, so to speak, accompany, and adjust the former. But should the legislator who is uncertain of his object flout the nature of the material in which he has to work, attempting to impose liberty in conditions which make for slavery, to favour the amassing of wealth where he should be giving his attention to problems of population, to plan conquest where a policy of peace is indicated — the authority of the laws will insensibly diminish, the structure of the community will change for the worse, and unrest will grow to a point at which the State will have to choose between death or change, and nature, which can never be defeated, will reassert her Empire.

(((XII)))

DIVISION OF THE LAWS

Many relations must be considered if the Commonwealth is to be properly organized, and that plan adopted which will be in the best interest of all. In the first place we have to bear in mind the way in which the body politic acts upon itself, or, in other words, the relation of the whole to the whole, or of the Sovereign to the State, and this relation is composed of that of its intermediate terms, as will be seen later.

The laws controlling this relationship are known as political, or basic, laws, and not without reason where they are wisely drawn. For if, in each State there is only one good method of regulating it, the people who have discovered that method ought to keep to it. But if the established order is bad, why should we regard as basic those very laws which themselves constitute the obstacle to its being good? Besides, in any case, it is always open to a People to change their laws, even when they are good. For if they like to injure themselves by what right can they be prevented from doing so?

The second set of relations are those subsisting between the members of the State, or between them and the whole of the body politic. The first should be as limited, the second as extensive, as possible. Every citizen should be completely independent of his neighbours, but wholly dependent upon the City. This is brought about always by the same means, for only where the State is strong are its members free. It is this second relation which produces civil law.

It may be held that there is yet a third type of relation between the individual and the law, that of punishable disobedience — and this gives rise to criminal law which, strictly speaking, is less an independent system of law than a means of bringing sanctions to bear on all the others.

To these three kinds of law a fourth should be added, and it is the most important of them all. It is to be found not graven on pillars of marble or plates of bronze but in the hearts of the citizens. It is the true foundation on which the State is built, and grows daily in importance. When other laws become old and feeble it brings them new life or fills the gaps they leave untenanted. It maintains a People in the spirit of their Founder, and, all unnoticed, substitutes for authority the force of habit. I refer to manners, customs, and, above all, opinion. This is a field unknown to our politicians, yet on these things depends the success of all the rest. With them the great legislator is unceasingly occupied in private, even when he seems to be confining his attention to matters of detail which, at best, are merely the arch, whereas manners, slow in their growth, are the keystone without which it will not stand.

Of all these different classes, political laws, which determine the specific forms of government, are alone relevant to my subject.

BOOK III

Before speaking of the various forms of government, let us make some attempt to establish the precise meaning of the word 'government' itself, for it has never, hitherto, been really well explained.

(((I)))

OF GOVERNMENT IN GENERAL

I warn the reader that he must apply his mind to this chapter slowly and deliberately. I have not the skill to make my meaning clear save to those who concentrate their attention upon it.

Two causes combine to produce every free action: the one moral, namely, the will, which determines the act: the other physical, namely, the strength which executes it. When I walk towards an objective, I must, in the first place, have made up my mind to reach it: in the second, my feet must be capable of carrying me thither. A paralytic may wish to run, an active man may wish not to. In either case the result is the same, for both men remain where they are. The body politic is controlled by similar springs of action, and the same distinction can be made, when speaking of it, between strength and will — the latter under the name of *legislative power*, the other under that of *executive power*. Nothing can, or should be done, without a combination of the two.

We have seen that legislative Power belongs to the People, and can belong to nobody else. It will be easily understood from the principles already established that the executive power, on the contrary, cannot belong to the generality as a legislating or supreme body, because it is concerned only with particular acts which do not fall within the competence of the law, nor, consequently, of the sovereign whose actions can take the form only of laws.

The *strength*, therefore, of the body politic cannot be exerted save through an appropriate agent who translates it into action in accordance with instructions issued by the general will, acts as a channel of communication for the State and Sovereign, and performs for public ends the same function as that fulfilled in the individual man by the union of mind and body. That is why the State needs a government. The word is wrongly confounded with Sovereignty. In fact, it is nothing but its minister.

What, then, is government? It is an intermediate body set up to serve as a means of communication between subjects and sovereign, and it is charged with the execution of the laws and the maintenance of liberty, both civil and political.

The members of such a body are called magistrates or *Kings*, in other words, *Governors*: and the body as a whole goes by the name of *Prince*.[1] Those, therefore, who maintain that the act by which a People submit to their rulers is not a contract have much right on their side. It is, strictly speaking, nothing but a *commission*, an employment in which those rulers, as simple officers of the Sovereign, do but exercise in its name the powers delegated to them, which can be limited, modified, or resumed as the Sovereign pleases. The alienation of such a right, being incompatible with the body social, is contrary to the whole object for which it has been established.

I call *government*, therefore, or supreme administration, the legitimate exercise of the executive power, and *prince* or *magistrate* the man or body charged with that administration.

It is in the government that those intermediate powers are to be found, the relations of which form the link connecting the whole with the whole, the sovereign with the State. It can be likened to that existing between the extremes of a continuous proportion, of which the mean proportional is the government. The government receives from the Sovereign the

1. Thus, in Venice, the title of *serenissime prince* is given to the College, even when the Doge is not present.

orders which it passes on to the People. If the balance of the State is to be preserved it is necessary, other things being equal, that the product or power of the government as a whole shall balance the product or power of the citizens, who are, at one and the same time, both Sovereign and subjects.

Furthermore, no one of the three terms can be altered without this balance being immediately destroyed. If the Sovereign wishes to govern, if the magistrate wishes to frame laws, or if the subjects refuse to obey, then disorder will be substituted for the rule of law, power and will must cease to act in concert, and the State, entering on a phase of dissolution, will fall either into despotism or into anarchy. And since there is but one true mean on which each set of relations can be established, there is but one good government possible for a State. But, because a thousand different events may change the balance within a nation, not only may different forms of government be good for different States, but also for the same State at different times.

That I may do what I can to give some idea of the different relations which may exist between the two extremes, I will take as an example the size of population, this being a term easy to handle.

Let us suppose, for the sake of argument, that a State has ten thousand citizens. The Sovereign can be regarded only as a collective entity, as an embodiment; while each citizen, taken as a subject, has to be viewed individually. The Sovereign, therefore, is to the subject in the proportion of ten thousand to one. In other words, each several member of the State enjoys but a ten-thousandth part of the sovereign authority, though he owes complete obedience to it. Should the size of the population be a hundred thousand, the position of its subjects is in no way changed, for each of them is equally with all the rest subject to the authority of the laws, while his own single voice, reduced to a hundred-thousandth part, has ten times less influence in their formulation. And so, since the subject is always a single individual, the proportion in which the Sovereign stands to him increases in the ratio of the size of the population. Whence it follows that the larger the State the less the liberty.

When I say that the proportion increases, I mean that it is removed from equality. Thus, the greater the ratio in the geometrical sense, the less is it in the commonly accepted meaning of the term. In the first, the ratio, viewed according to quantity, is measured by the exponent; in the second, viewed according to identity, it is estimated by similarity.

Now the smaller the ratio in which the wills of individual citizens stand to the general will, or, in other words, customs to laws, the greater must be the part played by repressive force. It follows, therefore, that the larger the population, the stronger, relatively, must the government be, if it is to function efficiently.

On the other hand, since the increase in State powers offers those who hold the public authority in trust added temptation to abuse their position, and more opportunities of doing so, it may be laid down that the more power a government has to coerce the People, the more should the Sovereign have to coerce the government. I do not mean absolute power, but such relative power as resides in the different parts of the State.

It follows from this double ratio that the unbroken proportion between Sovereign, Prince, and People is no arbitrary notion, but a necessary consequence of the nature of the body politic. It follows, further, that one of the extreme terms, to wit, the People as Subject, being fixed and represented by unity, every time that the double ratio increases or diminishes, the single ratio increases or diminishes in like manner, with the result that the middle term is changed. From which it is clear that there can be no single and absolute form of constitution, but that governments vary in their nature according to the size of the State in which they exist.

Should anyone, wishing to turn this system into ridicule, say that in order to establish a mean ratio and form the body of the government it is necessary, according to me, only to take the square root of the population, my answer would be that I have adopted this quantitative approach merely as an example, and that the ratio of which I have been speaking is not to be reckoned solely in terms of number, but, in general, by the quantity of action which results from many causes. I should add that if, in order to express my meaning in as few words as possible, I have temporarily borrowed the language of geometry, I know perfectly well that mathematical precision is not to be looked for when dealing with moral quantities.

Government is, on a small scale, what the body politic is on a large one. It is a moral person endowed with certain faculties, active when considered as Sovereign, passive when considered as the State, and capable of subdivision into other similar relations, giving rise to a totally different proportion; and, within this, another, reckoned in terms of the judicial function, and so on and so on, until we reach a single, indivisible middle term, to wit, one supreme chief or magistrate whom we may regard as standing in this progression as unity between the series of fractions and that of whole numbers.

Without letting ourselves be tied up in this multiplicity of terms, let us rest content with considering government as a new body in the State, distinct from the People and from the Sovereign, and occupying an intermediate place between them.

There is this essential difference between the two bodies, that, whereas the State exists in and by itself, government depends for its being on the Sovereign. Thus, the will of the prince, expressed in his acts as ruler, is, or should be, nothing but the general will, or, in other words, the Law. Such power as he has is but the power of the community concentrated in his person. The moment he tries to perform some absolute and independent action, the bond of union which holds the State together becomes loosened. If, finally, it should happen that the prince's will as an individual is more active than the will of the Sovereign, and that, in order to compel obedience to that individual will he makes use of the public powers under his control, so that, at one and the same moment there are two sovereigns, one *de jure*, the other *de facto*, all social unity will automatically vanish and the body politic will be dissolved.

Nevertheless, in order that the body of government may have an existence, a real life which distinguishes it from the body of the State: in order that all its members may act in concert and perform the function for which it was instituted, it must have an individual self, a consciousness in which all its members can share, as well as powers and a will of its own capable of maintaining it in being. This individual existence implies assemblies, councils, a competence to deliberate issues and to make resolutions, rights, titles, and privileges, all belonging to the prince exclusively, and conferring the greater honour on the magistrate the heavier the burden he has to bear. The real difficulty is how to insert this subordinate totality into the larger totality in such a way that, while not injuring the constitution in general, it may yet enjoy an adequate strength of its own, and may always hold the particular power which is designed to keep it alive and flourishing, distinct from the public power whose function it is to preserve the State, so that, in a word, it may always be ready to sacrifice government in the interests of the People, and not the People in the interests of government.

Furthermore, just because the artificial body of government is the work of another body no less artificial, and enjoys a life which is, in some sort, derivative and subordinate, that is no reason why it should not act with greater or less vigour and promptitude, and be in a more or less robust condition of health. Finally, without directly detaching itself from the object for which it was instituted, it can depart from it, more or less, according to the way in which it has been set up.

From these differences spring the different relations which a government may have with the body of the State, and these must be in harmony with the accidental and peculiar relations by which the State itself is modified. For it may often be that a government, excellent in itself, will become extremely vicious if the relations which bind it to the State are not altered to suit the defects of the body politic to which it belongs.

(((II)))

OF THE PRINCIPLE WHICH CONSTITUTES THE DIVERS FORMS OF GOVERNMENT

To explain the general cause of these differences, I must here distinguish the Prince from the Government, as formerly I distinguished the State from the sovereign.

The body of the magistracy may be composed of few or many members. We said that the ratio of the Sovereign to his subjects increases with the growth of the population. By an obvious analogy, we can say the same of government in regard to its magistrates.

Now, the total power of the government being always that of the State does not vary. Whence it follows that the greater the power exerted by the government on its own members, the less does it have left to exert on the people as a whole.

Consequently, the more numerous the magistrates, the weaker the government. Since this maxim is fundamental, I shall try to make my meaning still clearer.

We can distinguish in the person of the magistrate three essentially different forms of will. First, there is the will which belongs to him as an individual. This is concerned only with his own personal advantage. Second, there is the will which is common to all the magistrates. This considers only the advantage of the Prince, and may be called the will of the corporate government, such will being general in respect of the government itself, but particular in respect of the State of which the government forms part. Third, there is the will of the People, or the Sovereign Will, which is general in respect both of the State regarded as a whole and of the government considered as part of that whole.

Ideally, the particular, individual, will should play no part whatever in legislation, and the will of the corporate government, that is to say, of those whose collective function it is to carry out the acts of government, very little. Consequently, the general will must remain dominant as the sole rule of all the rest.

According to the natural order, however, these different wills become the more active the more concentrated they are. And so it is that the general will is always the weakest, the will of the corporate government coming next, and the will of the individual holding first place: so that, in the government, each member is primarily himself, secondly a magistrate, and only at third remove a citizen. This arrangement is directly contrary to the needs of the social order.

Where government is in the hands of a single man, we have the perfect example of the individual will and the will of the government as a body acting in complete unity, which means that the will of the government is seen in the highest intensity of which it is capable. Now, since the use of power depends upon the degree of will involved, and since the absolute power of government does not vary, it follows that the most active form of government is that of a single ruler.

On the other hand, where the executive is united with the legislative, where the Sovereign is identified with the Prince, and every citizen is a magistrate, the will of the corporate government, confounded with the general will, has its activity limited to that of the latter, in which case the individual will retains its full force, and the government, endowed with the same absolute power, will be at its lowest relative point. In other words, its activity will be at the minimum.

These facts are incontestable, and other considerations serve but to confirm my conclusions. It is clear, for instance, that any given magistrate is more active within the body of which he forms part than is any given citizen in the body politic, with the result that the will of the individual has much greater influence in the actions of government than in those of the sovereign. For each magistrate is, almost always, charged with some special function of government, whereas, each citizen, taken singly, performs no function of the sovereign. Again, the larger the State the greater is its real power, although that power does not increase in proportion to the size of the State. But while the State remains the same, it matters little whether the number of magistrates be increased. A multiplicity of officers does not confer on the government any increase of real power, because the power is the power of the State and does not vary. Thus, the relative power or activity of the government diminishes, while its absolute or real power cannot increase.

It is certain, too, that the pace at which affairs of state are handled becomes slower in proportion as the number of those engaged is increased. Where too much attention is paid to prudence, not enough account is taken of fortune, opportunities are missed, and, by excessive deliberation, the fruits of deliberation are lost.

I have just proved that government grows weaker in proportion as the number of magistrates increases, and earlier still I proved that the larger the figure of a nation's population, the greater should be the repressive power of government. Whence it follows that the relative number of magistrates to government should be in inverse ratio to that of subjects to sovereign. In other words, the larger a State becomes the more concentrated should its government be; so that the number of rulers should diminish as the size of the population grows larger.

I am speaking here not of the rectitude of government, but of its relative power, since, on the other hand, the more magistrates there are the more does the will of the governmental body approximate to the general will. But where there is only one magistrate the will of the government, as I have already pointed out, becomes identified with the will of a single man. Thus, what is gained in one direction is lost in another, and the art of the legislator consists in knowing the precise point at which the Power and the Will of government, always in a proportion of reciprocity, are combined in the ratio which will be of the greatest service to the State.

(((III)))

OF THE CLASSIFICATION OF GOVERNMENTS

We have seen in the foregoing chapter why it is that the different forms of government are distinguished according to the number of individuals who compose them. It remains here to see how the distinction is made.

The Sovereign can, in the first place, entrust the machinery of government to the whole people, or to most of the people, in which case the Commonwealth will contain more citizens acting as magistrates than simple members of the State. This form of government is known as *democracy*.

Government may, on the other hand, be restricted to a small number, so that the total of simple members of the State exceeds that of its magistrates. This form goes by the name of *aristocracy*.

Finally, all government may be concentrated in the hands of a single magistrate from whom all other officials derive their power. This third form, which is the commonest of all, is known as *monarchy*, or royal government.

It should be noted that all these forms, or, at least, the first two, may vary in degree, and are, in fact, extremely elastic. For a democracy may involve the whole of a people or be limited to half of it. Aristocracy, too, may extend to as much as one-half, though it may, alternatively, be limited to some smaller and indeterminate total. Even royalty can be shared. The Constitution of Sparta provided that two kings should be permanently in office, and there were times when the Roman Empire had as many as eight Emperors at the same time, without, for that reason, being in any sense divided. There is, therefore, a point at which each form of government merges into one of the others, and it must be obvious that, though there are but three denominations of government, the actual function may be susceptible of as many different forms as the State has citizens.

Nor is this all. Since the same government may, in certain

respects, be subdivided into a multiplicity of parts, each one
of which may differ from the others in the manner of its administration, from the mingling of the three main types a
number of mixed forms may emerge, each one of which is
capable of being multiplied by all the basic forms.

There has always, in all ages, been much argument about
the best form of government. Those who engage in such disputation do not sufficiently bear in mind that each may be
the best in certain circumstances, the worst in others.

If, in different States, the number of the supreme magistrates should be in inverse ratio to the number of citizens,
it follows that, speaking generally, democracy is best suited
to small states, aristocracy to those of medium size, and monarchy to the largest. This rule emerges clearly from the general principle. But how is it possible to reckon the multiplicity of circumstances which may produce exceptions?

(((IV)))

OF DEMOCRACY

He who makes the law knows better than any man how it
should be administered and interpreted. It would seem,
therefore, that every good constitution should provide for the
uniting of legislative and executive powers. But it is precisely
such a union that leads to inefficiency in government, since
matters which ought to be distinguished are not, and the
Prince and the Sovereign, being but the same person, form,
so to speak, a government without a government.

It is not good that he who makes the law should administer
it, nor that the body of the People should have its attention
diverted from general principles to particular instances.
Nothing is more dangerous than the influence exerted by
private interests on public affairs. The abuse of law by government is a lesser evil than the corruption of the legislator,
which is the inevitable result where private interests are
pursued. When that happens, the substance of the State

suffers a change for the worse, and all improvement becomes impossible. A People that was never guilty of abusing the powers of government would certainly never abuse their own independence. A People that always governed well would stand in no need of being governed at all.

If we take the term in its strict meaning, no true democracy has ever existed, nor ever will. It is against the natural order that a large number should rule and a small number be ruled. It is inconceivable that the People should be in permanent session for the administration of public affairs, and it is clear that commissions could not be set up for that purpose without the form of the administration being thereby changed.

Indeed, I think it may be laid down as a general rule that where the functions of government are parcelled out among a number of different official bodies, the smaller must, sooner or later, acquire the greater authority, if only because it is but natural that they should find it easier to transact business more quickly.

How difficult, too, to bring together the various elements made necessary by the democratic form of government. In the first place, the State must be sufficiently small to make it possible to call the whole people together without difficulty, and each citizen must be in a position to know all of his neighbours. In the second place, manners must be so simple that business will be kept to a minimum and thorny questions avoided. There should be, too, a considerable equality in fortune and in rank, for otherwise there will not long be equality in rights and authority. Finally, there must be little or no luxury, because either it is the product of wealth, or it makes wealth necessary. It corrupts both the rich and the poor, the rich through their possessions, the poor through their lust to possess. It sells the country in exchange for vanity and soft living. It takes from the State all its citizens to make each the slave of his fellows, and all the slave of opinion.

That is why a famous author has said that virtue is the

mainstay of the State, for only where there is virtue will all the above-mentioned conditions exist. But, through not making the necessary distinctions, this brilliant genius often falls into inaccuracies, and is at times guilty of confused thinking. He does not see that, since sovereign authority is everywhere the same, the same principle should hold for all well-constituted States, though in varying degrees, according to the form of their government.

It must be added that the democratic or popular system of government is, more than most, subject to civil strife and internal dissension, because no other is so violently and so continually exposed to the temptations of change, or demands so high a degree of vigilance and courage in maintaining itself. It is the one type of constitution above all others in which the citizen must arm himself with strength and constancy, and must forever be mindful of the truth which was once expressed as follows by a virtuous Prince when speaking to the Polish Diet: '*Malo periculosam libertatem quam quietum servitium.*'[2] Were there such a thing as a nation of Gods, it would be a democracy. So perfect a form of government is not suited to mere men.

(((V)))

OF ARISTOCRACY

We have here two quite distinct moral persons, to wit, the Government and the Sovereign: consequently, two general wills, the one of all the citizens, the other confined to the members of the administration. Thus, though the government can regulate its internal policy as it likes, it can never speak to the People save in the name of the Sovereign, or, in other words, of the People themselves. This should never be forgotten.

Primitive societies were governed aristocratically. The heads of families deliberated with one another about public

2. The Prince of Posnania, father of the King of Poland, and Duke of Lorraine.

affairs. The young bowed, without question, to the authority of experience: hence such names as *Priest, Ancients, Senate,* and *Gerontes.* The savages of North America are still governed in this way, and very well governed they are.

But as the inequality produced by institutions came to prevail over natural inequality, wealth and power grew to be accounted of more importance than age,[3] and aristocracy became elective. Finally, a time came when power, like property, was transmitted from father to son, with the result that certain families were recognized as patrician, government became hereditary, and it was no uncommon thing to find senators of twenty.

There are, then, three sorts of aristocracy: natural, elective, and hereditary. The first exists only among primitive peoples. The third is the worst of all forms of government: the second is the best. It is aristocracy in its strictest sense.

Not only has it the advantage of distinguishing between the two powers, but the further one of choosing its members. For while, in popular government, all the citizens are magistrates by right of birth, in an elective aristocracy the magistracy is confined to a small number of persons who exercise it as a result of selection,[4] a method by which honesty, wisdom, and the other reasons which lead to the choice and respect of the public are so many fresh guarantees that the State will be well governed. Furthermore, assemblies are more easily convoked, business is more efficiently discussed, and government is carried on more quickly and with a greater degree of order and diligence. The reputation of the State is better maintained abroad by a body of venerable

3. It is clear that the word *optimates* meant, in the ancient world, not the *best* but the *most powerful.*

4. It is very important that the method of electing magistrates be regulated by law. For, if their appointment is made dependent upon the will of the prince, an hereditary aristocracy is bound to develop, as happened in the Republics of Venice and of Berne. The first of these has long been in a state of dissolution, though the second, owing to the great wisdom of the Senate, still continues. It is an exception to the rule, as dangerous as it is honourable.

senators than by a multitude of unknown persons of little account.

In a word, it is the best and most natural arrangement that can be made that the wise should govern the masses, provided that they govern them always for their good, and not selfishly. Organs of government should never be multiplied unnecessarily, nor should twenty thousand men be employed to do what five hundred, carefully selected, can do better. But it should be noted that the executive body begins here to direct the public powers in a lesser degree according to the general will, and that another inevitable tendency begins to remove part of the executive power from the control of law.

But certain special points must be stressed. The State must not be so small, nor its people so primitive and upright, that the execution of the laws follows automatically upon the expression of the will of the People, as in a well-regulated democracy. Nor should it be so large that the various officials scattered over its extent for the carrying on of government may be in a position to trespass upon the domain of the Sovereign, each in his own territory, and, having achieved independence, end by becoming its masters.

But if aristocracy demands fewer virtues than popular government, many of those which it has — at its best — are found nowhere else, such as a spirit of moderation in the rich and of contentment in the poor. A strict insistence on equality would seem to be out of place in such a system. It certainly was not observed in Sparta. Finally, if this form of government involves inequalities of fortune, it is in order that the administration of public affairs may be in the hands of those best able to give all their time to it, and not because, as Aristotle affirms, the rich are always to be preferred to the poor. On the contrary, it is important that the occasional election of a poor man should serve as a reminder to the people that it is not wealth alone which marks a man out for preferment.

(((VI)))

OF MONARCHY

So far we have been considering the prince as a moral and collective person only, to whom the force of law alone imparts unity, and who holds the executive power in trust for the State. We have now to ponder the situation which arises when these powers are concentrated in the hands of a *natural* person, that is to say, of a real man, who has the sole right under the law to employ them. A man of this description is called a monarch or a King.

The situation is the very reverse of what we find in other forms of administration. For in them a collective being takes the place of the individual, whereas here an individual takes the place of a collective being, in such a way that the moral unity which constitutes the prince is, at the same time, a physical unity in which the various faculties which, in the other cases, are only, with much difficulty, concentrated in a single person, are here brought together by the processes of nature itself.

Thus, the will of the people and the will of the prince, the generalized powers of the State and the particular powers of government, all depend on the same machinery of motivation. All the springs of the machine are in the same hand, everything moves to the same end, and there are no opposed and mutually destructive elements. It would be impossible to devise any constitution in which so small an effort is capable of producing such large results. Archimedes seated quietly on the shore, and launching a great ship without the slightest difficulty, stands for me as the emblem of an able monarch ruling the whole vast extent of his territories from his cabinet, setting all in motion while himself remaining unmoved.

Of all forms of government the monarchical is the most vigorous. Nowhere else does the will of a single man sway a vaster empire or dominate more easily the wills of others. Everything, it is true, works to one end, but that end is not the public happiness, and the very strength of the executive continually operates to the disadvantage of the State.

Kings desire absolute power, and ancestral voices cry to them that the best way of attaining their desire is to be beloved of their people. All that is very fine and grand: to some extent, also, it is true. But, unfortunately, this excellent maxim is habitually laughed to scorn in the Courts of the world. Power which springs from the People's love is, assuredly, better than any other kind, but it is precarious, and exists only on conditions. Princes can never rest content with it. Even the best of monarchs likes to feel that he can behave badly if he wants to, without, for that reason, ceasing to be master in his own house. In vain will his political mentor remind him that, since his strength is but the strength of his people, it is to his interest that they should be flourishing, populous, and formidable. He knows only too well that this is not true, that his personal interests will best be served when they are weak, wretched, and incapable of resistance. Admittedly, assuming that the people are always perfectly submissive, it is *then* to the prince's advantage that they be also strong, since, their strength being his, he can the better strike fear into the hearts of his enemies. But, since this advantage is but secondary and subordinate, and the two assumptions are mutually irreconcilable, it is only natural that princes should give precedence to the maxim which is of more immediate use to them. It is this lesson which Samuel impressed upon the Jews, which Machiavelli taught and supported with evidence. While seemingly designing his instructions for the ears of kings, he did, in fact, give shrewd counsel to their peoples. His *Prince* is a book for the use of republicans.[5]

5. Machiavelli was an upright man and a good citizen, but, since he was a member of the Medicis' household, he was compelled by the circumstances of oppression to disguise his love of liberty. The mere fact that he chose as his hero the execrable Cesare Borgia is sufficient evidence of his hidden intention. If we compare what he says in *The Prince* with what he says in his *Discourses on Titus*

We have already drawn the conclusion, in general terms, that the monarchic form of government is suited only to large States, and a detailed examination will serve to confirm this view. The larger the number of citizens engaged actively in the administration of public affairs, the more does the ratio between prince and people diminish and approach equality, so that it is unity or equality, even in a democracy. The ratio is, however, increased in proportion as the powers of the Executive are concentrated in few hands, and it reaches its maximum when the government is confided to a single individual. When that is so, the gap separating prince and people is too large, and the State lacks adequate articulation. In order that the necessary binding structure may be built up, a hierarchy becomes essential. Only a system comprising princes, ministers, and nobles can give effect to the orders of government. But such an organization is wholly unsuited to a small State which cannot but be ruined by all these interlaced degrees of authority.

It is never easy to ensure good government in a large State, least of all when the government is conducted by a single individual. We all know what happens when a king acts through his representatives.

Monarchy has one fundamental and inevitable blemish which must ever make it inferior to the republican form of government. In the latter it is men of ability and intelligence only who are entrusted by the public vote with the duties of administration, whereas, in a monarchy, the places of power and privilege go always to intriguing and rascally meddlers whose inferior talents, though successful in procuring preferment in royal courts, are seen in their true light once their owners are installed in positions of authority. In choosing administrators the People are far less likely to go wrong than is the prince, and it is as rare to find a good man among the

Livius and in his *History of Florence*, it will at once be apparent that his profound political wisdom has hitherto received but very superficial and prejudiced attention. The Court of Rome has sternly forbidden the circulation of his book — and no wonder! — since the light shed upon it in that work is only too illuminating.

ministers of a royal master as a fool at the head of a Republic. Consequently, when, by some happy chance, a born statesman is at the helm of a monarchy which has been all but run aground by irresponsible and dishonest ministers, the public stands amazed at his resourcefulness, and his term of office takes a prominent place in the annals of his country.

That a monarchic State be well governed, its greatness and extent must be proportionate to the abilities of its ruler. It is easier to conquer than to reign. Given the right kind of lever, a man might, with one finger, rock the world on its foundations, but only a Hercules can carry its weight upon his shoulders. No matter how restricted may be the boundaries of a State, it is almost always too large for its prince. When, on the contrary, it happens that a country is too small for its ruler — and such an occurrence is rare — that does not prevent it from being badly administered, because the ruler, following the dictates of his great designs, is forgetful of his people's interests, and causes them no less misery by the abuse of talents which he may have in excess, than might one whose freedom of action should be curtailed by lack of them. A kingdom should, if I may so put it, expand and contract from reign to reign according to the capabilities of its prince, whereas a Republic, of which the Senate is less unstable, may remain within constant frontiers and yet be no less well administered.

The most obvious disadvantage of single-person government arises from that lack of continuity which, in the other two forms of administration, guarantees an unbroken unity. When a king dies he has to be replaced by another. There is a dangerous interval while elections are being held, and the elections are themselves likely to be stormy. Unless the citizens are more disinterested, and can show a greater degree of integrity than we have any right to expect in such a form of government, lobbying and corruption are bound to play a large part. It is only natural that he to whom the State has sold itself should sell it in his turn, and draw compensation from the weak for the money which has been extorted from him by the powerful. Sooner or later in a monarchy, everything becomes a matter of money, and when that happens, the peace enjoyed under a king is worse than the disorders which mark an interregnum.

What steps have been taken to remove these evils? Crowns have been made hereditary in certain families, and orders of succession have been established which prevent disputes arising on the king's death — which is no more than to say that by substituting regencies for elections, and valuing apparent tranquillity above wise administration, men have preferred to run the risk of being saddled with minors, monsters, and imbeciles as their monarchs to facing a discussion aimed at the election of good kings. It has not occurred to them that, in taking such a risk, they have almost all the chances of the game against them. When the father of the younger Dionysius once upbraided him for being guilty of some dishonourable action, with the words: 'I am sure that *I* never set you such an example!' the young man replied with considerable acuteness, 'But then your father was not a king!'

When a man has been raised to a position in which he issues orders to others, everything conspires to deprive him of the spirit of justice and good sense. Much trouble, we are told, is taken to instruct young princes in the art of government. It would not appear that they derive much benefit from their education. It were better that they should first be taught the art of obeying. The greatest monarchs known to history were never trained in kingly duties. The science of ruling others is least mastered when most studied. It is better learned through obedience than command. 'Nam utilissimus idem ac brevissimus bonarum malarumque rerum delectus, cogitare quid aut nolueris sub alio principe, aut volueris.' [6]

One result of this lack of cohesion is an absence of consistency in royal governments, which, being conducted first on one plan, then on another, according to the character of the ruling prince or of the ministers wielding authority in his name, never long pursue a fixed object or a coherent line of

6. Tacitus, *Histories*, I. xvi.

policy. This continual change of direction means that the State is ever oscillating between a variety of general maxims and particular projects, which is not the case in other forms of government where the prince is ever the same. Experience, too, shows, in general, that if there is more of cunning in a Court, there is more of wisdom in a Senate, and that Republics achieve their policies with a less shifting vision and less hesitation than do monarchies, since, in the latter every revolution in the administration produces one, too, in the State, the constant rule common to all ministers and well nigh to all kings, being ever to act in a way diametrically opposed to that of their predecessors.

This same lack of cohesion gives the lie to a sophism which is forever in the mouths of those who administer kingdoms, and which takes the form not only of comparing the government of a country to that of a family, and the nature of a prince to that of a father (an error already refuted), but of attributing liberally to the chief magistrate all those virtues with which, in fact, he *ought to be* endowed, and assuming that he is always the man he should be. Were this so, the royal form of government would clearly be preferable to any other, since it is incontestably the strongest of all, and would also be the best if the will of the administration were in true harmony with the general will of the State.

But if, according to Plato, a man born with the qualities of kingship is extremely rare, how much rarer must be the occasions where natural endowments and the accidents of fortune are at one to illustrate the head that wears a crown? And if the education of princes necessarily corrupts those who receive it, what may one hope from a line of individuals each one of whom has been trained to rule others? It is an act of deliberate blindness to confuse monarchical government in general with government as conducted by a good king. To understand what the true nature of such government may be, we must take into consideration good and bad princes alike. For bad men do mount the throne, or perhaps it is that the throne makes them bad.

Our authors have been aware of these difficulties, though it seems that they have not been embarrassed by them. The remedy, they say, is to give unmurmuring obedience. God, in His anger, sends bad kings to a country, and they must be endured as the scourge of Heaven. Such sentiments are, no doubt, edifying, but I have a feeling that they are better suited to the pulpit than to books on politics. What should we say of a doctor who promises miracles but can do no more than exhort the sick whom he attends to patience? Everyone knows that those who are saddled with bad governments must endure them. The question which concerns us is how good ones may be found.

(((VII)))

OF MIXED GOVERNMENTS

Strictly speaking there is no such thing as a simple government. If its head be a single man, he must have magistrates subordinate to him. If its form is popular, it must have a head. Thus, when it comes to dividing the Executive power, there must always be many degrees of administration, ranging from those systems in which it is wielded by many, to those in which it is wielded by few, with, however, this difference, that sometimes the many depend upon the few, sometimes the few upon the many.

There are cases in which the division is equal, either because the constituent elements are in a condition of mutual interdependence, as in England, or because the authority of each, though independent, is imperfect, as in Poland. This latter arrangement is bad, since it means that there is no unity in the government, with the result that the State is over-loosely knit.

Simple government is, in itself, the best form of government for the sole and sufficient reason that it *is* simple. But when the Executive power is not sufficiently dependent on the Legislative, in other words, when the relation between prince and sovereign is greater than that between people and prince, this defective proportion has to be remedied by dividing the government. For then all the parts have no less authority over the subjects, and the fact of division makes them all together less strong against the sovereign. The same blemish can be guarded against by the institution of intermediate magistrates who, leaving the government entire, serve solely to balance the two forms of power, and to maintain their respective rights. In such cases, we should speak not of mixed, but of modified, government.

Similar measures will serve also to remedy the opposite disadvantage, and, when government is too loose, to erect tribunals the object of which is to concentrate it. This is done in all democracies. In the first case, government is divided that it may be weakened, in the second, that it may be strengthened. For the maximum both of strength and of weakness is to be found in simple governments, while the mixed forms give a general average of strength.

(((VIII)))

THAT EVERY FORM OF GOVERNMENT IS NOT SUITED TO EVERY COUNTRY

Since liberty is a fruit that does not grow in all climates, it cannot be enjoyed by all peoples alike. The more one ponders this principle, which was laid down by Montesquieu, the more one realizes its wisdom. The more one tries to oppose it, the more opportunity one gives to establish its truth by fresh proofs.

In all the governments of the world, the public person consumes but does not produce. Whence, then, does it draw the substance it consumes? From the work of its members. It is the superfluity of individuals which provides the necessities of the public: whence it follows that the civil State can exist only when men produce by their labour more than they need for their own subsistence. Now this superfluity is not the same in all the countries of the world. In several it is considerable, in others mediocre, in some non-existent, and in a few, actually a minus quantity. The proportion depends upon the fertility of the climate, on the kind of labour that the soil demands, on the nature of its products, on the strength of the inhabitants, on the greater or less consumption needed to provide them with necessities, and on various other considerations.

On the other hand, not all governments are of the same nature, some being greedier than others. This difference between them is based upon yet another principle, to wit that the further public taxes are removed from the source, the more burdensome they are. The extent of this burden is not to be reckoned in terms of the *amount* of the taxes, but with reference to the distance which they have to travel before they return to the hands from which they have come. Where the circuit is rapid and well organized, it matters little whether the amount to be paid be large or small: the people are always rich and the public finances healthy. Contrariwise, no matter how small an amount the people be called upon to provide, if it does not return to them, and if they are called upon to be for ever giving, the exhaustion point is soon reached, in which case the State is never rich and the people are always out at elbows.

It follows that the farther the people are removed from their government, the heavier does taxation become. Thus, in a democracy, the burden upon the people is least, in an aristocracy greater, while under a monarchy it is heaviest of all. Monarchy, therefore, suits only very rich nations, aristocracy those of middling wealth as well as middling size, democracy such States as are small and poor.

In fact, the more one reflects, the more clearly does one see that the difference between free States and monarchies lies in this; that in the first, everything is utilized for the public good, while in the others, public and private resources are reciprocal, the one growing in strength as the other weakens. What it comes to in the long run is that despotism, instead of governing men in order to make them happy, makes them miserable in order to govern them.

There are, under all climatic conditions, certain natural causes in consideration of which we can say what form of government best suits any given country, and even what type of inhabitants it should have.

Unfruitful and barren soil, where the product is not worth the labour that goes to extracting it, should remain fallow and uncultivated, or else should be inhabited only by savages. Soil from which men's work can assure only the bare necessities, should be settled by none but a barbarous people, any true body politic being there impossible. Soils which give merely a small surplus are best suited to the free. Those that are rich, and where a small amount of labour produces great results, should be governed monarchically, so that the excess and superfluity of the subjects may be consumed by the luxury of the prince, since it is better that such excess be absorbed by government than wasted by individuals. That there are exceptions to these rules I know, but they serve merely to confirm them, in that sooner or later they give birth to revolutions which re-establish things in accordance with the natural order.

We must ever distinguish general laws from such particular causes as may modify their effects. Should all the South be covered with republics, and all the North with despotic States, it would still remain true that, as a result of climate, despotism is better suited to warm countries, barbarism to cold, and the good body politic to regions of an intermediate kind. But I see that though the general principle may be admitted, there are likely to be disputes over its application. It will be argued that some cold countries are very fertile, and some southern ones extremely unrewarding. But this fact offers difficulties only to those who do not examine the matter in all its aspects. We must, as I said before, take into account considerations of labour, strength, consumption, et cetera.

Let us assume for the sake of argument that of two areas

equal in size one gives a yield of five, the other of ten. If the inhabitants of the first consume four and those of the second nine, the surplus in the first case will be one-fifth, in the second, one-tenth. The ratio between these two surpluses being inverse to that of their products, the area yielding five only will give double the surplus of that yielding ten.

But it is not a question of double yield, and he would be a rash man, in my opinion, who should maintain that the fertility of cold countries is, as a rule, even equal to that of warm. Still, for the sake of argument I will grant that such a condition of equality does, in fact, exist. Let us, if you will, set England in the scales with Sicily, and Poland with Egypt. Farther to the south we shall have Africa and the Indies, farther to the north, nothing at all. But to obtain the same quantity of production what a difference there must be in the labour involved! In Sicily men have but to scratch the surface of the ground, while in England it has to be ploughed with much pains. Where more hands are needed in order to assure the same amount of product, the surplus must necessarily be less.

Consider, too, that the same number of mouths consume much less in a warm climate where a man, if he is to be healthy, must shun excess. Europeans who try to live in hot climates as they would do at home, all perish of dysentery and indigestion. 'In comparison with Asiatic peoples,' says Chardin, 'we are all of us carnivorous and wolfish. There are those who attribute the frugality of the Persians to the fact their country is under-cultivated. I, on the contrary, hold that it produces fewer crops because its inhabitants need them less. If their habits of moderation' — he goes on — 'were due to natural scarcity, it would be the poor only who would have too little to eat, whereas, in fact, the habit of temperance is seen in every class: men in the different provinces would eat more or less according as their own particular area was rich or poor, whereas it is the kingdom as a whole that is remarkable for its moderation. The Persians take much pride in their way of life, saying that it is only necessary to look at their complexions to see how superior it is to that of those who inhabit Christian lands. And, indeed, there is an even quality about their colouring; their skins are lovely, fine-grained, and smooth. The complexions of the Armenians, their subjects, who live in European fashion, are, on the contrary, rough and spotty, their bodies gross and heavy.'

The nearer one gets to the Equator, the smaller is the amount of subsistence that people need. They eat scarcely any meat, their staple diet being composed of rice, maize, *cuzcuz*, millet, and cassava meal. There are in the Indies millions whose food costs no more than a halfpenny a day. Even in Europe there is a marked difference in appetite between Northerners and Southerners. A Spaniard will live for a week on what serves a German for a single dinner. In countries whose inhabitants are remarkable for greediness, luxury has a way of being expressed in terms of food. In England this is to be seen in the way the tables are loaded with meat, while in Italy guests are regaled with sugar and flowers.

There is also a decided difference in the relative luxury of clothes. In climates where seasonal changes are rapid and violent, clothes are good and simple. Where clothes are merely an excuse for display, one finds showiness rather than utility. To have clothes at all is a luxury. In Naples one will see men walking daily to Posilippo dressed in gold-embroidered coats but stockingless. The same truth holds of buildings. Where there is nothing to fear from climate, everything may be sacrificed to magnificence. In Paris and London the first consideration is warmth and comfort. In Madrid the reception rooms are superb, but the windows are not made to shut, and most of the bedrooms are no better than rat-holes.

Foodstuffs are much more substantial and highly-flavoured in hot countries. This is a third difference which cannot but have an effect on the second. Why do people eat so many vegetables in Italy? Because they are good, nourishing, and of an excellent flavour. In France, where they are grown only on water, they provide no nourishment for those who eat them, and are little regarded as edibles. Not but what their cultivation takes as much room and costs at least as much in human labour. It is a well-known fact that the wheat of the Barbary Coast, though inferior to that of France, has a far higher yield in flour, and the same is true of French wheat compared with the northern variants. Whence it may be inferred that a similar progression is, as a rule, clearly marked if one works upwards from the Equator to the Pole. But is it not a definite disadvantage to be able to derive less nourishment from a similar quantity of natural products?

To these considerations I can add another which flows from, and, at the same time, confirms them. It is this, that warm countries have less need of inhabitants, and could support a much larger population than they have, a state of affairs which results in a double superfluity, and that is always to the advantage of despotism. Given a constant population, revolt becomes proportionately more difficult where the inhabitants are spread thinly over a large area, because it is impossible, in such circumstances, for men to take counsel together quickly and secretly, and it is always easy for the government to get wind of their plans and to disrupt their communications. But where there is a numerous population, the more closely packed it is, the less possible is it for the government to usurp the functions of the sovereign. The leaders can deliberate as safely in their own homes as can the prince in his Council, and a mob can assemble as rapidly in open spaces as can the soldiers in their barracks. The great advantage possessed by a tyrannical government is that it can act over great distances. By providing itself with fixed bases, it can ensure a preponderance of strength at the periphery, just as, the longer a lever, the greater does its power become.[7] The

7. This does not contradict what I said above (Book II, ch. ix) about the inherent disadvantage of great States. I was dealing there with the authority wielded by a government over its members, whereas here I am concerned with the power it can bring to bear on its subjects. Where its officers are widely scattered, they serve as bases from which pressure can be brought to bear on the people. But it has no bases from which it can act directly on its own officers. Thus, in the one case the length of the lever is a cause of weakness, in the other of strength.

strength of the people, on the contrary, is effective only when they are concentrated. Where it is dissipated by dispersal it vanishes away and gets lost — like gunpowder which, when scattered over the ground, takes fire only by single grains. The most thinly populated countries, therefore, are the best suited to tyrannies. Wild beasts reign only in the desert.

(((IX)))

OF THE MARKS OF A GOOD GOVERNMENT

He, therefore, who asks what, in an absolute sense, is the best sort of government, is putting a question which cannot be answered because it is indeterminate. In other words, it admits of as many good solutions as there are possible combinations in the absolute and relative situations of various peoples.

But if it be asked by what signs one may know whether a people be well or badly governed, the case is different, and the question of fact can be resolved.

It never is resolved, however, because each man wishes to answer the question in his own way. The subject boasts of public law and order, the citizen of the freedom enjoyed by the individual. The first prefers the security of property, the second that of the person. The first will maintain that the harshest government is the best, the second the gentlest. The first wants to see crime punished, the second to make crime impossible. The first thinks it a fine thing that a country should be feared by its neighbours, the second prefers that they should ignore it. The first is happy when money circulates, the second demands bread for the people. Even if agreement be reached on these and similar points, are we any nearer to an answer? There is no scale by which moral quantities can be assessed. We may agree about the signs, but can we agree about their relative value?

I am always amazed that one obvious mark should be consistently misconstrued, and that men should be of such bad faith as not to agree about it. What is the goal set before themselves by all political organizations? — surely it is the maintenance and the prosperity of their members. And what is the most certain sign that a people is being maintained and rendered prosperous? — the size of the population. There is no need to go further in our search. Other things being equal, the government under which, without recourse being made to extraordinary measures, such as naturalization and colonial settlements, the citizens do most increase and multiply, is infallibly the best. Similarly, the government under which a people diminishes in number and wastes away, is the worst. Experts in calculation! I leave it to you to count, to measure, to compare.[8]

8. We should use the same criterion when deciding which centuries are to be regarded as having best assured the prosperity of mankind. Too much admiration has been given to those in which arts and letters flourished, but without any real understanding of the secret object of their culture, or any true consideration of its fatal effects. 'Idque apud imperitos humanitas vocabatur, quum pars servitutis esset.'[*] Shall we never learn to see in an author's general maxims the vulgar self-interest which is the real inspiration of his work? No matter what writers may say, when a country, however brilliant its culture, shows a falling birth-rate, it is *not* true that all is well with it, nor is the fact that a poet has an income of 100,000 francs alone sufficient to make his century superior to all others. It is not so much the apparent peace and tranquillity of the rulers that should concern us, as the general well-being of their countries, especially where those countries are large and thickly populated. Hail may devastate a few cantons, but it rarely causes famine. Outbreaks of violence and civil wars may be the cause of much nervousness among rulers, but it is not in them that a people's true evils are to be sought. Indeed, to some extent, they are beneficial, since a nation can at least enjoy something of a respite while the question who shall tyrannize over it is still in suspense. It is from permanent conditions that a country's prosperous and calamitous times are born. When all lie supine beneath the yoke, then death is close at hand, and rulers can destroy their subjects at their ease. 'Ubi solitudinem faciunt, pacem appellant.'[†] When the quarrels of the great disturbed the kingdom of France, and the Co-adjutor of Paris attended Parliament with a dagger in his pocket, the people, nevertheless, lived happily and multiplied in decent, free, and prosperous conditions. In the old days, Greece flourished in the midst of cruel wars: blood flowed in torrents, but the land was thickly peopled. 'It seemed,' said Machiavelli, 'that in spite of murder, proscription and civil strife, our republic became stronger than ever. The virtues of its citizens, their manners and their independence did more to strengthen, than could dissension to weaken, it.' Some small amount of disturbance gives wings to the soul, and it is liberty rather than peace, which breeds genuine prosperity in a nation.

* Tacitus, *Agricola*, xx.
† Tacitus, *Agricola*, xxxi.

(((X)))

OF THE ABUSE OF GOVERNMENT, AND OF ITS TENDENCY TO DEGENERATE

As particular wills act constantly in opposition to the general will, so does Government make an incessant effort against Sovereignty. As this strife becomes more marked, the constitution changes for the worse. And since there is here no corporate will which, by resisting the will of the Prince, can achieve equilibrium, it must happen that, sooner or later, the Prince will oppress the Sovereign and break the social treaty. This is the inherent and inevitable vice of the body politic which, from the moment of its birth, tends consistently to its destruction, just as old age and death ultimately destroy the human body.

There are two general ways in which a government degenerates; when it contracts, or when the State becomes dissolved.

A government contracts when it passes from the hands of the many to those of the few, or, in other words, when it changes from democracy to aristocracy, and, by one further remove, to royalty. That is the direction it naturally takes.[9]

9. The slow formation and development of the Republic of Venice in its lagunes, provides an outstanding example of this process, and it is a remarkable fact that after more than twelve hundred years, the Venetians seem not to have progressed beyond the second stage which began with the *Serrar di Consiglio* in 1198. As for their former Doges, so often cast up at them in reproach, it is proved — no matter what the *Squittinio della liberta veneta* may say — that they never really exercised sovereign rights at all. Someone, no doubt, will quote against me the example of the Roman Republic which, so it will be argued, followed just the opposite course, since it passed from monarchy to aristocracy, and from aristocracy to democracy. But I am far from agreeing with this view. What Romulus founded was a mixed form of government, which rapidly deteriorated into despotism. From causes peculiar to itself, the State perished untimely, as a child will sometimes die before reaching man's estate. It is from the expulsion of the Tarquins that the birth of the Republic should really be dated. But its first form was unstable, only half the necessary work having been done, in that the Patrician Order was never abolished. For thus it came about that an hereditary aristocracy — which is the worst of all legitimate forms of administration — remained in conflict with the democracy, and the result was that the government, ever uncertain and unfixed, attained

Should the process be reversed, and a movement set in from smaller to greater, government might then be said to relax. But such a reverse tendency is impossible.

In fact, a government never changes its form save when its springs, weakened from over-use, are incapable of keeping the old arrangements in being. Now, if a government eased its severity while extending its sway, its powers would become null, and it would be still less able than before to maintain itself. It must, therefore, wind-up and concentrate the spring in proportion as it expands, otherwise the State, whose weight it bears, will fall in ruins.

The dissolution of the State may come about in two ways. First, when the prince no longer administers it in accordance with the laws, but himself usurps the sovereign power. When that happens, a remarkable change takes place, for it is not the government but the State that contracts. The greater State, I mean, dissolves, and a smaller one, composed only of members of the government, is formed within it. Its relation to the rest of the people is then merely that of master and tyrant. Consequently, no sooner has the government usurped the sovereignty than the social pact is broken,

its final form only, as Machiavelli has shown, with the establishment of the Tribunate. Not until that had been created was there a genuine government and a true democracy. The People were not only Sovereign, but Magistrate and Judge as well, the Senate being but a subordinate tribunal serving to temper and concentrate the government. Even the Consuls, Patricians though they were, the First Magistrates of the Republic, and, in time of war, commanders with powers of life and death, found themselves, within the city bounds, no more than the People's presidents.

From that point on we see the government taking its natural course, with a strong tendency towards aristocracy. But since the Patrician Order had, so to speak, pronounced its own death-sentence, the aristocracy was no longer identified with it as in Venice or at Genoa, but became co-extensive with the Senate — a Council composed of Patricians and Plebeians alike — and was actually found giving candidates to the Tribunate as soon as that institution began to arrogate to itself an active function. For words do not alter facts, and when the People have rulers who govern in their name, they are always, no matter how they be called, an aristocracy.

It was aristocratic abuses that produced the civil wars and the Triumvirate. Sulla, Julius Caesar, and Augustus became, in fact, veritable monarchs, and the State finally broke up under the despotism of Tiberius. The history of Rome, therefore, far from invalidating my theory, serves but to confirm it.

and the ordinary citizens, having recovered of right their natural liberties, are compelled, but not bound, to obey.

The same thing happens when the members of the government severally usurp the power which they ought to exercise only as a corporate body. This is no less an infraction of the laws, and produces an even greater disorder. For the State is then confronted by, so to speak, as many princes as there are magistrates, and itself, no less divided than the government, must perish or change its form. When a State dissolves, the abuse of government, of whatever kind it may be, goes by the general name of *anarchy*. To speak more accurately, *democracy* degenerates into *ochlocracy*, *aristocracy* into *oligarchy*, and, I would add, *royalty* turns to *tyranny*, were not this latter term in itself equivocal and in need of explanation.

In the vulgar sense a tyrant is a king who governs by violence, without regard for justice or the laws. In the precise sense, the tyrant is a private individual who arrogates to himself the royal authority without having any right to it. That is what the Greeks meant by the word *tyrant*, which they gave indifferently to good and bad princes when their authority was not legitimate.[10] Thus, the words *tyrant* and *usurper* are completely synonymous terms.

I, in order to give different names to different things, use the name *tyrant* for one who usurps the royal authority, *despot* for one who usurps the Sovereign Power. The tyrant gains authority in despite of the laws in order to govern in accordance with them. The despot sets himself above the laws. Thus, the tyrant cannot be a despot, but the despot is always a tyrant.

---

10. 'Omnes enim habentur et dicuntur tyranni qui potestate perpetua in ea civitate quae libertate usa est.' (Corn. Nepos, *In Miltiad.*, ch. viii). It is true that Aristotle (*Eth. Nic.*, Book VIII, ch. x) draws a distinction between the tyrant and the king, in that the first governs for his own advantage, and the second for the advantage of his subjects: but, apart from the fact that, generally speaking, all Greek authors take the word *tyrant* in quite another sense, as is clear, especially, if we consult the Hiero of Xenophon, it would follow from Aristotle's distinction that there has never been one genuine kingdom since the world began.

(((XI)))

OF THE DEATH OF THE BODY POLITIC

On such a slope will even the best constituted of governments naturally and inevitably find itself. If Sparta and
Rome perished, what State can hope to last for ever? If we
would build a durable form of government, let us not dream
of making it eternal. We can succeed only if we do not
attempt the impossible, or flatter ourselves that we can give
to the work of men's hands a solidity which is a stranger to
human enterprises.

The body politic, no less than the body human, begins to
die from the very moment of its birth, and carries within
itself the causes of its own destruction. But both may have a
constitution more or less robust, more or less capable of enduring. The physical make-up of a man is the handiwork of
nature: the constitution of the State is the product of art.
It is not in men's power to prolong their lives, but they can
prolong the life of the State for as long as possible by devis-
ing for it the best conceivable form. Even the best Constitution will one day have an end, but it will live longer than one
less good, provided no unforeseen accident bring it to an
untimely death.

The principle of political life is in the sovereign authority.
The Legislative Power is the heart of the State, the Executive is its brain, and gives movement to all its parts. The
brain may be struck with paralysis and the patient yet live.
A man may be an imbecile and yet not die. But once the
heart ceases to function, it is all over with the animal.

It is not by the laws that a State exists, but by the Legislative Power. Yesterday's law has no authority to-day, but
silence is held to imply consent, and the sovereign is deemed
to confirm all laws that it does not abrogate — the assumption being that it has power to do so. When once it has declared its will on some specific issue, that will is perpetually
valid, unless it be revoked.

Why, then, do men show such respect for ancient laws? The reason is this, that the mere fact of their having lasted so long bears witness to the excellence of the will that once brought them into being. Had the sovereign not seen that they were salutary to the State, it would have revoked them, not once but several times. That is why laws, instead of growing weaker with the lapse of time, gain a constantly increasing strength in all well-constituted States. The feeling in their favour, bred of their antiquity, makes them each day more venerable. Where, on the contrary, the hold of the laws grows weaker with age, it is a sure proof that there is no longer any Legislative Power, and that the breath of life has departed from the State.

(((XII)))

OF HOW THE SOVEREIGN AUTHORITY IS MAINTAINED

The Sovereign, having no force other than the Legislative Power, acts only in accordance with the law. And since laws are nothing but the authentic acts of the general will, the sovereign cannot act save when the People are assembled. But, I shall be told, the idea that the whole of a People can be assembled is a mere chimera. It certainly is to-day, but it was not so two thousand years ago. Has human nature changed?

The limits of the possible in matters of morals are less constricted than we think. It is our own weaknesses, our own vices and prejudices that hedge us in. Base minds do not believe in great men. Vile slaves smile with an air of mockery at the very mention of the word *liberty*.

It is well to consider what may be done by observing what was done once. I think I may claim without fear of contradiction that the Roman Republic was a great State, and the city of Rome a great City. The last census taken gave a total of four hundred thousand citizens capable of bearing arms, and the last analysis of the population of the Empire more than four million citizens, not counting subject peoples, foreigners, women, children, and slaves.

How difficult a task, one might think, to bring together into an assembly the whole vast population of the capital and of the adjoining districts. Yet scarcely a week passed but the Roman people met to transact business, and often more than once. Not only did they exercise the rights of sovereignty, but in part, too, those of government. With certain matters they dealt, in certain cases they judged, and the *whole* of the people met together in the public place as magistrates no less frequently than as citizens.

If we study the early periods in the histories of nations we shall find that most primitive governments, even when monarchic in form, like those of the Macedonians and the Franks, were conducted by means of similar Councils. However that may be, this one incontestable fact of Roman usage may furnish a reply to all objectors. To argue from what is to what may be, I hold to be sound practice.

(((XIII)))

OF HOW THE SOVEREIGN AUTHORITY IS MAINTAINED
(*continued*)

It is not enough that the Assembly of the People should fix once and for all the Constitution of the State, and should give its sanction to a body of laws. It is not enough that it should establish a perpetual government, or provide means for the election of magistrates. In addition to extraordinary sessions summoned to deal with specific problems, there should be fixed and periodic meetings which nothing must be allowed to abolish or to delay, in such wise that on a given day, the People may be legitimately convened by law without having to wait for any further act of formal convocation.

Except for these meetings, however, legitimized by the recurrence of certain fixed dates, assemblies of the People *not* called by the magistrates appointed for that purpose must be regarded as having no legal sanction. Any business transacted at them must be held to be null and void, since even the order to assemble must proceed from the law.

It is impossible to lay down precise rules concerning the frequency of the legal assemblies, because many considerations are involved. But it may be said in general terms that the stronger the government, the more frequent should be such manifestations of sovereignty.

Such an arrangement, it may be argued, may suit a single city, but what happens when a State contains many cities? Is the sovereign authority to be divided into parts, or is the whole of it to be concentrated in a single city, which will then lord it over all the others?

I would subscribe to neither solution. In regard to the first, the sovereign authority is one and indivisible: it cannot be divided without being destroyed. In regard to the second, a city no more than a nation can be legitimately subject to another, because the essence of the body politic resides in a just proportion between obedience and freedom, and because the words *subject* and *sovereign* are strictly complementary, the ideas which they express being united in the single word *citizen*.

I would say, further, that to unite several towns into one City is always an evil, and that he who would accomplish such a union should not plume himself on having avoided its natural disadvantages. The abuses to which large States are exposed should not be brought in argument against the man who desires to have only small ones. But how are small States to be assured of strength sufficient to resist their larger neighbours — as once the cities of Greece resisted the Great King, or, more recently, as Holland and Switzerland stood out against the House of Austria?

If a State cannot be kept within rational bounds, there is one resource always open to its inhabitants, namely that they should consent to the establishment of no one capital, but should let the machinery of government work from the different cities in turn, and should successively assemble the Estates of the Realm in each of them.

Only by apportioning its population in equal density over the whole extent of its territory, only by assuring to every part of it life and abundance, will a State become both strong and well-governed. Remember that the walls of cities are built only from the fragments of rural dwellings. For each palace that I see raised in the capital, I watch, in imagination, whole country communities laid in ruins.

(((XIV)))

OF HOW THE SOVEREIGN STATE IS MAINTAINED
(*continued*)

So soon as the People is convened as a sovereign body, all government jurisdiction ceases, the Executive Power is suspended, and the person of the meanest citizen is as sacrosanct and inviolable as that of the chief magistrate, because where the person represented is himself present, there is no longer any representative. Most of the violent scenes which took place in the Roman assemblies were due to the fact that this rule was either not known, or, if known, was neglected. The Consuls, at such times, were no more than the Presidents of the People: the Tribunes were but simple speakers: [11] the Senate was nothing at all.

These intervals of suspension during which the prince recognizes, or should recognize, an effective superior, have always been feared by him; and such assemblies of the People, being the aegis of the body politic and a brake on government, have, in all periods, been the terror of rulers, who have never been sparing of solicitude, objections, obstacles, and promises in their attempts to make the People out of love with them. When the latter are avaricious, cowardly, and pusilanimous, clinging to their ease more than to

11. In almost the same sense as this word bears in the English Parliament. The resemblance between their offices would have brought the Tribunes and the Consuls into conflict, even had all jurisdiction been suspended.

their liberty, they have not long resisted the concentrated efforts of the government. And thus it is that, the force of resistance constantly increasing, the sovereign power at last disappears entirely, so that the majority of cities fall and perish before their time.

But between the Sovereign Authority and Arbitrary Government there sometimes intervenes a middle term. About this it is now time to speak.

(((XV)))

OF DEPUTIES OR REPRESENTATIVES

As soon as the public service ceases to be the main concern of the citizens, and they find it easier to serve the State with their purses than with their persons, ruin draws near. If they are called upon to march to war, they pay for troops to take their place while they remain at home. If they are summoned to the Council Table, they nominate deputies in their stead, and, similarly, remain at home. As a result of laziness and money they end by having an army to enslave their country and representatives to sell it.

When they are preoccupied with commerce and the arts, and with the search for gain; when they become flabby and comfort-loving, then it is that men substitute payment for personal service. The citizen surrenders part of his profits that he may be left free to increase them at his ease. Once give money instead of service and you will soon be in chains. The word *finance* belongs to the language of slaves. In the true City it is unknown. In a genuinely free country, the citizens do all with their strong right arms, nothing with their money. So far from paying in order to be exempted from their duties, they will pay for the privilege of performing them. My view is not the common one. I hold that statute labour is less contrary to liberty than taxation.

The better constituted a State is, the more do public affairs occupy men's minds to the exclusion of their private

concerns. Actually, there are fewer private concerns, because the sum total of the general happiness furnishes a
larger proportion of the happiness of the individual, so that
he has less to seek by his own efforts. In a well-run City,
every citizen hastens to the assembly: under a bad government no one will move a step in order to attend it, knowing
that the general will will not prevail, and because, in the long
run, the cares of home drive out all others. Good laws breed
better: bad laws lead to worse. As soon as a man, thinking
of the affairs of the State, says: 'They don't concern me,' it
is time to conclude that the State is lost.

The cooling of patriotic fervour, the activity of private interests, the immense size of States, foreign conquests, and
the abuse by Government of its functions, all these things
have contributed to encourage that innovation by which
Deputies or Representatives are held to act for the People in
the Assemblies of the Nation. These Deputies or Representatives are what, in certain countries, men have had the
effrontery to call the Third Estate, which means no less than
that the special interests of two orders of Society are ranked
first and second, while those of the public as a whole come
but third.

Sovereignty cannot be represented, for the same reason
that it cannot be alienated. It consists essentially of the
general will, and will cannot be represented. Either it is itself
or it is different. There is no middle term. The Deputies of
the People are not, nor can they be, its representatives. They
can be only its Commissioners. They can make no definite
decisions. Laws which the People have not ratified in their
own person are null and void. That is to say, they are not
laws at all. The English people think that they are free, but
in this belief they are profoundly wrong. They are free only
when they are electing members of Parliament. Once the
election has been completed, they revert to a condition of
slavery: they are nothing. Making such use of it in the few
short moments of their freedom, they deserve to lose it.

The idea of representation is modern, and comes to us

from the feudal system, that iniquitous and absurd form of Government in which the human species was degraded and the name of man held in dishonour. In the republics of the ancient world, and even in monarchies, the People never had representatives. The very word was unknown. It is a remarkable fact that in Rome, where the Tribunes were sacrosanct, it was never so much as dreamed that they should usurp the People's functions. In the midst of that great multitude, they never attempted to pass of their own accord a single *plebiscitum*. We can, however, see what embarrassment the mob could cause by studying what happened in the time of the Gracchi when so great was the concourse that one whole section of the citizens had to record their votes from the house-tops.

Where right and liberty is everything, inconvenience matters little. In that wise nation everything was seen in its proper proportion. It was left to the Lictors to do what the Tribunes would never have dared to attempt. The People were haunted by no fear that the Lictors might wish to represent it.

That we may explain, however, in what way the Tribunes did sometimes represent the People, we must consider how the sovereign is represented by the government. Since law is nothing but the declaration of the general will, it is obvious that the People, in its legislative function, cannot be represented. But it may, and should, be represented in matters of Executive procedure, which is merely the application of force to law. From this we may see, on close examination, how few are the nations which have laws at all. However that may be, it is certain that the Tribunes, having no part in the function of the Executive, could never represent the Roman People by reason of the rights which they enjoyed as inherent to their office, but only by usurping those of the Senate.

Among the Greeks, all that the People had to do, they did themselves. They met constantly in public assembly. They lived in a mild climate. They were not greedy. Slaves did all the necessary work. The People's main concern was with liberty. Not having the same advantages, how can you preserve the same rights? Harder climatic conditions mean that your needs will be greater.[12] For six months in the year public places are unusable, and your hoarse voices cannot make themselves heard in the open air. You devote more time to gain than to liberty, and you fear slavery less than poverty.

What! can liberty be maintained only on a basis of slavery? Perhaps. Extremes meet. Everything that is not part of the natural order has its disadvantages, and civil society more than most. There are some situations so unhappy that liberty can be maintained by those who live in them only at the expense of the liberty of others, and the citizen can be perfectly free only if the slave is irremediably a slave. Sparta was a case in point. You, the peoples of the modern world, have no slaves to work for you, but you are yourselves slaves. Their liberty is paid for at the price of yours. You may, if you like, boast of this preference. I find in it more of cowardice than humanity.

I do not mean, by what I have said, that the institution of slavery is a necessity, nor yet that the right to enslave others is legitimate. I have, in fact, proved just the contrary. I am concerned only to explain why it is that the moderns, who think themselves free, have representatives, and why the ancients had them not. Be that as it may, the moment a People begins to act through its representatives, it has ceased to be free. It no longer exists.

Having examined the whole question thoroughly, I do not see how, henceforth, it will be possible for the sovereign to maintain among us the exercise of its rights, unless the City be a very small one. But, say you, if it is very small will it not fall a victim to its neighbours? No, I shall show later on how the external strength of a great People may be combined

---

12. To adopt in cold countries the luxury and soft ways of the life of the East is deliberately to court the fate of the Eastern slave. In fact, such submission would, in our case, be even more necessary than in theirs.

with the convenient polity and the solid order of a small State.[13]

(((XVI)))

THAT THE INSTITUTION OF GOVERNMENT IS NOT A CONTRACT

Once the Legislative Power has been firmly established, the next thing to be done is similarly to erect the Executive Power. For the latter, operating as it does, only through particular acts, and not being of the essence of the former, is naturally separate from it. Were it possible for the sovereign as such to wield the Executive Power, law and fact would be so inextricably confused that no one would be able any longer to distinguish between what was, and what was not, law. The body politic, thus unnaturally transformed, would soon become a prey to the very violence which it was originally instituted to combat.

The citizens being all equal by reason of the Social Contract, all may ordain what all may do, but none has the right to demand that another should do what he does not do himself. Now it is precisely this right — the very heart and centre of healthy life and activity in any State — that the sovereign makes over to the prince when a government is set up.

Many have argued that the very act of establishing a government is a contract between the People and such leaders as it may choose for itself, a contract in which it is stipulated as between the two parties on what conditions some shall command and others obey. This, as I think most men would agree, is a strange way of entering into a contract. But let us see whether such a view can be maintained.

In the first place, the supreme authority can no more modify than it can alienate itself. To limit it is to destroy it. To argue that the sovereign can impose a superior upon himself is absurd and contradictory. To admit the obligation to

13. I had intended to do this in a sequel to the present work, and in treating of external affairs I should have considered the nature of confederations — a new subject, and one of which the principles have yet to be established.

obey a master is tantamount to reverting to a condition of absolute liberty. Further, it is quite obvious that a contract between the People and separate persons would be a particular act, whence it follows that such a contract could not be either a law or an act of sovereignty, and that consequently it would have no legal sanction.

It is clear, too, that the contracting parties would be, as between themselves, subject only to the natural law, and that therefore they would have no guarantee that their mutual undertakings would be maintained — a situation in all respects repugnant to a civil society. Since he who wields the power is always the master when it comes to applying it, one might just as well give the name of contract to the behaviour of a man who says to another — 'I give you all my property on condition that you render back to me as much of it as you please.'

There is but one contract in the State, and that is the primitive contract of association. By reason of its existence it excludes all further contracts. It is impossible to conceive of any public contract which would not be a violation of the one originally entered into.

(((XVII)))

OF THE INSTITUTION OF GOVERNMENT

How, then, should we view the act by which a government is instituted? Let me begin by saying that such an act is complex, being composed of two others, to wit, the establishment of the law and its execution.

By the first, the sovereign ordains that there shall be a body of government established under such and such a form, and it is clear that this act is a law.

By the second, the People nominate those leaders who shall be charged with the administration of the government by law established. Now this nomination, being in itself a particular act, is not a second law, but only a consequence of the first, and a function of government.

The difficulty is to understand how it is possible to have an act of government before ever a government exists, and how a People, which can only be either sovereign or subject, can, in certain circumstances, become prince or magistrate.

It is here that there again comes to light one of those astonishing properties of the body politic by which it reconciles apparently contradictory operations. For this situation is brought about by a sudden conversion of sovereignty into democracy, in such sort that, without any noticeable change, and merely as a result of a new relation of all to all, the citizens, having become magistrates, pass from general acts to particular acts, from the law to the execution of the law. This change of relation is not a mere subtlety of speculative thought without any instance in fact. It happens every day in the English Parliament, where the Lower House, on certain occasions, turns itself into a Grand Committee the better to discuss affairs, and, by so doing, becomes, from being a Sovereign Court as it was before, a mere Commission which report back to itself as House of Commons on the business it has transacted as Grand Committee, and debate anew, under one title, what it has already decided under another.

This, then, is the specific advantage of democratic government, that it can be established in fact as the result of a simple act of the general will. This done, the provisional government thus set up remains in possession, should its form be the one adopted, or proceeds to establish, in the name of the sovereign, the form of government prescribed by law. This is the only way in which government can be legitimately instituted. To pursue any other course would be to renounce the principles above established.

(((XVIII)))

OF THE MEANS OF PREVENTING THE USURPATIONS OF GOVERNMENT

It follows from this elucidation of what was said in Chapter XVI, that the act as the result of which a government is set

up, is in no way a contract, but a law; that those who hold
the executive power in trust are not the People's masters but
its officers; that the People can appoint and remove them at
will; that for them it is a question not of contract but of obedience, and that, in assuming the functions which the State
lays upon them, they are merely carrying out their duties as
citizens, and have no sort of right to dispute about the conditions.

When, therefore, it happens that the People establish an
hereditary government, whether a monarchy vested in a
single family, or an aristocracy confined to one particular
order of society, they do not in any sense enter into an undertaking. What they do is to give provisional form to the administration until such time as they may see fit to determine
otherwise.

It is true that changes of this kind are always dangerous
and that violent hands should not be laid upon an established
government save when it has become incompatible with the
public good. But this attitude of caution is a maxim of politics only, and in no wise a rule of right. The State is no more
obliged to leave the civil authority in the hands of its rulers
than the military authority in those of its generals. Again, it
is true that, in such cases, the People can never be too careful to observe all the formalities needed if a regular and legitimate act is to be distinguished from a seditious rising,
and the will of all from the noisy clamour of a faction. It is
particularly important that no more be conceded to the un-
pleasant event than cannot, in law, be refused. It is from this
obligation that the prince derives one great advantage in
maintaining his power in despite of the People, without being
accused of usurpation. Though he may seem to be doing no
more than exercise his rights, it is easy for him to extend
them, and, while seeming only to ensure public peace, to
prevent those assemblies which might have as their object
the re-establishment of order. He avails himself, thus, of a
silence which he will not allow to be broken, or of irregulari-
ties which he causes to be committed. It is easy for him to

assume that he has the approval of those whom fear keeps silent, and to punish those who are courageous enough to speak. It was thus that the Decemvirs, having been originally elected for one year, and then continued in office for a second, attempted to retain their power in perpetuity by forbidding the *comitia* to assemble. It is in this simple fashion, too, that all the governments in the world, once armed with public power, sooner or later usurp the sovereign authority.

The type of periodical assemblies of which I spoke above are peculiarly fitted to prevent or defer this evil, especially when they need no formal act of convening. For the prince cannot then put obstacles in the way of their meeting without openly showing that he is infringing the law and is an enemy of the State.

The opening of these meetings, whose only object is the maintenance of the social treaty, should always take the form of enunciating two propositions which may not be suppressed, and should be made the objects of two separate votes.

The first is this: 'That it please the sovereign to uphold the present form of Government.'

And the second: 'That it please the People to leave the administration in the hands of those who at present conduct it.'

I am assuming here what I believe I have already proved, that there is no fundamental law of the State which cannot be revoked, not even the social pact. For should all the citizens assemble for the express purpose of breaking this pact by common accord, it would undoubtedly be broken by due form of law. Grotius goes so far as to hold that it is open to every man to renounce his allegiance to the State of which he is a member, and to recover his natural liberty as well as his property when he leaves its territory.[14] But it would be absurd if all the citizens assembled could not do what each was at liberty to do severally.

14. It being assumed that he does not leave his country in order to avoid doing his duty, and to escape from having to serve it just when it has most need of him. Flight thus motivated would be a criminal act punishable by law. It would be desertion, not retirement.

BOOK IV

(((I)))

THAT THE GENERAL WILL IS INDESTRUCTIBLE

So long as a number of men assembled together regard themselves as forming a single body, they have but one will, which is concerned with their common preservation and with the well-being of all. When this is so, the springs of the State are vigorous and simple, its principles plain and clear-cut. It is not encumbered with confused or conflicting interests. The common good is everywhere plainly in evidence and needs only good sense to be perceived. Peace, unity and equality are the foes of political subtlety. Upright and simple men are hard to deceive by the very reason of their simplicity. Lures and plausible sophistries have no effect upon them, nor are they even sufficiently subtle to become dupes. When one sees, in the happiest country in all the world, groups of peasants deciding the affairs of State beneath an oak-tree, and behaving with a constancy of wisdom, can one help but despise the refinements of other nations which, at so great an expense of skill and mystification, make themselves at once illustrious and wretched?

A State thus governed has need of very few laws, and when it *is* found necessary to promulgate new ones, the necessity will be obvious to all. He who actually voices the proposal does but put into words what all have felt, and neither intrigue nor eloquence are needed to ensure the passing into law of what each has already determined to do so soon as he can be assured that his fellows will follow suit.

What sets theorists on the wrong tack is that, seeing only those States which have been badly constituted from the beginning, they are struck by the impossibility of applying

269

such a system to *them*. The thought of all the follies which a
clever knave with an insinuating tongue could persuade the
people of Paris or of London to commit, makes them laugh.
What they do not know is that Cromwell would have been
put in irons by the people of Berne, and the Duc de Beaufort
sent to hard labour by the Genevese.

But when the social bond begins to grow slack, and the
State to become weaker; when the interests of individuals
begin to make themselves felt, and lesser groups within the
State to influence the State as a whole, then the common interest suffers a change for the worse and breeds opposition.
No longer do men speak with a single voice, no longer is the
general will the will of all. Contradictions appear, discussions arise, and even the best advice is not allowed to pass
unchallenged.

Last stage of all, when the State, now near its ruin, lives on
only in a vain and deceptive form, when the bond of society
is broken in all men's hearts, when the vilest self-interest
bears insolently the sacred name of Common-Weal, then
does the general will fall dumb. All, moved by motives un-
avowed, express their views as though such a thing as the
State had never existed, and they were not citizens at all. In
such circumstances, unjust decrees, aiming only at the satisfaction of private interests, can be passed under the guise of
laws.

Does it follow from this that the general will is destroyed
or corrupted? No; it remains constant, unalterable and pure,
but it becomes subordinated to other wills which encroach
upon it. Each, separating his interest from the interest of all,
sees that such separation cannot be complete, yet the part he
plays in the general damage seems to him as nothing compared with the exclusive good which he seeks to appropriate.
With the single exception of the particular private benefit at
which he aims, he still desires the public good, realizing that
it is likely to benefit him every whit as much as his neighbours. Even when he sells his vote for money, he does not
extinguish the general will in himself, but merely eludes it.

The fault that he commits is to change the form of the question, and to answer something which he was not asked. Thus, instead of saying, through the medium of his vote, 'This is of advantage to the State,' he says, 'It is to the advantage of this or that individual that such and such a proposition become law.' And so the law of public order in assemblies is not so much the maintenance of the general will, as the guarantee that it shall always be asked to express itself and shall always respond.

I might say much at this point on the simple right of voting in every act of sovereignty, a right of which nothing can deprive the citizen — and on that of speaking, proposing, dividing and discussing; a right which the government is always very careful to leave only to its members: but this important matter would require a whole treatise to itself, and I cannot cover the whole ground in this one.

(((II)))

OF VOTING

It is clear, from what has just been said, that the manner in which public affairs are conducted can give a pretty good indication of the state of a society's morale and general health. The greater the harmony when the citizens are assembled, the more predominant is the general will. But long debates, dissension and uproar all point to the fact that private interests are in the ascendant and that the State as a whole has entered on a period of decline.

This seems less evident when two or more social orders are involved, as, in Rome, the Patricians and the Plebs, whose quarrels so often troubled the *comitia* even in the best days of the Republic. But this exception is more apparent than real. For, in such circumstances, there are, so to speak, because of a vice inherent in political bodies, two States in one. What is not true of the two together is true of each separately. Indeed, even in the most stormy times, the *plebiscita* of the

Roman people, when the Senate did not interfere, were always passed quietly and by a large majority of votes. The citizens having but one interest, the people had but a single will.

At the other extremity of the scale unanimity returns; when, that is to say, the citizens, having fallen into servitude, have no longer either liberty or will. When that happens, fear and flattery transform votes into acclamations. Men no longer deliberate, they worship or they curse. In this base manner did the Senate express its views under the Emperors, sometimes with absurd precautions. Tacitus relates that, in the reign of Otho, the Senators, in heaping execrations on Vitellius, were careful to make so great a din that, should he chance to become their master, he would not be able to tell what any one of them had said.

From these various considerations spring those general rules which should regulate the manner of counting votes and comparing opinions, according as whether the general will is more or less easily to be discerned, and the State more or less in a condition of decline.

There is one law only which, by its very nature, demands unanimous consent, and that is the social pact. For civil association is, of all acts, the most deliberately willed. Since every man is born free and his own master, none, under any pretext whatsoever, can enslave him without his consent. To decide that the son of a slave is born a slave is tantamount to saying that he is not born a man.

If, then, when the social pact is made, voices are raised in opposition, such opposition does not invalidate the contract, but merely excludes from it those who voice it, so that they become foreigners among the general body of the citizens. When the State is instituted, residence implies consent. To live in a country means to submit to its sovereignty.[15]

15. This must always be understood to relate to a free State, for elsewhere family interests, property, the impossibility of finding a refuge abroad, necessity or violence, may all keep a man resident in a country in spite of his wish to leave it. When this is so, the mere fact of his living there does not imply his consent to the contract or to the violation of it.

In all matters other than this fundamental contract, a majority vote is always binding on all. This is a consequence of the contract itself. But, it may be asked, how can a man be free and yet constrained to conform to a will which is not his own? How comes it that the members of the opposition can be at the same time free and yet subject to laws which they have not voted?

My reply to this is that the question is wrongly put. The citizen consents to all the laws, even to those which have been passed in spite of him, even to those which will visit punishment upon him should he dare to violate any of them. The constant will of all the members of a State is the general will, and by virtue of it they are citizens and free men.[16] When a law is proposed in the assembly of the People, what they are asked is not whether they approve or reject the proposal in question, but whether it is or is not in conformity with the general will, which is *their* will. It is on this point that the citizen expresses his opinion when he records his vote, and from the counting of the votes proceeds the declaration of the general will. When, therefore, a view which is at odds with my own wins the day, it proves only that I was deceived, and that what I took to be the general will was no such thing. Had my own opinion won, I should have done something quite other than I wished to do, and in that case I should not have been free. True, this assumes that all the characteristics of the general will are still in the majority. When that ceases to be the case, no matter what side we are on, liberty has ceased to exist.

When I showed above how the wills of individuals come to be substituted for the general will in public deliberations, I made sufficiently clear what practical means existed for preventing this abuse. I shall have more to say on this point below. In regard to the proportional number of votes needed

16. At Genoa one can see written on the walls of the prisons and engraved on the irons of the Galley-slaves, the word *Libertas*. The use of such a device is excellent and just. In all States it is the malefactors only who prevent the citizens from being free. If all such folk were one and all confined to the galleys, it would be possible to enjoy perfect freedom.

to declare this will, I have also stated the principles on which it can be determined. The difference of a single vote destroys equality: one voice raised in opposition makes unanimity impossible. But between unanimity and equality there are many unequal divisions, at each of which this number can be fixed as the State and the needs of the body politic may demand.

Two general rules may serve to regulate this proportion: one, that the more important and solemn the matters under discussion, the nearer to unanimity should the voting be: two, that the more it is necessary to settle the matter speedily, the less should be the difference permitted in balancing the votes for and against. Where a verdict must be obtained at a single sitting, a majority of one should be held to be sufficient. The first of these rules seems to be more suited to the passing of laws, the second to the transaction of business. Be that as it may, only a combination of them can give the best proportion for the determining of majorities.

(((III)))

OF ELECTIONS

In regard to the election of the Prince and the magistrates — which, as I have said, are complex acts — there are two possible methods of procedure — choice and lot. Both have been employed in various republics, and the election of the Doge of Venice is still conducted by a very complicated mixture of the two. 'Election by lot,' says Montesquieu (*Esprit des lois*, Book II, ch. ii), 'is of the very essence of democracy.' With this I agree, but how does this come about? 'The drawing of lots,' he goes on, 'is a method of election which bears unfairly on no one. It gives to each citizen a reasonable hope that he may serve his country.' But that is not the real reason.

If we remember that the election of its rulers is a function of government and not of sovereignty, it will be clear why the method of drawing lots is more of the essence of democracy, in which administration is better in proportion as its acts are few.

In every true democracy, office is no benefit but a heavy charge which it would be unfair to lay on the shoulders of any one man rather than another. The law alone can put this obligation upon the man designated by lot. For then, the chances being the same for all, and the choice being independent of any human will, the universal nature of the law is not changed by the special application.

In an aristocracy, the Prince chooses the Prince, the government maintains itself, and to that, of all systems, the method of deciding by vote is best suited.

The example of the way in which the Doge of Venice is elected confirms rather than destroys this distinction, for its mixed character well becomes a government of the mixed sort. It is a mistake to regard the Venetian system as being a genuine aristocracy. The People, it is true, play no part in the government, but then, the nobility itself fills the role of the People. A large number of poor *Barnabotes* never hold any office at all. They have nothing of nobility save the empty title of *Excellency*, together with the right of taking part in the Great Council. This Great Council being as numerous as our own General Council in Geneva, its illustrious members enjoy no more privileges than do our simple citizens. It is certain that, discounting the extreme disparity between the two republics, the bourgeoisie of Geneva does, in fact, exactly represent the Patrician Order of Venice: our natives and residents are the equivalent of the city-dwellers and citizens of Venice: our peasants of the subjects of the mainland. However the Republic of Venice be viewed — its size apart — the government is no more aristocratic than our own. The only difference is that we, having no Head of the State who holds office for life, do not feel that same need of election by lot.

Elections by lot can have no disadvantage in a true democracy, for where all are equal in character and ability, as well as in principles and fortune, choice becomes a matter of indifference. But I have already said that there nowhere exists such a thing as a true democracy.

Where choice and lot are mixed, the former should be used for filling posts which demand special talents, such as commands in the army; the second for those appointments which demand only good sense, justice, and integrity — such as judicial posts, because in a well-constituted State these qualities are common to all the citizens.

Neither lot nor voting has any place in a monarchical government. Since the monarch is by right the sole Prince and the only Magistrate, the choice of lieutenants depends on him alone. When the Abbé de Saint-Pierre proposed to increase the number of the King's Councils, and to elect their members by ballot, he did not see that what he was suggesting would amount to a complete change in the form of government.

I should now speak of the manner of recording and counting votes in an assembly of the People, but perhaps an account of how the Roman system worked in this matter may afford a better exposition of the general principles than any which I could produce. It is not unworthy of a judicious reader that he should see in some detail how public and private affairs were dealt with in a Council consisting of two hundred thousand men.

(((IV)))

OF THE ROMAN COMITIA

We have no certain records of the earliest period of Roman history. It is reasonable to suppose that most of what we are told about that time consists of fables,[17] and that, in general, the most instructive part of the annals of a nation, to wit, the account of how it came to be founded, is what we most often

---

17. The name *Rome*, which some would have us believe comes from Romulus, is Greek, and means *strength*. *Numa*, too, is a Greek word and means *law*. It seems curious, to say the least, that the first two kings of the City should have been born with names so happily related to their future actions.

lack. Daily experience teaches us what causes lie behind the rise and fall of Empires, but, since no new nations are being established in our own time, we have little more than conjecture to guide us in our attempts to discover how such agglomerations came into existence.

The customs which we find already established when a nation's historical period begins are certain evidence that they must somewhere have had an origin, and those traditions relative to such origins are most likely to be true which find support in the best authorities, and are confirmed by even stronger reasons. On this assumption I have tried to act in my effort to discover how the freest and most mighty People that ever existed came to exercise its supreme power.

After the foundation of Rome, the infant Republic, that is to say, the founder's army, consisting of Albans, Sabines, and foreigners, was divided into three classes which, having been so divided, took the names of *tribes*. Each of these tribes was subdivided into ten *curiae*, and each *curia* into *decuriae*, at the head of which were set leaders who bore the names of *curiones* and *decuriones*.

In addition, a body of a hundred horsemen or Equites was taken from each tribe, and this was called a *century*, whence we may see that these divisions, unnecessary in the life of a City, were at first purely military. But it would seem that an instinct for greatness led the tiny city of Rome to give itself, from the earliest times, a system which would be suited to the Capital of the World.

One disadvantage of this primitive division soon became apparent, namely, that the tribes of the Albans (Ramnenses) and of the Sabines (Tatientes) remained ever constant, while that of the foreigners (Luceres) continually grew as the result of additions from outside. This latter, therefore, soon surpassed the other two in size. The remedy for this dangerous abuse, devised by Servius, took the form of changing the basis of division, and of substituting for the racial criterion (which he abolished) a quite different one derived from the localities in the city occupied by each of the tribes. Instead of three tribes, he made four, each occupying one of the hills of Rome and bearing its name. Thus, he not only found a way to remedy present inequality, but saw to it that no such inequality should arise in the future. That this division should be one not only of localities but of men, he forbade the inhabitants of each district to move to another, thereby preventing the different races from intermingling.

He also doubled the original three centuries of cavalry, and added to them twelve others, though retaining the ancient names. By this simple and wise step he managed to distinguish the body of horsemen from that of the People without provoking any outcry from the latter.

To these four urban tribes, Servius added fifteen others, called *Rural tribes*, because they consisted of those who lived on the land. These were divided into the same number of *Cantons*. At a later date a further fifteen were added, and the Roman People thus found themselves divided into thirty-five tribes, a total which remained unaltered down to the end of the Republic.

One consequence of this distinction between the Urban and the Rural tribes deserves notice, because there is no other example in history of this particular form of organization, and because Rome owed to it the preservation of her morals and the growth of her Empire. One would naturally assume that the Urban tribes would rapidly monopolize all power and privilege, and would reduce the Rural tribes to a subordinate status. In fact, the very reverse occurred. The taste of the primitive Romans for a country life is well known. This was bred in them by the wise founder who made country pursuits and military duty a part of freedom, and relegated, so to speak, to the city, the arts, the crafts, the intrigues of the great world, the making of money, and the institution of slavery.

Since, then, all who made Rome illustrious lived in the country and farmed their land, it became customary to seek among them alone the mainstays of the Republic, and this State, in which honourable Patricians played the leading part, grew to be respected by the whole world. The simple life and hard work of the villages was preferred to the lazy, flabby existence of town-dwellers. The man who, in the city, would have been no more than a wretched proletarian, became, as a farm-worker, an honoured citizen. 'It was not without reason,' said Varro, 'that our great ancestors made the village the nursery of those strong and valiant men who defended them in time of war, and, in time of peace, provided them with food.' Pliny tells us positively that the Rural tribes were honoured for the men who composed them, while the cowards whom it was intended to degrade were transferred, as a sign of ignominy, to those of the city. The Sabine, Appius Claudius, having established himself in Rome, was there loaded with honours and inscribed as a member of a Rural tribe which, later, took the name of his family. Finally, the freed slaves were always made members of the Urban, not the Rural, tribes, and there is no single instance during the lifetime of the Republic of any of these freed-men holding office, even though they were recognized as citizens.

This principle was an excellent one, but so far was it pushed that it gave rise ultimately to a change, and certainly to an abuse, in the political system.

First, the Censors who, for a long time, had arrogated to themselves the right to transfer arbitrarily the citizens of one tribe to another began to allow most of them to choose the tribe of which they wished to become members, a concession which did no manner of good, and deprived the office of Censorship of one of its main resources. Furthermore, since the great and the powerful all entered themselves as members of one or other of the Rural tribes, while the freed-men, when they were enfranchized, remained with the populace in the Urban ones, the tribes in general ceased to have a territorial basis and became so much intermingled that it was impossible to determine who belonged to which, save by scrutinizing the registers. The result was that the word *tribe* grew to have a personal, rather than a genuinely residential, significance, or, rather, became almost chimerical.

It happened, too, that the Urban Tribes, being closer to the centre of things, were often stronger in the *Comitia*, and sold the State to those who deigned to buy the votes of the rabble that composed them. The Founder having established ten curiae in each tribe, the whole of the Roman People at that time enclosed within the walls of the City were comprised in thirty curiae, each one of which had its own temples, its own gods, its officers, its priests, and its particular Feasts, called *Compitalia*, which bore a close resemblance to the *Paganalia* later held by the Rural tribes.

When Servius revised the division, he left this number of thirty untouched, because it did not admit of equal distribution among his four new tribes. Consequently, the Curiae were independent of the tribes and constituted yet another section of the City-dwellers. But this question of Curiae did not arise for the Rural tribes, or for the people who composed them, because, since the tribes had become a purely civilian institution — an entirely different system having been introduced for the levying of troops — the military divisions set up by Romulus were now superfluous. Thus, though every citizen was inscribed on the list of one of the tribes, it by no means followed that each was a member of a Curia.

Servius made also a third division which had nothing to do with the other two, though, because of the effects it produced, it became, in fact, the most important of all. He distributed the whole Roman People into six classes, the specific character of which derived neither from a residential qualification nor yet from the personal characteristics of those who composed them, but purely from property. The result of this was that the highest classes contained the rich, the lowest the poor, while those in between represented the citizens who enjoyed a middling situation. These six classes were subdivided into one hundred and ninety-three subsidiary bodies known as *Centuries*, so distributed that the first class accounted, of itself, for more than half of them, while the lowest class formed only one. It happened, therefore, that the class with fewest individual members had a majority in

Centuries, while the whole of the lowest class counted as no more than a subdivision though it contained more than half the population of Rome.

That the People might less perceive the consequences of this new arrangement, Servius pretended that it had a military purpose. In the second class he placed two Centuries of armourers, and in the fourth two Centuries of those engaged in making instruments of war. In each class, except the lowest, he made a distinction between the young men and the old, that is to say, between those who were under an obligation to bear arms, and those who, by reason of their age, were legally exempted — a distinction which more than the property qualification necessitated a constant revision of census lists. Finally, he ordained that the Assembly should be held on the Campus Martius, and that all those of military age should attend it armed.

The reason why he did not carry this differentiation of young and old into the lowest class was that the working-people of whom it was composed were not granted the privilege of bearing arms in the service of their country. A man must have a hearth of his own before he could be accorded the right to defend it. Of all the out-at-elbows rascals who to-day lend glitter to the armies of kings, there is not one who would not, probably, have been driven with contempt from the ranks of a Roman cohort in the days when soldiers were the defenders of liberty.

There was, however, a distinction made in the lowest class between *proletarians* and *capite censi*. The first, men not reduced to the most abject degree of penury, did at least furnish citizens to the State, and sometimes, even, at times of exceptional crisis, soldiers too. Those, on the other hand, who had absolutely nothing which they could call their own, and could be reckoned only by the counting of heads, were regarded as, to all intents and purposes, non-existent. Marius was the first who condescended to enrol them.

Without deciding whether this third principle of assessing the population was, in itself, good or bad, it is safe, I think, to assume that only the simple habits of the earliest Romans, their disinterested patriotism, their taste for agriculture, and their contempt for commerce and the feverish pursuit of wealth, could have made it practicable. Could such an arrangement have lasted for twenty years without overturning the State among any of the peoples of the modern world, suffering as they do from a grasping lust for money, from a lack of spiritual stability, from the lure of intrigue, from restlessness, and from the continual winning and losing of large fortunes? It should not be forgotten, either, that the morals of the Romans and the office of Censorship, being stronger than the actual system just described, did much to correct its weaknesses, and that many a rich man saw himself relegated to the lowest class for having made too great a public display of his wealth.

From what I have said it is not difficult to understand why it is that there is scarcely ever a mention in Roman history of more than five classes, though actually there were six. The sixth, because it furnished neither soldiers to the army nor voters in the Campus Martius, and thus had no real function to perform in the Republic, was rarely accounted of any importance.[18]

Such, then, were the various systems of differentiation in use among the Roman People. Let us now study the effect which they produced in the assemblies. These, when summoned according to law, were called *Comitia*, and generally used the Public Square of Rome or the Campus Martius, being distinguished as *Comitia Curiata*, *Comitia Centuriata*, and *Comitia Tributa*, according to which of the three forms of convocation was employed. The *Comitia Curiata* was instituted by Romulus, the *Comitia Centuriata* by Servius, while the *Comitia Tributa* owed its origin to the Tribunes of the People. No law was sanctioned, no Magistrate appointed,

18. I say in the *Campus Martius* because it was there that the *Comitia* was assembled by Centuries. When brought together in its other two forms, the People made use of the *forum* or of some other meeting-place, and when that occurred, the *capite censi* had as much influence and authority as the leading citizens.

save by the People in *Comitia*, and, since there was no citizen who was not inscribed in a Curia, a Century, or a Tribe, it followed that no citizen was excluded from the right of voting, and that the Roman People was truly Sovereign, *de jure* and *de facto*.

Before the Comitia could be legally assembled, and before what was determined in it could have the force of law, three conditions were necessary. First, that the Magistrate or the Body convoking it should have due authority to call it together. Second, that the assembly should be held on one of the days set aside by law for the purpose. Third, that the omens should be favourable.

There is no need to explain the intention of the first of these rules. The second was imposed by reasons of State. Thus, the Comitia could not be held on holidays or market-days when the country-folk who came into Rome to transact business could not spare time to attend public meetings. By means of the third the Senate kept a firm hold on a proud and excitable people, and tempered the ardour of the seditious Tribunes, though the latter found more than one way of freeing themselves from this check.

Laws and the appointment of magistrates were not the only matters dealt with by the Comitia. Since the Roman People had usurped the most important functions of government, it may be said that the fate of Europe was determined at these assemblies. The variety of public business decided the different forms in which they were convoked according to the nature of the business on which they were called upon to pronounce.

That we may judge of these different forms, it is necessary only that we compare them. Romulus, when he instituted the Curiae, had in view the checking of the Senate by the People, and of the People by the Senate, while himself retaining supreme power over both. By this arrangement he gave to the People the authority which numbers bestow, thus compensating them for not wielding the power of wealth which he left in the hands of the Patricians. But, true to the spirit of monarchy, he left, in fact, greater power with the Patricians because their 'clients' could always be relied upon to ensure a dominant majority when it came to the taking of votes. This admirable institution of patrons and clients was a triumph of political shrewdness and humanity, without which the Patrician Order, so contrary to the spirit of the Republic, could not have continued. To Rome alone belonged the honour of giving to the world this high example from which no abuse ever resulted, but which has never been imitated elsewhere.

This same form of Curiae continued under the kings down to the time of Servius, and, seeing that the reign of the last of the Tarquins was held not to have been legal, the royal laws were styled *leges curiatae*. Under the Republic, the Curiae, which were still limited to the four Urban tribes and contained only the populace of Rome, suited neither the Senate — which was at the head of the Patricians — nor the Tribunes of the People who, though plebeians, were the leaders whom all citizens in easy circumstances followed. They fell, therefore, into discredit; so low, in fact, that their thirty lictors did as a body what should have been done by the *Comitia Curiata*. The division into Centuries was so favourable to the aristocracy that it is not easy to see at first why it was that the Senate did not always carry the day in the Comitia whenever it was assembled in that form. To it alone belonged the right to elect the Consuls, the Censors, and the other Curule magistrates. Actually, of the one hundred and ninety-three Centuries which made up the six classes into which the whole Roman People were divided, the first class contained ninety-eight. Since, therefore, the voting went by Centuries only, this single class had a majority over all the others. When all these Centuries were in agreement, the rest of the votes were not even counted, and what had been decided by a minority passed for the decision of the mass. It may be said that when the Comitia was called by Centuries, business was transacted as the result of a money, rather than a voting, majority.

But these excesses of power were tempered in two ways. First, the Tribunes as a rule, and a great number of plebeians always, were in the class of the rich, and served to balance the influence exercised by the Patricians in its ranks. Second, the Centuries were not always called upon to vote in their order, which would have meant starting with the first, but lots were drawn as a result of which the Century designated proceeded alone to the business of election. The other Centuries were called together on a different day by order of rank. They then proceeded to renew the election and usually confirmed it.[19] Thus the power of example was taken from high rank and left at the disposition of the lot, in strict accordance with the principles of democracy.

There followed from this custom yet another advantage, which was that the country voters had time between the two elections to inform themselves of the merit of the candidate who had been provisionally chosen, and could thus be sure of declaring their decision with full knowledge of the issue. Ultimately, however, this system was discontinued on the plea of quickening procedure, and both elections took place on the same day.

The *Comitia Tributa* was, strictly speaking, the Council of the Roman People. It could be convoked only by the Tribunes who were themselves elected by it, and, in accordance with its decisions, passed their *plebiscita*. Not only did the Senate have no standing in it, but no Senator could even be present at its deliberations. Compelled, therefore, to submit to laws on which they had not been able to vote, the Senators were, in this respect, less free than the poorest of the citizens. This injustice was the result of an ill-contrived piece of machinery and was, by itself, enough to invalidate the decrees of a body from which a section of the citizens was excluded. Had all the Patricians taken part in the meetings of this Comitia in accordance with their civic rights, they could scarcely have influenced decisions made by a count of heads

19. The Century thus designated by lot was called *praerogativa*, because it was the first to cast its vote: whence comes our own word 'prerogative.'

which enabled the meanest proletarian to carry as much weight as the leader of the Senate.

Thus we may see that, besides the order resulting from these different divisions for the counting of votes, the various methods employed, far from being immaterial and interchangeable, were each carefully calculated to suit the particular type of business to be considered.

Without going into the matter in any greater detail, it should be clear from what has been said above that the *Comitia Tributa* was especially favourable to popular government, whereas the *Comitia Centuriata* was best suited to an aristocracy. As to the *Comitia Curiata*, in which the city populace formed the majority, this served only to favour tyranny and subversive schemes. It was bound to fall into disrepute, since even the seditious refrained from using a piece of machinery which made their intentions uncomfortably obvious. It is certain that the real majesty of the Roman People was to be found only in the *Comitia Centuriata*, the only assembly in which all could play a part, seeing that the Rural Tribes were excluded from the *Comitia Curiata*, the Senate and the Patricians from the *Comitia Tributa*.

The actual method of recording votes was, among the primitive Romans, as simple as their manners, though, even so, less simple than it had been in Sparta. Each man announced his will in a loud voice, and this was duly entered in writing by a clerk. A plain majority within each tribe determined the tribal vote, and the same system held good for the Curiae and the Centuries. This method was a good one so long as honesty prevailed among the citizens, and so long as each was ashamed to give his vote publicly in support of an unjust decision or an unworthy candidate. But when the People became corrupted, and votes were bought and sold, it was well that the ballot should be secret so that the purchaser might be restrained by uncertainty, and rascals given a chance of not becoming traitors.

I know that Cicero finds fault with this change, and attributes to it, in part, the ruin of the Republic. But, though I am fully aware of the weight which should be given to the authority of Cicero on a point such as this, I cannot agree with him. On the contrary, I hold the opinion that the lack of similar changes is bound to accelerate the destruction of the State. Just as a diet which is suited to those in good health is not to be recommended to the ailing, so a corrupt People cannot be governed by laws designed for an upright one. Nothing better proves the truth of this maxim than the continuance of the Republic of Venice, only the semblance of which now remains simply and solely because its laws are suited to none but worthless men.

The citizens, therefore, were given tablets on which each could record his vote without anyone knowing how he had cast it. New formalities, too, were introduced for the collection of these tablets, for the counting of the votes, the checking of totals, &c. These, however, did not alter the fact that the reliability of the officers entrusted with these functions [20] was often suspect. Finally, as a protection against lobbying and the sale of votes, edicts were issued the very multitude of which proves their inefficacy.

As the Republic drew towards its end, the Romans were often constrained to have recourse to extraordinary expedients in order to make up for the inadequacy of the laws. Sometimes miracles were invoked, but this step, though it might impose upon the People could not deceive their governors. Sometimes assemblies were hastily convoked before the candidates could have time to start canvassing. Sometimes a whole session was given up to talk when it was clear that the People had been won over already and was ready to support a bad cause. But finally, ambition eluded all attempts to control it. What is really surprising is that, notwithstanding these abuses, this great People, by reason of its ancient institutions, continued to elect magistrates, to pass laws, to sit in judgement in the Courts, to carry on business, both public and private, with almost as great a facility as might have been shown by the Senate itself.

20. Custodes, diribitores, rogatores suffragiorum.

(((V)))

OF THE TRIBUNATE

When it is found impossible to establish an exact balance between the constituent bodies in the State, or when irreme-
diable causes act in such a way as constantly to change the relations existing between them, it is thought advisable to set
up an *ad hoc* office which shall have nothing in common with
those already existing, and may restore the ratio, and, at the
same time act as a bond of union, or middle term, between
Prince and People or Prince and Sovereign. If necessary, it
may do both at once.

This body, which I shall call the *Tribunate,* is the guardian
of the laws and of the Legislative Power. It serves sometimes
to protect the Sovereign against the Government — as the
Tribunes of the People did in Rome; sometimes to support
the Government against the People, as the Council of Ten in
Venice does, in our own time; sometimes to maintain the
proper balance of the State, as was the case with the Ephors
in ancient Sparta.

The Tribunate is not a constituent part of the City, and
should play no part in either the Legislative or Executive
functions. The very fact that it does not do so increases its
power, for though it can initiate nothing, it can stop anything from being done. It is more sacrosanct and more deeply
revered as protector of the laws than either the Prince who
administers them or the Sovereign who ordains them. This
truth emerges very clearly when we consider the history of
Rome and see how the proud Patricians, who were filled with
contempt for the common people, were compelled to bow
before one of their officers who controlled no patronage and
wielded no jurisdiction.

The Tribunate, wisely tempered, is the strongest possible
buttress of a good constitution: but if its power grows even
a little beyond what it should be, it may well overturn every-

thing. It is not in its nature to be weak. If it is anything at all, its power never falls below what is necessary for its operation. It degenerates into tyranny whenever it usurps the Executive Power whose moderator it is, and tries to make laws instead of confining itself to its proper function of protecting them. The enormous power exercised by the Ephors, which was fraught with no danger so long as Sparta retained its moral standards, did but increase the process of corruption once that corruption had started. The blood of Agis, who was murdered by these tyrants, was avenged by his successors. Both the crime of the Ephors and its punishment served equally to hasten the death of the Republic, and, after Cleomenes, Sparta no longer counted for anything. Rome pursued much the same path to its ultimate eclipse as a democracy, and the excessive power of the Tribunes, usurped by decree, was used in conjunction with the laws which had been originally framed to ensure civic liberty, to bolster up the very Emperors who destroyed it. As to the Council of Ten in Venice, it is a bloodstained tribunal, a cause of horror to Patricians no less than to the People. Far from maintaining the laws at a high level, it serves no other purpose, once they have become degraded, than to strike in secret blows on which no one dare let in the light of day.

The Tribunate, like the Government, becomes weak as soon as it contains too many members. When the Tribunes of the People in Rome, at first limited to two, then to five, wished to double this latter number, the Senate showed itself agreeable to the change, being convinced that it could always play off some of them against the others — which, in fact, is precisely what it did.

The best means of preventing usurpation by so redoubtable a body, though one which no government seems hitherto to have considered, would be so to arrange matters that it was never permanent, and to institute regulations by which it would be wholly suppressed for certain definite periods. These periods, which should never be long enough to per-

mit abuses to grow strong, could be fixed by law with a pro-
viso that they be curtailed or terminated in cases of necessity
by an extraordinary Commission.

This piece of suggested machinery seems to me to have no
disadvantage, because, as I have already said, the Tribunate,
since it forms no part of the Constitution, can be removed
without the infliction of any damage on the body politic.
That it would be efficacious follows from the fact (or so it
seems to me) that an Office suppressed and then re-estab-
lished is endowed not with the authority wielded by its pred-
ecessor, but only with such as may be bestowed upon it by
law.

(((VI)))

OF THE DICTATORSHIP

The very fact that the laws are inflexible, and are not, therefore, adaptable to the movement of events, may, in certain
cases, render them pernicious, and the cause, in times of
crisis, of the State's destruction. The existence of an established order, and the slowness which is the inevitable ac-
companiment of things done by due procedure, necessitates,
if the law is to function properly, a margin of time which, in
certain circumstances, it is impossible to guarantee. A
thousand cases may arise for which the Legislator has not
been able to provide in advance, and the ability to foresee that
some things cannot be foreseen is a very necessary quality.

The political institutions of a State should not, therefore,
be made so rigid that the effect of them cannot be suspended.
Even in Sparta the laws were allowed to lie dormant.

But only the gravest dangers can justify any fundamental
change in public order, and the sacrosanct nature of the laws
never should be interfered with save when the safety of the
State is in question. In such rare and obvious instances,
public security must be assured by an *ad hoc* decision which
entrusts it to him who is most worthy of the charge. A commission of this kind can be operated in two ways, according
to the nature of the danger. If, in order that it may be coun-

tered, a mere increase in government activity is likely to be sufficient, this may be obtained by concentrating executive power in the hands of one or two of its members. In this way it is not the authority of the laws that is altered, but only the method of their administration. But where the peril is of such proportions that the machinery of law is an actual obstacle in dealing with it, then a single ruler must be appointed who can reduce all law to silence and temporarily suspend the sovereign authority. In a case of this kind, the general will is not in doubt, and it is obvious that the People's first concern must be to see that the State shall not perish. Thus, the suspension of legal authority does not imply its abolition. The magistrate in whose power it is to impose silence on it, cannot make it speak. He dominates, but cannot represent, it. Laws are the one thing he cannot make.

The first method was the one employed by the Roman Senate when it charged the Consuls, in a formula consecrated by custom, to provide for the safety of the Republic. The second was adopted when one of the two Consuls nominated a Dictator — a custom learned by Rome from Alba.[21]

In the early days of the Republic frequent recourse was had to the Dictatorship, because the State was not then sufficiently well established to maintain itself by the mere strength of its Constitution.

The high level of morals then obtaining made superfluous many of the precautions which might have been necessary in another age. There was no fear that the Dictator would abuse his powers, nor that he would be tempted to prolong them beyond their due term. It seemed, on the contrary, that such power laid so heavy a weight on the man who was invested with it, that he hastened to lay it down, as though to replace the laws was a duty too onerous or too much fraught with danger.

It is not the risk of its abuse, but of its being made cheap, that leads me to find fault with the indiscreet employment of

21. Such nomination was made at night and in secret, as though it were felt to be a shameful thing to elevate a man above the law.

this supreme magistracy during the early period. For when it was too often used at elections, at ceremonies of dedications, and on other purely formal occasions, there was no small danger that it might lose much of its authority when real need for it arose, and that men might grow accustomed to regard as an empty title what had been so often used for purposes of vain display.

Towards the end of the Republic, the Romans, grown more circumspect, were as foolishly niggardly in their recourse to it as they had been prodigal before. It was easy to see that their fears were ill-founded, that the very weakness of the Capital was, at that time, a sure guarantee against the magistrates in its midst; that a Dictator might, in certain circumstances, defend the public liberty without ever constituting a serious threat to it, and that Rome's fetters would be forged not in the City but in the armies. The poor resistance put up by Marius to Sulla, and by Pompey to Caesar, was proof enough of what might be expected from authority at home when faced by an attack from without.

This error was the cause of the commission by the Romans of many grave faults. One such was their failure to appoint a Dictator during the Catiline affair. For, since the matter at issue was confined within the walls of the Capital, or extended at most to a few of the Italian provinces, they could easily, if armed with the boundless authority conferred by law on a Dictator, have put an end to the conspiracy which, as things turned out, was suppressed only by a happy combination of chances which no amount of human foresight could have anticipated.

But instead of having recourse to the Dictatorship, the Senate handed over all its powers to the Consuls, with the result that Cicero, in order to act effectively, had to exceed his legitimate powers on a point of capital importance. If, in the first transports of joy, his conduct was approved, he was later justly called upon to render an account of all the blood shed by the citizens in contravention of the laws, though such a reproach could never have been levelled against a man in-

vested with the Dictator's authority. But the Consul's eloquence carried all before it, and he himself, Roman though
he was, just because he was more concerned with his own
frame than with the well-being of his country, sought not so
much the surest and most legitimate way of saving the State,
as to win for himself the honour and glory of having brought
the business to a successful end.[22] Thus, he was rightly
honoured as the liberator of Rome, and no less rightly
punished as one who had broken its laws. His recall, though a
brilliant personal triumph, was undoubtedly an act of pardon.

For the rest, in whatever way this important commission
might be conferred, it was essential that it be limited to the
shortest possible time, and that no extension ever be permitted. In such crises as might call for its employment, the
State was likely to be destroyed or saved in a matter of days,
and once the urgent need was past, the office of Dictator became either tyrannical or meaningless. At Rome, the Dictatorship was conferred for six months only, and most of
those who held it, abdicated before that time-limit was
reached. Had the period been longer, they might have been
tempted to extend it still further, as did the Decemvirs when
given power for no more than one year. The Dictator had
time only to deal with the need which had led to his appointment, and none in which to make other plans.

(((VII)))

OF THE CENSORSHIP

Just as the declaration of the general will is made by the laws,
so the declaration of public judgement is made by the Censorship. Public Opinion is a kind of law whose administration is in the hands of the Censor. He is called upon to apply
it only to particular cases, as is the Prince.

22. Of this he could not have been certain had he proposed the nomination of a
    Dictator, because he dared not put forward his own name, and could not feel
    confident that it would be advanced by his colleagues.

Far, then, from being the arbiter of Public Opinion, the Censor's Tribunal is but the instrument used in declaring it. Once it goes beyond that, its decisions are null and of no effect.

It is useless to distinguish the moral standards of a country from the objects of its esteem, for both are based upon the same general principle, and must, of necessity, be intermingled. In all the countries of the world, it is opinion, not nature, that decides men in the choice of their pleasures. Reform their opinions, and their morals will automatically be purified. All men love what is lovely, or what they judge to be so; but it is precisely in this matter of judging that they may be led astray. Whoso judges of manners, judges of honour; and whoso judges of honour makes opinion his touchstone.

The opinions of a nation are born of its Constitution. Though the law does not control manners, it is in legislation that they have their origin. When legislation grows weak, manners degenerate. But when that happens, no amount of judgement on the part of the Censors will do what the laws have failed to do.

It follows that though the Censorship may be useful for the purpose of conserving manners, it can never re-establish them. Install your Censorship, therefore, while the laws still have their full vigour. Once that has been lost, there is room only for despair. No power based on law can be strong when law itself has lost its strength.

Censorship maintains manners by preventing opinions from growing corrupt, by intervening to keep them on the right lines, and sometimes, even, by giving fixity to standards which suffer from too great fluidity. The employment of 'Seconds' in the conduct of duels, a custom which, in the kingdom of France, was carried to wild extremes, was there abolished as the result of just a few words embodied in a Royal decree: 'As for those who are cowardly enough to call upon Seconds . . .' This judgement, anticipating that of the public, at once put an end to the custom. But when the same edicts went on to declare that duelling in any form is no less cowardly — which is perfectly true, though at variance with commonly held opinions — the public merely laughed at a decision about which it had already made up its mind.

I have said elsewhere [23] that, since public opinion is not subject to constraint, even the faintest shadow of such a thing should be absent from the tribunal appointed to represent it. We can never too much admire the art with which this check-mechanism, fallen into complete desuetude among the moderns, was utilized by the Romans, and, with even greater skill, by the Lacedaemonians.

A man of evil reputation having made an admirable proposal in the Council at Sparta, the Ephors ignored it, but had the same motion brought forward by a virtuous citizen. What honour for the one, what a disgrace for the other! — and all without a single word of praise or blame to either! Certain drunkards from Samos [24] once fouled the tribunal of the Ephors. The very next day a public edict was issued giving permission to the Samians to be filthy. No real punishment could ever have been so severe as a licence thus granted. When Sparta pronounced on what was or was not honourable, the rest of Greece did not appeal from her decision.

(((VIII)))

OF CIVIL RELIGION

There was a time when men's only kings were the Gods. Theocracy then was the one form of government that they knew. They followed the reasoning of Caligula, and, at the time, they reasoned rightly. Only when feelings and ideas have passed through a long period of degeneration, will men submit to take as masters those who are in all respects like themselves — and feel pride in doing so.

23. I only refer in this chapter to what I have dealt with at length in my *Letter to M. d'Alembert.*
24. Actually, they were from another island which the delicacy of our language forbids me to name.

But because a God was set at the head of every separate
political society, it followed that there must needs be as
many Gods as Peoples. Two communities, in ignorance of,
and almost always at enmity with, one another could not for
long recognize the same master. Two armies ranged opposite
one another in battle, could not obey the same general. Thus,
from national divisions came polytheism, and thence developed theological and civil intolerance — the two being
naturally the same thing, as will be explained later.

The fancy which led the Greeks to discover their own
Gods among the nations of the barbarians, came from the
fact that they had also to regard themselves as being the
natural overlords of those nations. But we have learned to
regard as foolish a form of erudition which turns upon the
identity of different People's Gods, as though Moloch,
Saturn and Chronos could all be the same! — as though the
Baal of the Phoenicians, the Zeus of the Greeks, and the
Jupiter of the Latins could be identical! — as though some
common characteristic could be found in purely imaginary
beings all bearing different names!

If it be asked how it came about that, in the pagan world,
where each State had its own form of worship and its own
Gods, there were no such things as wars of religion, I should
reply that it was because each State having its own religious
forms as well as its own system of government, no distinction was made between its Gods and its Laws. Political and
theological wars were the same. The limits within which the
Gods were sovereign, were, so to speak, coterminous with a
country's frontiers. The God of one nation had no rights
over other nations. The Gods of the pagans were not jealous
Gods, but shared among themselves the Empire of the
World. Even Moses and the Jews at times leaned towards
this view, as when they spoke of the God of Israel. They
regarded, it is true, as of no account the Gods of the Canaan-
ites, a proscribed People, condemned to destruction, whose
place they were destined to take. But note in what terms they

spoke of the deities of those neighbouring nations whom they were forbidden to attack: 'Are you not entitled by law to possess what belongs to Chamos, your God?' said Jephthah to the Ammonites. 'We, on similar grounds, possess the lands which our conquering God has won.' [25] This, it seems to me, proves that the claims of Chamos and of the God of Israel were regarded as equally valid.

But when the Jews, after they had been forced to submit to the kings of Babylon, and, later still, to the kings of Syria, persisted in their determination to recognize no God but their own, this refusal was regarded as an act of rebellion against the conqueror, and brought down upon them the persecutions of which we read in their history, and of which there is no other example prior to the rise of Christianity.[26]

Since, then, each religion was part and parcel of the laws of the State which subscribed to it, the only way to convert a People was to overwhelm them in war, nor could there be other missionaries than successful conquerors. To change their religion being an obligation forced upon the vanquished by the law of conquest, it was no use talking about it until conquest was an established fact. Far from men doing battle for their Gods, the Gods, as in Homer, did battle for their followers. Each side sought victory from its patron deity, and paid the price in altars. The Romans, before assaulting a beleaguered city, called upon the Gods within to leave it. When they allowed the people of Tarentum to retain their angry Gods, it was because they regarded

25. 'Nonne ea quae possidet Chamos deus tuus, tibi jure debentur?' — so runs the text of the Vulgate. This has been translated by Père de Carrières as follows: 'Do you not think that you have a right to possess what belongs to Chamos, your God?' I am ignorant of the full force of the Hebrew text, but I can see that, in the Vulgate, Jephthah recognizes positively the rights of the God Chamos, and that the French translator has weakened this recognition by inserting a phrase 'do you not think?' which is not in the Latin.

26. There is very strong evidence to show that the war of the Phocaeans, generally known as the 'Sacred War,' was not a war of religion at all. Its object was to punish certain sacrilegious acts, not to subdue unbelievers.

them as having been conquered by their own, and forced to do them homage. They left the vanquished their Gods, just as they left them their laws. The obligation to present a crown to Jupiter Capitolinus was often the only tribute they imposed.

When, in later ages, the Romans carried their religious observances and their Gods into their remoter territories, and not seldom adopted those of the people they had over-run, granting to these alien deities the rights of citizenship, it happened that the various Peoples of their vast Empire found that, almost unbeknownst to themselves, they had acquired a multitude of Gods who were more or less the same every-where. That is how it came about that the paganism of the whole world took on a uniformity and became everywhere identical.

Such were the conditions in which Jesus established on earth a Kingdom of the Spirit. The result of this was that a schism developed between the theological and the political systems, and that the State ceased to be one and indivisible, and developed those domestic divisions which have never ceased to disturb Christian Peoples. Now, this new idea of a Kingdom in another world had never taken form in pagan minds. Consequently, the non-Christian Peoples always re-garded Christians as, in reality, rebels who, beneath an hy-pocritical show of humility, were seeking only an oppor-tunity to make themselves independent and dominant, and, by the use of cunning, to usurp that authority which, in their days of weakness, they had pretended to respect.

This lay behind the policy of persecution.

What the pagans had feared came to pass. The whole face of things was changed. The humble Christians now spoke in quite a different tone, and a time soon came when they saw the kingdom which had always proclaimed itself to be of another world, becoming, under the leadership of a visible leader, the most violent of despotisms in this.

But since there have always been Princes and civil laws, this double seat of authority gave rise to a perpetual state of conflict between opposing jurisdictions. Any good ordering of life has become impossible in Christian States, nor has it ever been finally established whether a man owes ultimate obedience to ruler or to priest.

Many Peoples, however, even in Europe, or in the lands abutting on it, have wished to maintain, or to re-establish the ancient system, but without success. The spirit of Christianity has been everywhere victorious. The sacred cult has remained, or once more become, independent of the sovereign, and is without any true bond of union with the body of the State. Mahomet, in his wisdom, knit his political system into a strong whole, and, so long as the form of government which he laid down persisted under the Caliphs who were his successors, it was completely unified, and, in so far as it was unified, good. But no sooner had the Arabs become rich, educated, polite, soft and cowardly, than they were subjugated by the barbarians. Then the division between the two powers began again. It may be less apparent among the Mohammedans than it is among the Christians, but it exists all the same, especially in the sect of Ali; and there are States, like ·Persia, where it has never ceased to make itself felt.

Among us, the Kings of England have established themselves as Heads of the Church, as, too, have the Czars. But by assuming this title they have become not so much the Church's masters as her ministers. They have acquired less the right to change her nature than to maintain her in being. They are not Legislators, but merely Princes. Wherever the clergy constitute a corporate body they are the masters and the legislators within their sphere of influence.[27] There are,

27. It should be noted that what knits the clergy together into a corporate body is not so much the existence of formal assemblies, as in France, but the communion of churches. Communion and excommunication form the social pact of the clergy, and armed with this, they will for ever be masters both of the kings and of the People. All priests who are in communion with the Church, no matter whether they come from the ends of the earth, are fellow citizens. This invention is a political triumph. There never was anything at all resembling it in the pagan priesthood, where a corporate body of clergy was unknown.

then, in England and in Russia, as elsewhere, two powers and two sovereigns.

Of all the Christian authors, the philosopher, Hobbes, alone has seen the evil clearly, and the remedy too. He only has dared to propose that the two heads of the eagle should be united, and that all should be brought into a single political whole, without which no State and no Government can ever be firmly established. But he should have seen that the arrogant spirit of Christianity is incompatible with his system, and that the interest of the priest will ever be stronger than that of the State. It is not the horrible and false aspects of his political theory that makes it so detestable, but precisely those parts of it which are true.[28]

I do not doubt but that anyone, developing the facts of history from this point of view, could, without difficulty, equally refute the opposed attitudes of Bayle and of Warburton, one of whom claims that no religion is ever useful to the body politic, while the other maintains, on the contrary, that Christianity forms its strongest support. It would be easy to prove to the first that no State was ever yet founded save on a basis of religion, and, to the second, that the Christian law is, fundamentally, more harmful than useful to the firm establishment of the community. To make what I mean clear, I need only give a little more precision to the rather over-vague ideas of religion in its relation to my subject.

Religion, viewed in reference to Society, (the relation being either general or particular) may also be divided into two kinds — the religion of man as man, and the religion of the citizen. The first, without temples, without altars, without rites, and strictly limited to the *inner* worship of the Supreme God, and to the eternal obligations of morality, is the pure and simple religion of the Gospels. It is Theism in its truest form, what may be called natural divine law.

28. Read, among other things, what Grotius said in a letter written to his brother, dated 11th April 1643, from which it is easy to see what that learned man approves and what he blames in the book *De Cive*. It is true that he is inclined to be indulgent and, seemingly, to forgive the author his good qualities in consideration of his bad ones: but others are not so merciful.

The other, inscribed in a single country, gives to it its God, its special and tutelary patron. Its dogmas, its rites, its forms of worship, are all prescribed by law. Everything outside the boundaries of the nation which professes it, is regarded as infidel, foreign, barbaric. It limits men's rights and duties to the territories in which its altars reign supreme. Such were all the religions of primitive peoples, religions to which we can give the name of divine law, civil or positive.

There is a third, and more extraordinary, type of religion which, by giving to men two sets of laws, two heads, two countries, imposes upon them two contradictory systems of duty, and makes it impossible for them to be at the same time devout individuals and good citizens. Such is the religion of the Lamas, such is the religion of the Japanese, such is Roman Christianity. Religion of this kind may be called priestly religion, and from it results a sort of mixed and unsocial law which has no name.

Considered politically, each of these three types of religion has its faults. The third is so obviously bad that to demonstrate the fact, though it might be amusing, would be merely a waste of time. Everything that disrupts the social bond of unity is valueless. All institutions which set a man in contradiction with himself are of no worth.

The second is good in that it links divine worship with a love of the laws. By making their country an object of adoration to the citizens, it teaches them that to serve the State is to serve its tutelary God. It is a species of Theocracy in which there is no Pontiff but the Prince, no priests but the magistrates. Then to die for one's country is to suffer martyrdom: to violate the laws is to be guilty of impiety, and to expose an evil-doer to public obloquy is to subject him to the wrath of God: *Sacer estod.*

But it is also bad in so far as, being founded on error and lies, it deceives men, making them credulous and superstitious, and smothers the true worship of the Divinity in a welter of empty ceremonial. It is bad, too, when, becoming exclusive and tyrannical, it makes a people bloody-minded and intolerant, so that they breathe nothing but murder and massacre, and hold themselves to be performing a sacred act when they kill all who do not recognize their God. Such things put people in a natural state of war with their neighbours, and this spells danger to their own safety.

There remains, then, the religion of man, or Christianity, not as we see it to-day, but as we find it in the Gospels — which is quite a different thing. By virtue of this holy, sublime and true religion, men, as all being children of the same God, look on one another as brothers, and the society which unites them remains firmly knit even in death.

But this religion, since it has no particular relation to the body politic, leaves to the laws the force which they derive from themselves, and adds nothing to it. In so far as that is so, one of the chief bonds of the social fabric remains ineffective. But the evil goes farther, because, so far from attaching the hearts of the citizens to the State, it weans them from it, as from all merely earthly concerns. I know of nothing more at odds with the spirit of society.

We are told that a people of true Christians would constitute the most perfect society imaginable. I see only one great difficulty in the way of accepting this statement, namely, that a society of true Christians would cease to be a society of men. I will go further, and maintain that this supposed society, for all its perfection, would be neither the strongest nor the most durable. By the mere fact of being perfect it would lack unity. Its very perfection would constitute the vice to which it would eventually succumb.

Every member of it would do his duty. The people would be subject to laws: their rulers would be just and moderate, their magistrates honest and incorruptible. Their soldiers would hold death in contempt. There would be neither vanity nor luxury. All this we may set on the credit side. But let us extend our gaze a little farther.

Christianity as a religion is wholly spiritual. It is occupied only with the thought of Heaven. The Christian's country is no longer of this world. True, he does his duty, but he does it in a mood of profound indifference to the success or failure of his efforts. Provided he has nothing with which to reproach himself, it matters little to him whether things here below go well or ill. If the State flourishes he scarcely dares to enjoy his share of the public happiness, and fears lest the glory of his country may make him proud. If the State perishes, he blesses the land of God for lying heavy on His people.

That a Society may live in peace, that its harmony may be maintained, it is needful that all good citizens, without exception, be good Christians. But should it be so unfortunate as to contain but one ambitious man, one single hypocrite, a Catiline, for instance, or a Cromwell, he will certainly get the better of his pious compatriots. Christian charity does not easily permit a man to think evil of his neighbour. Should one of them, as the result of some trickery, impose upon his fellows and become possessed of part of the public authority, he will be at once loaded with honours. It is God's will that he be respected. Should he become powerful, it is God's will that he be obeyed. Should he who wields this power abuse his trust, he is seen as the scourge with which God punishes His children. A Christian would have an uneasy conscience about driving out a usurper. It would mean disturbing the public peace, using violence, shedding blood — all of which accords ill with Christian mildness. Besides, what matters it if a man be free or a slave in this valley of sorrows? The essential thing is to get to Paradise, and resignation is but one means more for attaining that end. Should a foreign war break out, the citizens will make no ado about marching to battle. Not one among them will dream of flight. They will do their duty, but with no passionate desire for victory. They know better how to die than how to conquer. What does it signify whether they win or lose? Does not Providence know better than they do themselves what is best for them? It is not hard to imagine how a proud, impetuous and passionate enemy will turn this stoicism of theirs to his own account.' Set against them one of those generous peoples whose hearts are devoured by an ardent love of glory and of country. Imagine a Christian Republic at grips with Sparta or with Rome! The pious Christians would be beaten, crushed, destroyed before ever they had time to collect their wits, or else would owe their safety only to the contempt which they inspired in the breasts of their enemy. The oath taken by the soldiers of Fabius was, to my mind, a fine one. They did not swear to 'conquer or to die,' but to 'conquer and return,' and they kept their word. No Christian would ever have sworn the like. To do so, he would have thought, would mean tempting God. But I am guilty of error in speaking of a Christian Republic, for the words are mutually exclusive. Christianity preaches only servitude and dependence. Its spirit is over-favourable to tyranny, and the latter always draws its profit from that fact. True Christians are made to be slaves! They know it, and care little, for, in their eyes, this brief life counts for nothing.

Christian troops, we are told, are excellent. That I deny. I challenge anyone to show me them. I do not know of any such thing as a body of Christian troops. The Crusades will be quoted against me. I have no wish to dispute the valour of the Crusaders, but I would point out that, far from being Christians, they were soldiers in the service of a priest; they were citizens of the Church. The country for which they fought was a spiritual one, though, in some way that I do not understand, the Church had made it temporal. Strictly speaking, this particular instance comes really under the heading of paganism. Since the Gospel established no national religion, any form of Holy War is, among Christians, an impossibility.

Under the pagan Emperors the Christian soldiers were gallant fighters. That is a fact borne out by all Christian authors, and I am prepared to believe it. They were competing in a matter of honour with non-Christian troops. When the Emperors became Christian, this competition ceased. Once the Cross had put the Eagle to flight, Roman valour disappeared.

But let us lay all political considerations aside and, return-
ing to the question of 'Right,' determine the principle of this
important point. The Right which the social pact confers on
the Sovereign over his subjects does not, as I have already
pointed out, extend beyond the realm of public utility.[29] The
subject is, let it be stated, in no way obliged to render an
account of his opinions of the Sovereign, save in so far as
they effect the community. Now, it is of considerable concern to the State whether a citizen profess a religion which
leads him to love his duties. But the dogmas of that religion
are of no interest to the State or to its members except as
they have a bearing on the morals and duties which the citizen professing it should hold and perform in dealing with
others. That consideration apart, it is open to each to enter-
tain what opinions he pleases, and it is no part of the business
of the State to have cognizance of them, since, not being
competent in the affairs of the other world, no matter what
be the fate of its members in the life to come, it has no sort
of concern with such matters, provided the citizen fulfils his
duties in this one.

But there is a purely civil profession of faith, the articles
of which it behoves the Sovereign to fix, not with the precision of religious dogmas, but treating them as a body of
social *sentiments* without which no man can be either a good
citizen or a faithful subject.[30] Though it has no power to
compel anyone to believe them, it can banish from the State

29. 'In the Republic,' says the Marquis d'Argenson, 'each man is perfectly free
   in all things that do no harm to others.' This is the unalterable criterion, and
   it could not be more precisely stated. I have not been able to resist the pleasure of quoting more than once from this manuscript — albeit unknown to the
   public — in the hope that thereby I may give honour to its illustrious author,
   a man ever worthy of respect who never, even when a Minister, fell short of
   true citizenship, nor ceased to promulgate sane and upright views on the
   government of his country.

30. Caesar, when speaking in defence of Catiline, tried to establish the dogma
   that the soul is mortal. Cato and Cicero, in rebuttal, did not involve themselves in the pleasing complexities of philosophical disputation, but confined
   their efforts to proving that Caesar had pleaded as a bad citizen, having advanced a doctrine pernicious to the State. That, indeed, was what the Roman
   Senate was called upon to decide, not a point of theological theory.

all who fail to do so, not on grounds of impiety, but as lacking in social sense, and being incapable of sincerely loving
the laws and justice, or of sacrificing, should the need arise,
their lives to their duty. Any man who, after acknowledging
these articles of faith, proceeds to act as though he did not believe them, is deserving of the death penalty. For he has committed the greatest of all crimes, that of lying before the law.

The dogmas of this civil religion should be few, clear and
enunciated precisely, without either explanation or comment.
The positive clauses are: — the existence of a powerful, intelligent, beneficent and bountiful God: the reality of the life to
come: the reward of the just, and the punishment of evil-
doers: the sanctity of the Social Contract and of the Laws.
The negative element I would confine to one single article:
— intolerance, for that belongs to the creeds which I have
excluded.

Those who draw a distinction between civil and theological intolerance are, in my opinion, guilty of error. The
two things are inseparable. It is impossible to live in peace
with those whom we believed to be damned. To love them
would be to hate God who punishes them. It is essential that
they be either converted or punished. Wherever theological
intolerance enters it cannot but have an effect on civil life,[31]
and when that happens the Sovereign is no longer sovereign,

31. Marriage, for instance, being a civil contract, has civil consequences; and
without them it is impossible for society even to subsist. If we assume that the
clergy succeed in arrogating to themselves the sole right to perform the act
of marriage, a right which, of necessity, they will usurp whenever they serve
an intolerant religion, is it not obvious that, by establishing the authority of
the Church in this matter, they will render that of the Prince null, and create
a situation in which the Prince will have as subjects only such as the clergy
shall see fit to give him? Being in a position to permit or to refuse marriage,
according as whether those concerned do, or do not, hold certain doctrines,
whether they admit or denounce the validity of this or that formula, whether
they be more or less devout, the Church, surely, if only it use a little tact and
refuses to yield ground, will be the sole controller of inheritances, offices,
citizens, and the State itself, which could not continue were it composed only
of bastards. But, I shall be told, men will appeal against abuses, will adjourn
decisions, will issue decrees and lay hold on the temporal power. How sad!
The clergy, no matter how little they may have of, I do not say courage,
but good sense, will stand aside from all such agitations and will quietly go

even in temporal affairs. From then on, the priests are the real masters, the kings no more than their officers.

Now that there are, and can be, no longer any exclusive national religions, we should tolerate all creeds which show tolerance to others, so long as their dogmas contain nothing at variance with the duties of the citizen. But anyone who dares to say 'Outside the Church there can be no salvation,' should be banished from the State, unless the State be the Church and the Prince the Pontiff. Such a dogma is good only where the government is theocratic. In any other it is pernicious. The reason for which, according to the popular story, Henry IV embraced the religion of Rome would make any honest man leave it: and especially any Prince who was capable of using his brain.[32]

(((IX)))

CONCLUSION

Having thus laid down the true principles of political right, and striven to establish the State on a durable foundation, I have now but to strengthen it on the side of its relations with other powers, a subject which would include such matters as the Law of Nations, Commerce, the Right of War and Conquest, Public Right, Leagues, Negotiations and Treaties, etc. But all this forms a new field which is too vast for my limited vision. It is better that I confine myself to things nearer at hand.

their own way. They will blandly acquiesce in claims and adjournments, in decrees and seizures — and will still be masters in the end. It is not, I think, any great sacrifice to surrender a part when one is sure of getting possession of the whole.

32. We are told by an historian that the king, having ordered a conference to be held in his presence between the doctors of the two Churches, and hearing a Protestant pastor admit that a man might be saved even though he were a Catholic, interrupted the debate with these words: 'What, do you then agree that a man may be saved even if he holds to the religion of these gentlemen opposite?' The pastor replied that there was no doubt he could, provided he lived a good life. The King then continued as follows: 'In that case, if I listen to the voice of prudence, I shall profess their religion and not yours, thereby making certain that I shall be saved in the eyes of both of you. For were I to become a Protestant, I might be saved in your view, but not in theirs, and prudence ordains that I take the safest road.'